Praise for
Arminian and Baptist

What a breath of fresh air Matt Pinson has been to me. While being enriched by and appreciative of the heritage of Reformed theologians, I could never buy into the thoroughgoing Calvinistic paradigm. Pinson has shown that it is possible to harness the rich heritage of Reformed Theology without jettisoning a balanced and biblically grounded Arminianism.

—Ajith Fernando, Teaching Director and
former president, Youth for Christ, Sri Lanka

I know of no other person in the history of theology whose views have been as distorted as the thinking of Arminius. And, I know of no other theologian who has as thoroughly researched these issues as J. Matthew Pinson has. I highly recommend this book to those who consider themselves to be Arminian in their theology. Most Arminians will encounter some surprises here. I also recommend it to Calvinists. Our first obligation to those with whom we disagree is to find out what the other person is actually saying. If this happens, Arminianism will be given a new face in the theological world.

—F. Leroy Forlines, Professor Emeritus and
former Dean of Students, Welch College

Pinson gives in these essays a compelling account of an Arminianism that is at once Reformed, classical, and evangelical. Some Calvinists will find here a set of first cousins they never knew they had, and some Arminians will discover a sturdier faith that comes within the "hair's breadth" of difference Mr. Wesley talked about.

—Timothy George, founding dean,
Beeson Divinity School of Samford University

As one in a more Reformed stream of the Baptist tradition, I disagree with much of Arminianism. But I thank God for the resurgence of grace-oriented, gospel-focused Arminianism represented in this book. This is an Arminianism with a deep sense of radical human depravity, the sovereign initiative of God, penal substitutionary atonement, and the imputation of the active and passive obedience of Christ to the believer. In short, this is the Arminianism of Thomas Helwys and the heroic orthodox General Baptists of old, not that of the TV evangelists. We may sometimes disagree on the "how" and the "when" of salvation, but we agree on the "what" and the "Who."

—*Russell Moore, President, Ethics and Religious Liberty Commission, Southern Baptist Convention*

I enthusiastically recommend this book. It represents the happy blending of church history and theology, and Pinson is at home in both fields. Anyone who has the slightest interest in understanding a thoroughly evangelical Arminianism, and seeing it in the context of its Reformation roots, will want to read this book. The name "Arminianism" covers a broad and varied spectrum. Theologians must therefore explain what kind of Arminianism they espouse and how it differs not only from other kinds of Reformed theology but also from other kinds of Arminian theology. These essays will answer the reader's questions about the Arminianism that is part of the tradition of those of us whose heritage lies in the English General Baptists of the seventeenth century. I've been acquainted with each of these essays in their original circumstances, reading them or hearing them read. It will be very useful, now, to have them together in one volume. Kudos to Pinson and to Randall House for bringing them to us in this format.

—*Robert E. Picirilli, Professor Emeritus and former Academic Dean, Welch College*

This book is a timely, thoughtful, and thorough presentation of the Arminian Baptist theological tradition. It will make a significant contribution to perpetuating, persevering, and promoting the theological traditions of Free Will Baptists. They as well as others will profit greatly by reading this book.

—*Melvin L. Worthington, Executive Secretary Emeritus, National Association of Free Will Baptists*

ARMINIAN
AND BAPTIST

Explorations in a Theological Tradition

J. MATTHEW PINSON

randall house

114 Bush Rd | Nashville, TN 37217
randallhouse.com

35.74

Published by Randall House
114 Bush Road
Nashville, TN 37217
www.randallhouse.com

Printed in the United States of America

ISBN 13: 9780892656967

9194 75036

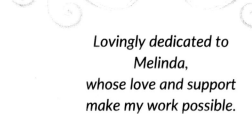

Lovingly dedicated to
Melinda,
whose love and support
make my work possible.

Table of Contents

Preface

Recently there has been a resurgence of interest in Arminianism. This renewed fascination probably results from the fact that traditional Calvinism has
become more popular in evangelicalism, and people who demur from it are
looking for resources that will enable them to frame their soteriology in non-
Calvinist ways. Free Will Baptists have been at the forefront of production of
such resources. Chief among these are F. Leroy Forlines and Robert E. Picirilli.[1]
Stephen M. Ashby and I have entered the field with some writings of our own,
building on the foundation of our elders.[2] This approach to Arminianism, which
has roots in our English General Baptist forebears as well as Arminius himself,
has been variously known as Reformed Arminianism, Reformation Arminianism, or Classical Arminianism.[3]

Reformed Arminianism, unlike most Arminianism, posits a traditional Reformed notion of original sin and radical depravity that only the grace of God
via the convicting and drawing power of the Holy Spirit can counteract. It puts
forward a thoroughgoing Reformed, penal satisfaction view of atonement, with
the belief that Christ's full righteousness is imputed to the believer in justification. Thus, it diverges from the perfectionism, entire sanctification, and crisis-
experience orientation of much Arminianism, believing that one perseveres in
salvation through faith alone. While believers can apostatize from salvation and
be irremediably lost, this apostasy comes about through defection from faith
rather than through sin.

Over the past couple of decades, I have written a number of essays on this
sort of Arminianism and how Arminian Baptists may locate themselves within
the Christian tradition. Increasingly, with the resurgence of interest in Arminianism, I have had many requests for this material, some of which has never

appeared in published form but which I have referred to in various published writings. Many have suggested that I collect them in one volume for ease of reference and to make them more accessible and available to a new audience. The book you hold in your hand is the result of my decision to take their advice.

These are mostly essays that were written several years ago. With few exceptions, I have for the most part reprinted them here unchanged. In at least one chapter, "Thomas Grantham and the Diversity of Arminian Soteriology," I have included here a combination of two previous essays. The basis of that chapter is an unpublished paper I wrote for Professor Richard Greaves in a doctoral seminar at Florida State University twenty years ago. I used part of that paper in a presentation at New Orleans Baptist Theological Seminary, later published in their *Journal for Baptist Theology and Ministry*.[4] The chapter puts the other material from the earlier paper with the new material in the latter article. Similarly, the book's first chapter adapts some material found previously in "Will the Real Arminius Please Stand Up?" that was originally published in *Integrity: A Journal of Christian Thought*, augmenting it with new content.[5]

Most of the other chapters here are mostly unchanged reprints of earlier published articles, reprinted here with permission, and one is published here for the first time. "Atonement, Justification, and Apostasy in the Theology of John Wesley" was originally published in *Integrity: A Journal of Christian Thought*.[6] "The First Baptist Treatise on Predestination: Thomas Helwys's *Short and Plaine Proofe*" and the review essay on *Whosoever Will* were published in the *Journal for Baptist Theology and Ministry*.[7] "The Nature of Atonement in the Theology of Jacobus Arminius" and the review of *Arminian Theology: Myths and Realities* were published in the *Journal of the Evangelical Theological Society*.[8] "Confessional, Baptist, and Arminian" was published as a chapter in *Evangelicals and Nicene Faith* edited by Timothy George.[9]

The only essay in this book that has never been published in some form is "Sin and Redemption in the Theology of John Smyth and Thomas Helwys." Its having never been published is ironic, given that it and its thesis regarding the divergence of Thomas Helwys's more Reformed Arminianism from the semi-

Pelagian Anabaptist soteriology of his mentor John Smyth lies at the heart of my account of the sort of Arminianism my tradition espouses.

I recently told a colleague that all my thinking on the contents of this book is essentially what it looks like when a person standing on the shoulders of Leroy Forlines and Robert Picirilli starts to try to do historical theology using materials from the sixteenth and seventeenth centuries. That is what I have done. What I found was that there is a lively output of literature from General Baptist preachers in England in the seventeenth century that says things very similar to what Forlines and Picirilli have said, ideas the latter remember taking shape in the course in "Arminian Theology" they took under Dr. L. C. Johnson in the early 1950s. When I traced the history of southern Free Will Baptists back as far as I could (standing on the shoulders of historians such as William F. Davidson, Michael R. Pelt, and George Stevenson), I bumped into these same General Baptists, because the earliest Free Will Baptists in America were simply English General Baptists who had moved to this side of the Atlantic.[10] Then I read Arminius and found similar themes in his writings.

This is not to say that everything every English General Baptist said, or everything Arminius said, is the same as the contemporary Reformed Arminian account. It is simply to say that we find in Arminius and the seventeenth-century English General Baptists precursors to what is now being called Reformed Arminianism. We discover in their writings themes that are not typically found in most other forms of Arminianism or non-Calvinism—whether Wesleyan, Anabaptist, Stone-Campbell-Restorationist, or the more common Finneyesque variety of frontier-holiness theology that has been popular in American evangelicalism.

I trust that the bringing together of all these essays into one volume will be of help to those who wish to understand the Arminian Baptist theological tradition and the unique stream of Arminian theology associated with it, thus complementing a growing body of literature from this theological vantage point.

I wish to thank a few individuals without whom this book would not have been possible: Leroy Forlines and Robert Picirilli for the foundation they have laid and interest they have shown in my work, Darrell Holley and Stephen Ashby for the myriad conversations about this subject matter over the last twenty-five years, my editor Michelle Orr and her team for their excellent work, my executive assistant Martha Fletcher for help with the indices, my wife Melinda for her loving encouragement and wise feedback on these ideas, and my children Anna and Matthew and parents John and Linda Pinson for their loving support of my research and writing.

[1]See, e.g., F. Leroy Forlines, *Classical Arminianism: A Theology of Salvation*, ed. J. Matthew Pinson (Nashville: Randall House, 2011); Robert E. Picirilli, *Grace, Faith, Free Will: Contrasting Views of Salvation—Calvinism and Arminianism* (Nashville: Randall House, 2002).

[2]See, e.g., Stephen M. Ashby, "Reformed Arminianism," in J. Matthew Pinson, ed., *Four Views on Eternal Security* (Grand Rapids: Zondervan, 2002); Ashby, "Introduction" to *The Works of James Arminius* (Nashville: Randall House, 2007); J. Matthew Pinson, *A Free Will Baptist Handbook: Heritage, Beliefs, and Ministries* (Nashville: Randall House, 1998); and the articles reprinted in this book.

[3]Forlines prefers "Classical Arminianism." The term "Reformed Arminianism" was first used by Picirilli in his preface to Forlines's commentary on *Romans* (Nashville: Randall House, 1987), but by the time Picirilli wrote *Grace, Faith, Free Will*, he had begun preferring the term "Reformation Arminianism." Ashby and I prefer "Reformed Arminianism" because it emphasizes that Arminius was self-consciously Reformed; that this sort of Arminianism is closer to Reformed theology on the meaning of original sin and depravity, the nature of atonement, justification, and sanctification; and that our General Baptist forefathers self-consciously saw themselves in their seventeenth-century milieu as "reformed according to the Scriptures" (more reformed, they would have argued, than the Calvinists in the established churches).

[4]"Thomas Grantham's Theology of Atonement and Justification," *Journal for Baptist Theology and Ministry* 8 (2011), 7-39 (with responses and rejoinder). The original paper was entitled, "The Diversity of Arminian Soteriology: Thomas Grantham, John Goodwin, and Jacobus Arminius."

[5]"Will the Real Arminius Please Stand Up? The Theology of Jacobus Arminius in Light of His Interpreters," *Integrity: A Journal of Christian Thought* 2 (2003), 121-39.

[6]"Atonement, Justification, and Apostasy in the Thought of John Wesley," *Integrity: A Journal of Christian Thought* 4 (2008), 73-92.

[7]"The First Baptist Treatise on Predestination: Thomas Helwys's *A Short and Plaine Proofe*," *Journal for Baptist Theology and Ministry* 6 (2009), 139-51; "Whosoever Will: A Review Essay," *Journal for Baptist Theology and Ministry* 7 (2010), 25-41.

[8]"The Nature of Atonement in the Theology of Jacobus Arminius," *Journal of the Evangelical Theological Society* 53 (2010): 173-85; A Review of *Arminian Theology: Myths and Realities* by Roger Olson, *Journal of the Evangelical Theological Society* 49 (2006), 877-81.

[9]"Confessional, Baptist, and Arminian: The General-Free Will Baptist Tradition and the Nicene Faith," in Timothy George, ed., *Evangelicals and Nicene Faith: Reclaiming the Apostolic Witness* (Grand Rapids: Baker Academic, 2011), 100-15.

[10]See, e.g., William F. Davidson, *The Free Will Baptists in History* (Nashville: Randall House, 2001); Michael R. Pelt, *A History of Original Free Will Baptists* (Mount Olive College Press, 1998); George Stevenson, "Benjamin Laker," in *Dictionary of North Carolina Biography*, ed. William S. Powell (Chapel Hill: University of North Carolina Press, 1991), 4:3, 4.

1

JACOBUS ARMINIUS: REFORMED AND ALWAYS REFORMING

ARMINIUS AND HIS INTERPRETERS

Jacobus Arminius has been the object of much criticism and much praise during the past four centuries. Arminians have usually poured praise on him as the progenitor of their theological tradition, while non-Arminians, specifically those within the Reformed-Calvinistic tradition, have heaped criticism on him for departing from the Reformed faith. Both praise and criticism, however, have mostly proceeded from partisan biases and rest on misinterpretations of Arminius's theology. Most Reformed critics have portrayed him as a semi-Pelagian and a defector from Reformed theology, while most Arminians—Wesleyans and Remonstrants—have cast him in Wesleyan or Remonstrant terms, failing to take seriously his theology itself and the context in which it was spawned.[1]

Both Reformed and Arminian scholars have traditionally portrayed Arminius's thought as a departure from Reformed theology, or, as Richard A. Muller described it, "a full-scale alternative to Reformed theology."[2] Many Reformed thinkers have portrayed Arminius as "a clever dissembler who secretly taught doctrines different from his published writings."[3] Most writers commit the *post*

1

hoc ergo propter hoc fallacy by attributing to Arminius theological movements that came after him. Roger Nicole, for example, described Arminius as the originator of a slippery slope that started with Episcopius and Limborch (who were "infiltrated by Socinianism") and ended with Unitarianism, Universalism, and the philosophy of E. S. Brightman.[4] Reformed writers traditionally described Arminius as a semi-Pelagian, an appellation that persists to this day. Several Reformed authors have recently characterized Arminius's thought as "semi-Pelagian"[5] or even "similar to Pelagianism."[6] These comments are remarkable given Arminius's often stated aim to maintain "the greatest possible distance from Pelagianism."[7]

Most Arminians, while praising Arminius, have viewed him in the light of either Remonstrant or Wesleyan theology, thus describing him in more synergistic or semi-Pelagian terms. The tendency of most Arminians is to give a brief biographical sketch of Arminius, with the customary discussion of "Arminius as the Father of Arminianism," and then to offer an exposition of the five points of the Remonstrance. Or, as Carl Bangs says, the biographical sketch is many times followed by "copious references to Arminius's successor, Simon Episcopius, who, although in many ways a faithful disciple of Arminius, is not Arminius."[8]

None of these things, however, is true of Arminius, and only when one brings certain assumptions to his writings will one interpret him in these ways. Bangs summarizes this problem well:

> It is evident that such accounts of Arminius assume a definition of Arminianism which cannot be derived from Arminius himself. It means that the writers begin with a preconception of what Arminius should be expected to say, then look in his published works, and do not find exactly what they are looking for. They show impatience and disappointment with his Calvinism, and shift the inquiry into some later period when Arminianism turns out to be what they are looking for—a non-Calvinistic, synergistic, and perhaps semi-Pelagian system.[9]

Those who bring presumptions into the study of Arminius by reading later Arminian themes into his thought fail to realize perhaps the most important thing about his theology: that it is distinctively Reformed, and that it is a *development* of Reformed theology rather than a *departure* from it. By focusing on Arminius's doctrine of predestination and its differences with both Calvin and post-Dort Calvinism, people have tended to emphasize Arminius's differences with Calvin and the Reformed tradition rather than his similarities with them. Both Arminians and Calvinists have thought of Arminius's theology as essentially a reaction against Reformed theology rather than the self-consciously Reformed theology that it is.[10] William den Boer is correct when, discussing Arminius in his Reformed context, he favorably cites Willem J. Van Asselt's comment that there were "different trajectories" in sixteenth-century Reformed theology, and that it was "not monolithic." Thus, den Boer places Arminius's thought in the "spectrum" of sixteenth-century Reformed theology—a movement that was "multi-faceted, dynamic, and ever-developing." He thus rightly criticizes the view that there was "*the* Reformed theology."[11]

Those who see predestination as the essential core of Reformed theology find it easy to say that, since Arminius did not articulate predestination in the same way Calvin did, he is a semi-Pelagian. Then they transfer this alleged semi-Pelagianism to all of his theology. Generations of theological students have received this picture of Arminius. But this approach fails to take his theology seriously. The best way to understand Arminius, and thus to benefit from his unique and substantial contribution to Protestant theology, is to understand his theological context, his stated view of Reformed theology (specifically that of Calvin), his confessional beliefs, and his published writings. If one believes Arminius to be an honest man, rather than a treacherous one, one will see a picture of him emerge that is radically different from the one(s) above.[12]

ARMINIUS'S LIFE

Before discussing the theological milieu in which Arminius taught and wrote, it will be helpful to give a brief sketch of his life.[13] Arminius, born in

3

1559 and named Jacob Harmenszoon, grew up in Oudewater, Holland, and later studied at the newly established University of Leiden. After graduation from Leiden in 1581, he was brought to Geneva to study under Theodore Beza, Calvin's successor and son-in-law. He left there to study at Basel for a year but returned and studied at Geneva until 1586. Arminius's second stint at Geneva went smoothly. Beza gave a glowing report to the Amsterdam burgomasters, who were inquiring if Arminius was fitting in well.

In 1587, Arminius was assigned a pastorate in Amsterdam and was ordained in 1588. Before assuming his pastorate, Arminius traveled with his friend Adrian Junius to Italy and studied philosophy for seven months with James Zabarella at the University of Padua. Arminius took this journey without the permission of the Amsterdam burgomasters. Though he said that the experience made the Roman Church appear to him "more foul, ugly, and detestable" than he could have imagined,[14] some of his later enemies used the trip to suggest that he had sympathies with Rome, "that he had kissed the pope's shoe, become acquainted with the Jesuits, and cherished a familiar intimacy with Cardinal Bellarmine."[15]

In 1590, Arminius married Lijset Reael, a daughter of a member of the city council. About this time, he became involved in theological controversy. Arminius was asked to refute the teachings of Dirk Coornhert, a humanist who had criticized Calvinism, and two ministers at Delft who had written an anti-Calvinist pamphlet. The traditional view was that Arminius, in his attempt to refute these anti-Calvinist teachings, converted from Calvinism to anti-Calvinism. Yet Bangs has shown there is no evidence that he ever held strict Calvinist views. At any rate, he became involved in controversy over the doctrines of the strong Calvinists. In 1591, he preached on Romans 7, arguing against the Calvinists' view that the person described in vv. 14-24 was regenerate. A minister named Petrus Plancius led the charge against Arminius. Plancius labeled Arminius a Pelagian, alleging that Arminius had moved away from the Belgic Confession of Faith and the Heidelberg Catechism, advocating non-Reformed views on predestination and perfectionism. Arminius insisted his theology was in line with that of the Reformed Church and its Confession and Catechism, and the Amsterdam burgomasters sided with him. About a year later, after a sermon on Romans 9, Plancius again led the charge against Arminius. The latter insisted his teachings were in line with Article 16 of the Belgic Confession, and the consistory accepted Arminius's explanation, urging peace until the matter could be decided by a general synod.

For the next ten years, Arminius enjoyed a relatively peaceful pastorate and avoided theological controversy. During this decade, he wrote a great deal on theology (things that were never published in his lifetime), including extensive works on Romans 7 and 9 as well as a long correspondence with the Leiden Calvinist Francis Junius. In 1602, after Leiden professor Lucas Trelcatius the elder died from the plague, there was a move to get Arminius appointed to his position, but there was also opposition to Arminius's appointment, led by Leiden professor Franciscus Gomarus. Despite this opposition, the Leiden burgomasters appointed Arminius as professor of theology in May 1603. Soon he was awarded a doctorate in theology.

Arminius would spend the last six years of his life at Leiden, struggling with tuberculosis but always in a firestorm of theological controversy. The primary source of the controversy was predestination, and this is what Arminius and the movement that was named after him became known for. Another issue of dispute was the convening of a national synod. Arminius's side wanted a national synod convened with power to revise the Confession and Catechism, while the strict Calvinists relied more on local synods. In 1607, the States General brought together a conference to prepare for a national synod. Arminius recommended the revision of the confessional documents but was voted down. He continued to be accused of heresy and false teaching, which resulted in his petitioning the States General to inquire into his case. Eventually, Arminius and Gomarus appeared before the High Court in 1608 to make their respective cases. This was the occasion for Arminius's famous *Declaration of Sentiments*.[16]

In his *Declaration of Sentiments*, Arminius forthrightly argued against the Calvinist view of unconditional election.[17] He concluded his declaration by asking again for a national synod with hopes for a revision of the Confession. Gomarus appeared before the States General and accused Arminius of errors on not only original sin, divine foreknowledge, predestination, regeneration, good works, and the possibility of apostasy, but also the Trinity and biblical authority. While the States General did not support Gomarus, the controversy became more heated.

In August of 1609, the States General invited Arminius and Gomarus back for a conference. They were each to bring four other colleagues. Arminius's illness, which had been worsening, made it impossible for him to continue the conference, which was dismissed. The States General asked the two men to submit their views in writing within two weeks. Arminius never completed his, owing to his illness, and he died on October 19, 1609.

ARMINIUS'S THEOLOGICAL CONTEXT

An awareness of the theological situation in the Dutch Reformed Church before and during Arminius's lifetime enhances one's understanding of his theology. Most of the interpretations of Arminius's theology have been based on misconceptions about his situation.[18] Bangs mentions six misunderstandings that are common among interpreters of Arminius:[19] (1) that Arminius was reared and educated amidst Calvinism in a Calvinist country; (2) that his education at the Universities of Leiden and Basel confirmed his acceptance of Genevan Calvinism; (3) that as a student of Theodore Beza he accepted supralapsarianism; (4) that, while a pastor in Amsterdam, he was commissioned to write a refutation of the humanist Dirck Coornhert, who "attacked predestination, and who had declared that the doctrine of original sin is not in the Bible;"[20] (5) that while preparing his refutation, he changed his mind and went over to Coornhert's humanism,[21] and (6) that thus his theology was a polemic against Reformed theology. None of these six points, as Bangs has shown, are true.[22]

Arminius was not predisposed to a supralapsarian view of predestination. He rather shared the views of numerous Reformed theologians and pastors before him. He was not reared in a "Calvinist country." A brief look at the Reformed Church in the sixteenth century will reveal this. The origins of the Reformed Church were diverse, both historically and theologically. When Calvin came out with his views on predestination in the 1540s, there was a strong reaction from many within the Reformed Church. When Sabastien Castellio exhibited disagreement with Calvin's view of predestination, he was banished from Geneva but was given asylum by the Reformed in Basel and soon offered a professorship there. It was said that, in Basel, "if one wishes to scold another, he calls him a Calvinist."[23] Another Reformed theologian who reacted negatively to Calvin's doctrine of predestination was Jerome Bolsec, who settled in Geneva in 1550. When Calvin and Beza sent a list of Bolsec's errors to the Swiss churches, they were disappointed with the response. The Church of Basel urged that Calvin and Bolsec try to emphasize their similarities rather than their differences. The ministers of Bern reminded Calvin of the many biblical texts that refer to God's universal grace. Even Bullinger disagreed with Calvin, though he later changed his mind. Bangs notes that "the most consistent resistance to [Calvin's] predestination theory came from the German-speaking cantons,"[24] but that even in Geneva there was a fair amount of resistance. This is evidenced by the presence of the liberal Calvinist Charles Perrot on the faculty of the University of Geneva, even during Beza's lifetime.

"From the very beginnings of the introduction of Reformed religion in the Low Countries," says Bangs, "the milder views of the Swiss cantons were in evidence."[25] Because of Roman Catholic persecution, the first Dutch Reformed synod was held at the Reformed church in Emden, where Albert Hardenberg was pastor. Hardenberg, who was closer to Melanchthon than to Calvin on predestination, exerted great influence on the early leaders in the Dutch Reformed Church—most notably Clement Martenson and John Isbrandtson, who "publicly resisted the introduction of Genevan theology into the Low Countries."[26] At the Synod of Emden, the Heidelberg Catechism and the Belgic Confession of Faith were adopted. Both these documents allowed room for disagreement on the doctrine of predestination, but some ministers who had been educated in Geneva began attempts to enforce a supralapsarian interpretation of these documents.

Soon there arose two parties in the Dutch Reformed Church. Those who were less inclined to a Calvinistic view of predestination were more inclined toward a form of Erastianism and toleration toward Lutherans and Anabaptists, while the Genevan elements wanted strict adherence to Calvinism and Presbyterian church government. The lay magistrates and lay people tended toward the former, while more clergy tended toward the latter. However, a significant number of clergy clung to the non-Calvinistic view of predestination. As late as 1581, the magistrates at Leiden supported Jasper Koolhaes, a Reformed pastor in Leiden, after he was declared a heretic by the provincial Synod of Dort because of his non-Calvinistic interpretation of predestination.[27] The provincial Synod of Haarlem of 1582 excommunicated him. This action was opposed by the magistrates and some ministers of Leiden, The Hague, Dort, and Gouda. The Synod also attempted to force the Dutch churches to accept a rigid doctrine of predestination but did not succeed. As Bangs says, "Koolhaes continued to write, with the support of the States of Holland and the magistrates of Leiden. A compromise reconciliation between the two factions was attempted, but it was not successful. This indicates something of a mixed situation in the Reformed churches of Holland at the time that Arminius was emerging as a theologian."[28] Thus, there was no consensus on the doctrine of predestination in the Dutch Reformed Church of Arminius's time.

ARMINIUS, THE CONFESSIONS, AND CALVIN

It is within this historical context that Arminius worked out his Reformed theology. As a devout Dutch Reformed theologian, Arminius was loyal to the symbols of his church: The Heidelberg Catechism and the Belgic Confession of Faith. He reaffirmed on numerous occasions his faithfulness to these documents. Responding to the consistory in Amsterdam in 1593, Arminius felt it necessary to affirm his loyalty to the Catechism and Confession. He repeatedly reiterated this loyalty, as in 1605, when he responded to deputies of the Synods of North and South Holland.[29] In 1607, at the meeting of the Preparatory Convention for the National Synod, Arminius and some other delegates, emphasizing the priority of the Word of God as the church's rule of faith and practice, argued that the Confession and Catechism should be open to revision by the Synod, to clarify certain doctrines (e.g., the use of the plural when discussing original sin in the Catechism). This did not mean, however, that Arminius disagreed with anything the documents said. Arminius made this clear in a letter to the Palatine Ambassador, Hippolytus à Collibus, in 1608: "I confidently declare that I have never taught anything, either in the church or in the university, which contravenes the sacred writings that ought to be with us the sole rule of thinking and of speaking, or which is opposed to the Dutch [Belgic] Confession or to the Heidelberg Catechism, that are our stricter formularies of consent."[30]

In his *Declaration of Sentiments* that same year, he challenged anyone to prove he had ever made doctrinal pronouncements that were "contrary to God's Word or to the Confession and Catechism of the Belgic Churches."[31] Arminius lived and died with complete loyalty to the Heidelberg Catechism and the Belgic Confession of Faith. It is hard to believe that one could consistently lie both in public statements and in writing after writing (when it would have been much easier to do as Koolhaes did and enter some other occupation that was less psychically strenuous). If Arminius was not a dishonest, surreptitious, treacherous man, it may be confidently believed that he was a loyal defender of the symbols of his church to his dying day.

In light of the fact that most interpreters have cast Arminius as a foe of Calvin, Arminius's statements on Calvin are most interesting. Arminius made explicit references to Calvin throughout his writings—most of the time favorable ones. He had a high regard for Calvin as an exegete and theologian. His only important disagreement with Calvin was on the particulars of the doctrines of predestination and the resistibility of grace. Arminius, however, did not think predestination was the essential core of either Reformed theology or Calvin's theology. He expressed his high esteem for Calvin in a letter to the Amsterdam Burgomaster Sebastian Egbertszoon in May of 1607. The occasion of the letter was a rumor that Arminius had been recommending the works of the Jesuits and of Coornhert to his students. Arminius said: "So far from this,

9

after reading the Scripture . . . I recommend the *Commentaries of Calvin* be read. . . . In the interpretation of the Scriptures Calvin is incomparable, and . . . his *Commentaries* are more to be valued than anything that is handed down to us in the writings of the Fathers. . . . His *Institutes* . . . I give out to be read after the [Heidelberg] Catechism. But here I add—with discrimination, as the writings of all men ought to be read."[32]

In his *Declaration of Sentiments*, Arminius, setting forth his doctrine of justification, says, in essence, that if he is wrong, then Calvin too must be wrong: "Whatever one might say about this, no one among us accuses Calvin or considers him heterodox on this point, and my position is not so different from his as to prevent my signing my name to the positions he takes in Book III of his *Institutes*. To these opinions, I am prepared to state my full approval at any time."[33] Arminius's opinion of Calvin in these passages does not sound like that of an antagonist, but rather like one who has great respect for Calvin and is in agreement with him on most things. It is a mistake to exaggerate the importance of the doctrine of predestination to the point that it is the only doctrine that matters. Though Arminius differed with Calvin on predestination, Arminius was, and believed he was, consistently Reformed.

Though an examination of Arminius's historical and theological context, his confessional loyalties, and his opinion of Calvin do a great deal to establish his theological position, the final court of appeal are his writings. An analysis of them will show that he was in essential agreement with the Augustinian, Calvinistic, and Reformed expressions of the Faith with regard to original sin, the radical depravity and inability of humanity, the nature of atonement, and justification. Arminius differed from the strong Calvinists on *how one comes to be* in a state of grace, but not on *what it means to be* in a state of grace. A study of his writings shows that Arminius should not be described as semi-Pelagian or synergistic, but rather that he articulated the reality of original sin and total depravity and the necessity of divine grace in salvation just as strongly as any Calvinist.

ARMINIUS AND PREDESTINATION

Before undertaking that discussion, however, it will be instructive to summarize the primary doctrinal difference between Arminius and his strict Calvinist interlocutors: how one comes to be in a state of grace or not, that is, the doctrine of predestination.

Predestination as Conditional, Christocentric, and According to Foreknowledge

Robert E. Picirilli encapsulates Arminius's view of predestination when he says that, for Arminius, "the unconditionality of God's sovereign 'decisions' (plan, purpose) does not necessarily mean that all the ends God has purposed are achieved unconditionally or necessarily."[34] God *unconditionally* decrees that election and reprobation are *conditioned* on belief or unbelief.

F. Stuart Clarke and William den Boer are correct when they argue that Christ's satisfaction of divine justice is the driving force behind Arminius's doctrine of predestination, not free will.[35] As den Boer says, Arminius's view of freedom of the will "flows from" his doctrine of divine justice "as a consequence."[36] For Arminius, the primary problem with the strong Calvinist views on predestination, whether supralapsarian or infralapsarian,[37] was that they did not root predestination in the mediatorial work of Christ. It was as though Christ and his work were an afterthought. In both supralapsarianism and infralapsarianism, God decreed first which individuals would be elected and which would be reprobated. Only then did he decree to appoint Christ as mediator for the salvation of the elect. This is backward, Arminius argued. It "inverts the order of the gospel."[38] Instead, predestination must be grounded in Christ and "with respect to" his mediatorial work and the believer's union with him. In his *Examination of Perkins's Pamphlet*, Arminius argued that "God acknowledges no one for His own in Christ and on account of Christ, unless that same person be in Christ." Yet he argued that, in Calvinism, election is "without respect to Christ" and his mediatorial work. On the contrary, he said, Scripture "puts Christ as the foundation, not of the execution only, but also of the making of election itself."[39]

11

In his discussion of predestination in his *Declaration of Sentiments*, Arminius began by responding to the Calvinist doctrine that God has necessarily decreed certain people to eternal life and other people to eternal destruction "whom he was not viewing as already created or even as fallen," without reference to their belief or unbelief.[40] Arminius objected to (1) the view that God unconditionally decreed the fall, and (2) the view that God unconditionally decreed that certain people would be saved without regard to their belief and that He unconditionally decreed the rest would be damned without regard to their sin or unbelief. Arminius disagreed with supralapsarian Calvinism because he believed that it makes God the author of sin because God decrees that the fall of man must necessarily occur. He disagreed with both supralapsarian and infralapsarian Calvinism because he believed they remove election from its grounding in Christ's satisfaction of divine justice.[41]

In his *Declaration of Sentiments*, Arminius advanced an alternative schema of the divine decrees that upholds God's justice and righteousness and places Christ and the gospel at the center of predestination. First, Arminius argued, God decrees unconditionally to appoint Jesus Christ as "Mediator, Redeemer, Savior, Priest and King," who by His obedience and death obtains salvation. Second, God unconditionally decrees to save those who repent and believe in Christ but to leave impenitent unbelievers in sin and thus under divine wrath. Third, God unconditionally decrees to administer the means of salvation according to His wisdom and justice. Fourth, God unconditionally decrees "to save and to damn certain particular persons" according to His foreknowledge "through which God has known from all eternity those individuals who through the established means of his prevenient grace would come to faith and believe, and through his subsequent sustaining grace would persevere in the faith. Likewise, in divine foreknowledge, God knew those who would not believe and persevere."[42]

Thus Arminius taught *conditional, individual election* and *conditional, individual reprobation*. Those individuals whom God lovingly foreknew as believers, He elected as his own.[43] Those individuals whom He foreknew to be unbelievers, He reprobated.

Predestination, Foreknowledge, and Free Will

Arminius's views on predestination comport with a libertarian free will perspective on divine sovereignty and human freedom. Key to his approach was his distinction between necessity, contingency, and certainty. In his "Apology Against Thirty-One Defamatory Articles," he explained, "No contingent thing—that is, nothing which is done or has been done CONTINGENTLY—can be said to be or to have been done NECESSARILY, *with regard to the Divine decree.*"[44] Contingent things are things that did not have to turn out the way they in fact did. Necessary things are things that did have to turn out the way they in fact did. In God's universe, Arminius believes, there are necessities and contingencies, and for an act to be truly free, it has to be a contingency—it has to have been able to go one of two or more ways.[45]

Thus Arminius agreed with the idea that is now known (somewhat redundantly) as "libertarian freedom."[46] This is freedom, not from the power of sin or depravity, but from necessity. God has created His universe in such a way as to maintain creaturely freedom. Therefore, Arminius taught that the fall of man was contingent and not necessary. That is, God did not decree that Adam and Eve would fall by necessity. They fell as a result of their free choice to disobey God.

Arminius also distinguishes between events that are necessary and those that are "certain" or "infallible." While contingent events cannot be necessary, they can be certain. Arminius says,

> Because God, in virtue of His boundless knowledge, saw from eternity that man would fall at a certain time, hence the fall happened infallibly, in respect only of that foreknowledge, not in respect of any act of God's will, either affirmative or negative. For whatever happened infallibly in respect of God's will, the same happened also necessarily. . . . Hence it may be allowed to note briefly the difference between what comes to pass *infallibly*, and what *necessarily*: for the former is from the infinity of God's knowledge, the latter from the act of God's will: the former respects God's knowledge

13

alone, to which it appertains to know contingencies infallibly and certainly: the latter belongs to the very existence of the things: the necessity for which arose from God's will."[47]

Thus, Arminius believed that an action can be both contingent and certain, but not both contingent and necessary.[48] For the Calvinistic determinists of his day, God's foreknowledge was causal. Arminius replied that God foreknows all things that will come to pass; thus it is certain that they will come to pass. But this does not mean God made it so they must necessarily come to pass: "For a thing does not come to pass because it has been foreknown or foretold; but it is foreknown and foretold because it is yet (futura) to come to pass."[49] Some events have to be the way they are, because God foreordained them. Other events fall out a certain way but could have been another way. If free human actions had occurred in an alternative way because of free human choice, then God would have had foreknowledge of them instead.

Arminius would have disagreed with what has come to be known as "open theism," the idea that God does not have exhaustive foreknowledge of future free contingencies. The reason he would have opposed this notion is that he did not believe, like both open theists and classical Calvinists, that God's foreknowledge of future free contingencies causes them or makes them necessary.

Arminius's views also militate against a Molinist account of predestination, as presented, for example by recent scholars such as William Lane Craig and Kenneth Keathley.[50] While Arminius showed awareness of Luis de Molina's concept of middle knowledge, he did not utilize it in his doctrine of predestination. Arminius nowhere intimates that, in eternity past, God, knowing what everyone would do given certain circumstances, selected the possible world, from among all possible worlds, in which exactly what He desires to occur will occur, while at the same time human beings retain freedom. Instead, Arminius argued that God knew the future infallibly and certainty. Thus, He knew what everyone was freely going to do in the actual (not possible) world. This includes each individual's union with Christ through faith or rejection of Him through impenitence and unbelief.[51]

14

It is crucial to emphasize, as will be further discussed below, that Arminius believed human free will was freedom from necessity, not freedom from the bondage of sin. He said, if left to themselves, without divine grace, human beings will be completely sinful: "The will, indeed, is free, but not in respect of that act which cannot be either performed or omitted without supernatural grace."[52]

Predestination and Romans 9

Arminius responded to Calvinist exegetical arguments with his own *Analysis of the Ninth Chapter of St. Paul's Epistle to the Romans*. He taught that Paul's intent in Romans 9 was to show that believers are justified by faith alone, not to teach unconditional election and reprobation. Stephen M. Ashby is correct when he notes: "Arminius felt constrained by the text to address the redemptive-historical dilemma facing the Apostle Paul, rather than merely attaching himself to the commonly held interpretation of the Reformed divines."[53] Paul had been preaching that salvation comes through faith in Christ alone. This entailed that most Jews were not part of the covenant. Thus, the Jewish response Paul anticipates was that if God had rejected most of the Jews, God's word or covenant with Abraham was of no effect. According to Arminius, Paul's burden is to show that God's word still stands even if Jews who do not have faith in Christ are excluded, just as some descendants of Abraham have always been excluded.

For Arminius, the question of the text is not whether people are elected unconditionally but whether God's Word fails if Jews who seek righteousness by the law instead of by faith are excluded from the covenant. This is Paul's real question in Romans 9.[54] Arminius argued that Paul's point is that God's Word has not failed simply because some Jews have been excluded from the covenant, because Paul argues in verses 6 through 8 that not everyone who is physically an Israelite or child of Abraham is spiritually an Israelite or child of Abraham (vv. 6b-8).

Thus, Arminius interpreted Ishmael and Isaac, and Esau and Jacob, as types—the former in each pair represents children of the flesh, the latter children of the promise. Arminius quotes Galatians 4:21-31 to show that Paul himself sees these pairs as types or allegories: "the primary sense which God wished to signify . . . is not literal, but allegorical."[55] In that passage, Paul had contrasted Hagar and Sarah and Ishmael and Isaac, and then expressly stated that they were symbolic or allegorical (v. 24), and specified, "Now we, brethren, as Isaac was, are children of promise" (v. 28, NKJV). So Arminius concludes: "Isaac is reckoned in the seed: Isaac is the type of all the children of the promise: Therefore, all the children of the promise are reckoned in the seed. . . . Ishmael is not reckoned in the seed: Ishmael is the type of all the children of the flesh: Therefore none of the children of the flesh are reckoned in the seed."[56]

Ashby correctly states that, according to Arminius, "when man had failed in performing the demands of the Creation covenant, and indeed had 'by the fall incurred inability to perform it,' God transferred the condition of this covenant to faith in Christ."[57] God was, Arminius averred, "at liberty to fix in that [subsequent] covenant whatever conditions He might have thought fit. . . . It is free to Him to make a decree according to election, by which He may ordain to have mercy on the children of promise, but to harden and punish the children of the flesh.'"[58] Arminius was simply saying that God has mercy on the children of the promise (believers who seek righteousness through faith) and hardens and punishes the children of the flesh (unbelievers who seek righteousness by the works of the law) (vv. 31-32).

How did Arminius interpret the "vessels of wrath" and "vessels of mercy" in Romans 9? He said that God determined to make people vessels of mercy "who should perform the condition [of the covenant]" and vessels of wrath "those who should transgress it, and should not desist from transgressing." In essence, Arminius remarked, "God makes man a vessel: man makes himself a bad vessel, or sinner: God decrees to make man, according to conditions pleasing to Himself, a vessel of wrath or of mercy; which in fact He does, when the condition has been either fulfilled, or wilfully neglected."[59]

> God has the power of making men out of shapeless matter, and of enacting a decree about them, by the mere judgment and pleasure

of His will, ratified by certain conditions, according to which He makes some men vessels to dishonor, others vessels to honor: and that therefore man has no just ground of expostulation with God because He has made him to be hardened by His irresistible will; since obstinacy in sins intervenes between the determination of His will and the hardening itself; on account of which God wills, according to the same pleasure of His will, to harden man by His irresistible will. If any simply say that God has the power of making man a vessel to dishonor and wrath, he will do the greatest injustice to God, and will contradict clear Scripture."[60]

In other words, whom does God will to harden? Arminius believed God wills to harden those whom He foreknows will not meet the faith-condition of the covenant: the children of the flesh. On whom does God will to have mercy? Those whom He foreknows will meet the faith-condition of the covenant: the children of the promise.

Arminians and Calvinists alike have been fairly clear on Arminius's teaching on *how one comes to be* in a state of grace; Arminians agree, and Calvinists disagree. The primary misconceptions regarding Arminius have traditionally surrounded his understanding of *what it means to be* a sinner and *what it means to be* in a state of grace. An examination of Arminius's doctrines of original sin, human depravity and inability, and of the nature of atonement and justification reveal an agreement, not only with the Reformed confessions and catechisms, but also with the mainstream of Reformed thought in his day.

ARMINIUS AND ORIGINAL SIN

Arminius has usually been associated with semi-Pelagianism, and sometimes with outright Pelagianism. Most writers, both Arminian and Calvinist, have tended to dissociate Arminius's theology with that of Augustine. An investigation of Arminius's theological writings, however, reveals that he held to an Augustinian view of original sin that was within the bounds of Reformed confessional theology.

17

Before examining Arminius's writings, it will be beneficial to investigate his confessional beliefs. A look at the Heidelberg Catechism will reveal the Reformed hamartiology that characterized his theology. Questions seven, eight, and ten of the Catechism read thusly:

Q. 7. *Where, then, does this corruption of human nature come from?*
A. From the fall and disobedience of our first parents, Adam and Eve, in the Garden of Eden; whereby our human life is so poisoned that we are all conceived and born in the state of sin.

Q. 8. *But are we so perverted that we are altogether unable to do good and prone to do evil?*
A. Yes, unless we are born again through the Spirit of God.

Q. 10. *Will God let man get by with such disobedience and defection?*
A. Certainly not, for the wrath of God is revealed from heaven, both against our in-born sinfulness and our actual sins, and he will punish them accordingly in his righteous judgment in time and eternity, as he has declared: "Cursed be everyone who does not abide by all things written in the book of the Law, and do them."[61]

The Belgic Confession of Faith, in Article 15, "The Doctrine of Original Sin," says: "We believe that by the disobedience of Adam original sin has been spread through the whole human race. It is a corruption of all nature—an inherited depravity which even infects small infants in their mother's womb. . . . Therefore we reject the error of the Pelagians who say that this sin is nothing else than a matter of imitation."[62]

Thus, if Arminius was telling the truth when he stated his agreement with the confessional documents of his church, the doctrines of the Heidelberg Catechism and the Belgic Confession of Faith may rightly be said to have been Arminius's doctrine. These confessional statements provide the backdrop of his writings on the doctrine of original sin.

In his *Apology Against Thirty-One Theological Articles,* Arminius was arguing against teachings that certain individuals had ascribed to him or his colleagues, but which neither he nor they had ever taught. In the essays on Articles 13-14, Arminius was arguing against the condemnation of infants based on original sin. However, he stopped far short of a disavowal of original sin itself, rather attempting to defend his position on Reformed grounds. Arminius began the essay with a saying that had been attributed to Borrius, but which, Arminius argued, Borrius never said: "Original sin will condemn no man. In every nation, all infants who die without [having committed] actual sins, are saved."[63] Arminius proceeded to say that Borrius denied ever having taught either statement.[64] Arminius's primary aim here was to deny infant damnation. The doctrine of original sin and its imputation to the race was tangential to his argument. Yet he discussed the doctrine of original sin, and, while disagreeing with Augustine on infant damnation, he was thoroughly Augustinian on the doctrine of original sin, saying with Borrius that all infants "existed in Adam, and were by his will involved in sin and guilt."[65] Arminius argued that Francis Junius said the same thing Borrius said, that the infants of unbelievers may be saved only by "Christ and his intervention."[66]

Arminius discussed his views on original sin in a more systematic manner in his *Public Disputations,* explaining his doctrine of original sin in the passage entitled "The Effects of This Sin." It is clear here that Arminius was Augustinian. He said that the violation of the divine law results in two punishments: *reatus,* two deaths—one physical and one spiritual; and *privatio,* the withdrawal of man's primitive righteousness.[67] Arminius believed that Adam's sin caused physical death for the entire race and spiritual death for those who are not in Christ. His position on the effect of Adam's sin on the race was that "the whole of this sin . . . is not peculiar to our first parents, but is common to the entire race and to all their posterity, who, at the time when this sin was committed, were in their loins, and who have since descended from them by the natural mode of propogation."[68] According to Arminius, all sin in Adam and are guilty in Adam, apart from their own actual sins.

In the *Private Disputations*, Arminius echoed the sentiments of his *Public Disputations*. In Private Disputation 31, he stated, "All men who were to be propagated from [Adam and Eve] in a natural way, became obnoxious to death temporal and death eternal, and *(vacui)* devoid of this gift of the Holy Spirit or original righteousness."[69]

Statements such as these make it impossible to understand why so many interpreters have believed, like James W. Meeuwsen, that Arminius's view of original sin "shatters Adamic unity" and "implies that original sin is nothing more than a habit which was eventually acquired by man."[70] How can Arminius's clear affirmations cited above be reconciled with such statements? Arminius insisted that human beings deserve the punishment of God (eternal death) because of original sin and original guilt, not merely their own actual sin and their own actual guilt.[71] Meeuwsen went on to say that Arminius denied humanity is guilty because of Adam's sin.[72] But Arminius made it clear that he did not. When asked the question, "Is the guilt of original sin taken away from all and every one by the benefits of Christ?" Arminius said the question is "very easily answered by the distinction of the *soliciting, obtaining,* and the *application* of the benefits of Christ. For as the participation of Christ's benefits consists in faith alone, it follows that, if among these benefits 'deliverance from this guilt' be one, believers only are delivered from it, since they are those upon whom the wrath of God does not abide."[73] Furthermore, Arminius said to Francis Junius that God "imput[ed] the guilt of the first sin to all Adam's posterity, no less than to Adam himself and Eve, because they also had sinned in Adam."[74]

Arminius's treatment of original sin and guilt was clearly Reformed. Meeuwsen and other scholars too often read later theology into Arminius's thought, mistaking later Arminian theology for Arminius's. Only when this is done can Arminius be labeled as semi-Pelagian or Pelagian in his doctrine of sin. An objective examination of either Arminius's confessional beliefs or his writings shows that such allegations cannot be sustained.

ARMINIUS: *SOLA GRATIA AND SOLA FIDE*

With Arminius cleared from the charge of semi-Pelagianism with regard to original sin, it will be beneficial to examine what he believed about human inability in salvation and how he believed people may be rescued from this state. On the subjects of grace and faith, again, Arminius has been charged with holding semi-Pelagian and synergistic views that make God's foreknowledge of a person's merit the basis of redemption or that view individuals as sharing with God in their salvation. A brief look at Arminius's perspectives on grace, free will, and human inability, followed by an examination of Arminius's doctrine of justification, will reveal Arminius's loyalty to Reformed categories.

Human Inability

Arminius believed that people have no ability to seek God or turn to Him unless they are radically affected by His grace. It is commonly assumed that Arminius held a doctrine of free will that makes individuals totally able to choose God. However, Arminius's view of human freedom does not mean freedom to do anything good in the sight of God or to choose God on one's own. For Arminius, the basic freedom that characterizes the human will is freedom from necessity. Indeed, "it is the very essence of the will. Without it, the will would not be the will."[75] This has sounded to some like semi-Pelagianism. Yet, though Arminius averred that the human will is free from necessity, he stated unequivocally that the will is not free from sin and its dominion: "The Free Will of man towards the True Good is not only wounded, maimed, infirm, bent, and (*attenuatum*) weakened; but it is also (*captivatum*) imprisoned, destroyed, and lost: And its powers are not only debilitated and useless unless they be assisted by grace, but it has no powers whatever except such are excited by divine grace."[76]

Fallen humanity has no ability or power to reach out to God on its own. Arminius detailed "the utter weakness of all the powers to perform that which is truly good, and to omit the perpetration of that which is evil."[77] He argued at length that the whole person—mind, affections, and will—is completely sinful. One would be hard-pressed to find a more thorough definition of total depravity than what Arminius articulated. He stated that the human mind "is dark, destitute of the saving knowledge of God, and, according to the Apostle, incapable of those things which belong to the Spirit of God," having no perception of the things of God.[78] The affections and the heart are perverse, with a hatred and aversion to the true good and to what pleases God, and with a love for evil and the pursuit of it. In their deceitful, perverse, uncircumcised, hard, and stony hearts, unregenerate people have set themselves up as enemies of God.[79] The will has no power to perform the true good or keep from committing evil, because the unregenerate are slaves to the devil and under his power.[80] The entire life—mind, heart, and will—is submerged under sin and dead in sin.[81] These views led Moses Stuart to aver, "The most thorough advocate of total depravity will scarcely venture to go farther in regard to man in his unregenerate state, than . . . Arminius goes."[82]

Divine grace is the only power that can bring persons out of this state. Arminius was not a synergist; he did not believe individuals share with God in their salvation.[83] Human beings are saved by grace alone through faith alone. This excludes human merit of any kind. The faith that is the instrument of justification (not the meritorious cause or ground) could not be had without the grace of God. The grace of God alone gives individuals the power to come to Him.[84] Grace for Arminius was necessary and essential to salvation from start to finish. However, Arminius differed from Calvin and many Reformed theologians of his day by stating that this grace of God "which has appeared to all men" can be resisted. Arminius denied the distinction between a universal call and a special call. He insisted that the divine call is universal. However, the grace of God through this call can be and is resisted by individuals. Arminius said, "The whole of the controversy reduces itself to this question, 'Is the grace of God a certain irresistible force?'" He answered, "I believe that many persons resist the Holy Spirit and reject the grace that is offered."[85] Rather than an "irresistible force," grace, from Arminius's perspective, is a "gentle and sweet persuasion . . . not by almighty action or motion, which they neither will nor can resist, nor can will to resist."[86]

22

Key to Arminius's understanding of divine grace in salvation is that God desires the salvation of all people and provides atonement for every individual, not just for the elect. Arminius maintained against Perkins that "Christ stood in the stead of all men universally . . . and not in the stead of the elect only."[87] Arminius charged Perkins with confusing the obtaining of redemption with its application. Believers "were not redeemed" at the time Christ died, but "by those actions redemption was obtained, and then applied to them by faith, and so at length they were redeemed."[88] Arminius emphasized the importance of distinguishing "between redemption *obtained* and *applied*; and I affirm that it was *obtained* for all the world, and for all and every man; but *applied* to believers and the elect alone."[89]

Arminius's main argument for that assertion was that, unless God obtains redemption for all people, He cannot require faith in Christ from all people, nor can He blame people for "refusing the offer of redemption. For He refuses what cannot be His."[90] Thus, "if Christ has not obtained redemption for all, He cannot be the Judge of all."[91] For Arminius, this was the only way to explain the New Testament passages that indicate God's desire for all to be saved and come to the knowledge of the truth (1 Tim. 2:4). Arminius spends several pages responding to Perkins's explanation of the meaning of "all" in New Testament passages that teach God's desire for all to be saved. Arminius believed this is the clear teaching of Scripture, and he wondered how those who believe Christ died only for the elect can explain Scripture passages like 1 John 2:2; John 1:29; John 6:1; Romans 14:15; and 2 Peter 2:1, 3.[92]

Though Arminius differed from Calvin and the mainstream of Reformed theology on the particulars of grace, he still maintained that salvation is *sola gratia*. Arminius cannot be considered a semi-Pelagian or a synergist.[93] This fact is further attested in Arminius's doctrine of justification.

Justification by the Imputed Righteousness of Christ

Justification is another doctrine on which Arminius has been grossly misunderstood. As with the doctrines of original sin and grace, Arminius's doctrine of justification is usually interpreted through the lens of later Arminian theology.[94] Many Reformed writers have harshly criticized Arminian soteriology because, by and large, it has rested on the governmental theory of atonement as articulated by the Remonstrant theologian Hugo Grotius.[95] However, to read Arminius in light of Grotius is to misread Arminius.[96]

Arminius agreed with the Belgic Confession statement on justification. Article 22, after stating that justification is "by faith alone, or faith without works," says, "We do not mean that faith itself justifies us, for it is only an instrument with which we embrace Christ our Righteousness. But Jesus Christ, imputing to us all his merits, and so many holy works, which he hath done for us and in our stead, is our Righteousness."[97]

The Heidelberg Catechism states: "God wills that his righteousness be satisfied; therefore payment in full must be made to his righteousness, either by ourselves or by another." However, individuals cannot make this payment themselves. Only Jesus Christ, God incarnate, can make the payment for them. Thus, He pays the "debt of sin" and satisfies God's righteous requirements. Through saving faith, believers are "incorporated into [Christ] and accept all his benefits." They are in union with Christ, which means Christ bears their sins and they have the benefit of His righteousness.[98] The Catechism goes on to say, in question sixty, that "God, without any merit of my own, out of pure grace, grants me the benefits of the perfect expiation of Christ, imputing to me his righteousness and holiness as if I had never committed a single sin or had ever been sinful, having fulfilled myself all the obedience which Christ has carried out for me, if only I accept such favor with a trusting heart." Question sixty-one reads: "Why do you say that you are righteous by faith alone?" The answer is: "Not because I please God by virtue of the worthiness of my faith, but because the satisfaction, righteousness, and holiness of Christ alone are my righteousness before God, and because I can accept it and make it mine in no other way than by faith alone."[99] This is the same conception as that of the Belgic Confession. Arminius claimed to agree with both these documents, and, as will be seen, his writings are fully consonant with them.

Arminius's view of justification is summarized in his *Public Disputations.* There he said that justification is the act by which one, "being placed before the

24

throne of grace which is erected in Christ Jesus the Propitiation, is accounted and pronounced by God, the just and merciful Judge, righteous and worthy of the reward of righteousness, not in himself but in Christ, of grace, according to the Gospel, to the praise of the righteousness and grace of God, and to the salvation of the justified person himself."[100]

Justification for Arminius was forensic or imputative in nature. Arminius stated: "In his obedience and righteousness, Christ is also the Material Cause of our justification, so far as God bestows Christ on us for righteousness, and imputes his righteousness and obedience to us."[101] Arminius went as far as to say in his letter to Hippolytus à Collibus that God "reckons" Christ's righteousness "to have been performed for us."[102] In his *Declaration of Sentiments*, he averred: "I believe that sinners are accounted righteous solely by the obedience of Christ, and that the obedience and righteousness of Christ constitute the only meritorious cause through which God pardons the sins of believers and accounts them as righteous, as if they had perfectly fulfilled the law."[103]

Like the Reformed, Arminius believed that God must punish sin with eternal death unless one meets the requirement of total righteousness before Him. So he portrayed God as a judge who must sentence individuals to eternal death if they do not meet His requirements. In typical Reformed fashion, Arminius employed the analogy of "a judge making an estimate in his own mind of the deed and of the author of it, and according to that estimate forming a judgment and pronouncing sentence."[104] The sentence pronounced on the sinner who cannot meet the requirements of God's justice is eternal death. Yet, since no one has this righteousness, it must come from someone else. It can come only from Christ, who pays the penalty for sin on the cross—"the price of redemption for sins by suffering the punishment due to them."[105] When an individual exhibits saving faith, Arminius maintained, he comes into union with Christ; this union results in his being identified with Christ in His death and righteousness.[106] Hence, justification takes place when God as judge pronounces believers just or righteous because they have been imputed this righteousness of Christ, which is theirs through faith alone.

25

For Arminius, this emphasis on justice does not militate against God's mercy, as some later Arminians held. God never had to offer Christ for the redemption of humanity in the first place. If God had not made a way of satisfaction for His justice (through mercy), *then*, Arminius said, is when humanity would have truly been judged according to God's "severe and rigid estimation." Those who are under the law, according to Arminius, are judged in this severe and rigid way; those who are under grace, through faith, are graciously imputed the righteousness of Christ, which in turn justifies them before God the Judge.[107]

Arminius's enemies had charged him with teaching we are not justified by the imputation of Christ's righteousness, which is ours through faith, but it is our faith itself that justifies us. In the *Apology Against Thirty-One Defamatory Articles*, Arminius dealt with the statement his enemies had attributed to him: "The righteousness of Christ is not imputed to us for righteousness; but to believe (or the act of believing) justifies us."[108] Arminius's reply was that he never said the act of faith justifies a person. Arminius held that Christ's righteousness is imputed to the believer by gracious imputation *and* that our faith is imputed for righteousness. The reason he held both of these was because he believed they were both taught by St. Paul.

> I say that I acknowledge, "The righteousness of Christ is imputed to us;" because I think the same thing is contained in the following words of the Apostle, "God hath made Christ to be sin for us, that we might be made the righteousness of God in him." . . . It is said in the third verse [of Romans 4], "Abraham believed God, and it was imputed unto him for righteousness;" that is, *his believing* was thus imputed. Our brethren therefore do not reprehend ME, but the APOSTLE. . . . [109]

Arminius thought his foes were wrong to place the two concepts in opposition to one another, since Holy Scripture did not. He argued that faith is not the meritorious cause, the ground or basis, of justification, but rather the instrument *through which* one is imputed the merits of Christ.[110] Faith is necessary for Christ's righteousness to be imputed, and Arminius did not see a necessary opposition between the phrases "the righteousness of Christ imputed to us" and "faith imputed for righteousness."

Arminius's view of justification by grace through faith and the imputed righteousness of Christ is thoroughly Reformed and bears no influence of semi-Pelagianism or synergism. In another place, to clear himself of any misunderstanding, Arminius states his full agreement with what Calvin had said with regard to justification in his *Institutes.* Calvin wrote: "We are justified before God solely by the intercession of Christ's righteousness. This is equivalent to saying that man is not righteous in himself but because the righteousness of Christ is communicated to him by imputation. . . . You see that our righteousness is not in us but in Christ, that we possess it only because we are partakers in Christ; indeed, with him we possess all its riches."[111] This phrase is almost identical to many of Arminius's statements on justification in the *Public Disputations.*

CONCLUSION

An examination of Arminius's writings shows that his theology must be cleared of the charge of semi-Pelagianism, Pelagianism, and synergism. For Arminius, humanity is dead in trespasses and sin, is guilty before God, and can be saved only by grace alone, by the imputed righteousness of Christ alone, through faith alone.

This examination of Arminius's historical and theological context in the Reformed Church of his day, his loyalty to the Belgic Confession of Faith and the Heidelberg Catechism, his stated views of Calvin, and most importantly his writings has shown that Arminius's understanding of the nature of sin and salvation, rather than semi-Pelagian and synergistic, was broadly Reformed. Most interpreters of Arminius have viewed him in light of later Arminianism, most of which has tended toward a denial of the Reformed view of original sin and total depravity, and toward an espousal of synergism in the plan of salvation, the governmental view of atonement, and perfectionism.[112] It has been shown that it is irresponsible to read these later Arminian themes back into Arminius simply because his name is attached to the Arminian theological systems. A thorough analysis of Arminius's theology itself reveals that it was more a nuanced development of Reformed theology than a radical departure from it.[113]

[1]The best, most accessible source for becoming acquainted with Arminius's soteriology in the context of the Arminian-Calvinist debate is Robert E. Picirilli, *Grace, Faith, Free Will: Contrasting Views of Salvation—Calvinism and Arminianism* (Nashville: Randall House, 2002).

[2]Richard A. Muller, *God, Creation, and Providence in the Thought of Jacob Arminius* (Grand Rapids: Baker, 1991), 281.

[3]Bangs, "Arminius and the Reformation," *Church History* 30 (1961), 156. Muller resurrects this specter, seeming to leave Arminius's honesty open to question; see his "Arminius and the Reformed Tradition," *Westminster Theological Journal* 70 (2008), 41. Cf. Stephen M. Ashby, "Notes on Arminius" (unpublished notes).

[4]Roger Nicole, "The Debate over Divine Election," *Christianity Today*, October 21, 1959, 6.

[5]Carl Trueman, "Post-Reformation Developments in the Doctrine of the Atonement," in *The Precious Blood: The Atoning Work of Christ*, Richard D. Phillips, ed., (Wheaton: Crossway, 2009), 184; Trueman, *John Owen: Reformed Catholic, Renaissance Man* (Burlington: Ashgate, 2007), 26; David Dockery, *Southern Baptist Consensus and Renewal* (Nashville: B&H, 2008), 67; Alan F. Johnson and Robert Webber, *What Christians Believe* (Grand Rapids: Zondervan, 1993), 223-24; W. Robert Godfrey, review of *Jacob Arminius: Theologian of Grace* at Reformation21.com (*http://www.reformation21.org/shelf-life/jacob-arminius-theologian-of-grace.php*).

[6]Paul Enns, *The Moody Handbook of Theology* (Chicago: Moody, 2008), 323-24. Ralph Keen, in *The Christian Tradition* (Lanham: Rowman and Littlefield, 2008), says that Arminius believed "the human will is capable of doing good" and "the believer cooperated with grace" (234). See Olson, *Arminian Theology*, for more examples.

[7]Jacobus Arminius, *The Works of James Arminius*, 3 vols. Trans. James Nichols and William Nichols (Nashville: Randall House, 2007), 1:764. "Apology against Thirty-One Defamatory Articles" (this edition of Arminius's *Works* is hereafter cited as "Arminius, *Works*").

[8]Carl Bangs, "Arminius and Reformed Theology," Ph.D. diss., University of Chicago, 1958, 23. The best comparison and contrast of Arminius and the later Remonstrants (and one of the best treatments of Arminius I recommend) is Hicks, "The Theology of Grace in the Thought of Jacobus Arminius and Philip Van Limborch: A Study in the Development of Seventeenth-Century Dutch Arminianism," Ph.D. diss., Westminster Theological Seminary, 1985. This dissertation may be downloaded free from *http://evangelicalarminians.org/wp-content/uploads/2013/07/Hicks.-The-Theology-of-Grace-in-the-Thought-of-Arminius-and-Limborch.pdf*. See Hicks's briefer article, "The Righteousness of Saving Faith: Arminian versus Remonstrant

Grace," *Evangelical Journal* 9 (1991), 27-39. See also Mark A. Ellis, *Simon Episcopius' Doctrine of Original Sin* (New York: Peter Lang, 2006); and Sarah Mortimer, *Reason and Religion in the English Revolution* (Cambridge: Cambridge University Press, 2010). Mortimer is correct in saying that the Remonstrants "did not feel themselves bound to preserve Arminius's system in its entirety, and from the start they began to alter and reshape it" (26). In her important book, she ties Henry Hammond's Anglican Arminianism more to the Grotian strand of Remonstrantism and to Socinus, and not to Arminius, arguing that early Remonstrants Hugo Grotius and Simon Episcopius diverged radically from Arminius. See especially pp. 25-26, 119-25.

[9] Bangs, "Arminius and Reformed Theology," 14.

[10] Recent scholars have taken one of two broad positions on the soteriology of Jacobus Arminius. One group holds that his theology was a *development* of the Dutch Reformed theology of his day, while the other says that it was a radical *departure* from Reformed categories. Following Carl Bangs, scholars such as Hicks, Picirilli, Roger E. Olson, F. Stuart Clarke, William G. Witt, William den Boer, G. J. Hoerdendaal, Ellis, and Mortimer fall into the first category. Muller, Keith Stanglin, and Thomas McCall fall into the second. See Bangs, *Arminius: A Study in the Dutch Reformation* (Nashville: Abingdon, 1971); Bangs, "Arminius and the Reformation"; Bangs, "Arminius and Reformed Theology"; Hicks, "The Theology of Grace"; Picirilli, *Grace, Faith, Free Will*; Picirilli, "Arminius and the Deity of Christ," *Evangelical Quarterly* 70 (1998), 51-59; Roger E. Olson, *Arminian Theology: Myths and Realities* (Downers Grove: InterVarsity, 2006); William G. Witt, "Creation, Redemption, and Grace in the Theology of Jacobus Arminius," Ph.D. diss., University of Notre Dame, 1993; William den Boer, *God's Twofold Love: The Theology of Jacob Arminius (1559-1609)* (Gottingen: Vandenhoeck and Ruprecht, 2010); G. J. Hoerdendaal, "The Debate about Arminius outside the Netherlands," in *Leiden University in the 17th Century* (Leiden: Brill, 1975), 137-59; Mark A. Ellis, *Simon Episcopius*; Mortimer, *Reason and Religion in the English Revolution*; Muller, *God, Creation, and Providence*; Keith D. Stanglin, *Arminius and the Assurance of Salvation* (Leiden: Brill, 2007); Keith D. Stanglin and Thomas H. McCall, *Jacob Arminius: Theologian of Grace* (New York: Oxford University Press, 2012).

[11] *God's Twofold Love*, 43-44. Den Boer's perspective has much to commend itself over against the tendencies of Muller and colleagues to see Reformed theology as more of a monolith. Cf. Den Boer, "'Cum delectu': Jacob Arminius's Praise for and Critique of Calvin and His Theology," *Church History and Religious Culture* 91 (2011), 73-86. Cf. Wilhelm Pauck, who described Arminius's theology as an outgrowth of Reformed theology: "Indeed, there are many Calvinist theological traditions. The Reformed theologies of the Swiss, the German, the French, the Dutch, the Scotch, etc., are not so uniform as the theologies of the various Lutheran bodies are. The Arminians belong as definitely to the Calvinistic tradition as the defenders of the decisions of the Synod of Dort" (*The Heritage of the Reformation* [Boston: Beacon, 1950], 272. Quoted in Bangs, "Arminius and Reformed Theology," 25).

[12] Richard Muller and his students (e.g., Stanglin, McCall, and Raymond Blacketer) place more emphasis on Arminius's differences with Reformed orthodoxy than do most scholars. I disagree with them on this, yet in most respects they avoid the conventional stereotypes of Arminius characterized above. They are astute interpreters of Arminius and are more attentive to his historical and theological context than are most scholars (e.g., Stanglin's setting of

Arminius's thought in the context of that of his academic colleagues at Leiden). In particular, students of Arminius should be grateful to Muller (*God, Creation, and Providence*) for correcting the notion that Arminius was a humanist rather than a scholastic thinker. Arminius can be properly interpreted only in the context of the Reformed scholastic theology of his day. Muller has argued that Arminius's view of creation and providence and his intellectualism vs. voluntarism differ somewhat from Reformed Scholasticism. This is perhaps responsible for his divergent view of predestination. This observation, however, does not obscure the fact that there was no consensus on predestination, free will, etc., in the Dutch Reformed Church of Arminius's time. Nor does it detract from Arminius's inherently Reformed views on original sin, total depravity, human inability, the penal satisfaction nature of the atonement, or the imputative nature of justification. (See also Raymond Blacketer, "Arminius' Concept of Covenant in Its Historical Context," *Nederlands archief voor kerkgeschiedenis* 80 [2000], 193-220.)

[13]This brief summary information relies on Carl Bangs, *Arminius*. For two valuable shorter introductions to Arminius's life, but longer than this sketch, see Stephen M. Ashby, "Introduction" to *The Works of James Arminius* (Nashville; Randall House, 2007) and Robert E. Picirilli, "Arminius and the Calvinists," *Dimension* (Spring 1985), 7-15.

[14]Arminius, *Works*, 1:26.

[15]Caspar Brandt, *The Life of James Arminius, D.D.*, trans. John Guthrie (London: Ward and Company, 1854), 28.

[16]The references to the *Declaration of Sentiments* in this book are from the recent translation from the Dutch: W. Stephen Gunter, *Arminius and His Declaration of Sentiments: An Annotated Translation with Introduction and Theological Commentary* (Waco: Baylor University Press, 2012).

[17]He also was cautious in his statement regarding perseverance, insisting that he "never taught that a true believer either totally or finally falls away from the faith and perishes; but I do not deny that there are passages of Scripture that seem to indicate such" (Gunter, *Declaration of Sentiments*, Kindle locations 3292-3294; cf. Arminius, *Works*, 1:667; lit. "Ingenue tamen affirmo, nunquam me docuisse, quod vere credens aut *totaliter* aut finaliter a *fide deficiat, sicque pereat*," in Iacobi Arminii, *Opera Theologica* [Leiden: Godefridus Basson, 1629], 123). It is difficult, if not impossible, to decipher where Arminius comes down on perseverance. Scholars such as Picirilli, Olson, and Clarke seem to think Arminius was agnostic on the possibility of apostasy, while Stanglin thinks Arminius believed one could apostatize by committing sin and then regain salvation through penitence (see Stanglin, *Arminius and the Assurance of Salvation*, 133-39). Stephen M. Ashby and I have emphasized Arminius's statement that only when one declines from belief (and thus union with Christ) can one decline from salvation (see Pinson, "Introduction" and Ashby, "Reformed Arminianism," in Pinson, ed., *Four Views on Eternal Security* [Grand Rapids: Zondervan, 2002], 15, 137, 187). Arminius is so ambiguous on the subject that Reformed Arminians (who emphasize irremediable apostasy only by renouncing Christ through unbelief), conventional Arminians (who emphasize apostasy through sinning and regaining salvation through repentance), and once-saved, always-saved advocates all claim him as their own. I have almost given up on the possibility of ascertaining Arminius's position.

[18]The historical information in this section relies on Bangs, "Arminius and the Reformation," 155-160.

[19]These misconceptions arise from the Peter Bertius's funeral oration for Arminius and Caspar Brandt's *Life of James Arminius*.

[20]Ibid., 156.

[21]Ibid.

[22]See Bangs, *Arminius*, 141-42.

[23]Bangs, "Arminius and the Reformation," 157.

[24]Ibid., 158.

[25]Ibid.

[26]Ibid., 159.

[27]Koolhaes taught at the University of Leiden while Arminius was a student there. The first rigid predestinarian did not teach at the University until the arrival of Lambert Daneau.

[28]Bangs, "Arminius and the Reformation," 160.

[29]Carl Bangs, "Arminius as a Reformed Theologian," in *The Heritage of John Calvin*, ed. John H. Bratt (Grand Rapids: Eerdmans, 1973), 216.

[30]Arminius, *Works*, 2:690. "Letter to Hippolytus à Collibus."

[31]Gunter, *Declaration of Sentiments*, Kindle locations 2324-2325; cf. Arminius, *Works*, 1:600.

[32]Quoted in Bangs, "Arminius as a Reformed Theologian," 216.

[33]Gunter, *Declaration of Sentiments*, Kindle locations 3437-3440; cf. Arminius, *Works*, 1:700. Arminius's doctrine of justification will be dealt with later in this essay.

[34]Picirilli, *Grace, Faith, Free Will*, 45.

[35]The Christocentricity of election is the theme of Clarke's book, *The Ground of Election*, while the centrality of divine justice is the theme of den Boer's book, which is entitled *God's Twofold Love*, with reference to, first, God's love for His justice, and second, God's love for people.

[36]Den Boer, *God's Twofold Love*, 120.

[37]Supralapsarians said that God had decreed the fall ("lapse"), while infralapsarians said that He had not. But both held that God had unconditionally decreed the election of individuals without regard to their status as believers.

[38]Gunter, *Declaration of Sentiments*, Kindle location 2908; cf. Arminius, *Works*, 1:632.

[39]Arminius, *Works,* 3:296, 303. "Examination of Perkins's Pamphlet."

[40]Gunter, *Declaration of Sentiments*, Kindle location 2537; cf. Arminius, *Works*, 1:614.

[41]Cf. Arminius, *Works*, 2:698-700. "Letter to Hippolytus à Collibus."

[42]Gunter, *Declaration of Sentiments*, Kindle locations 3168-3170; cf. Arminius, *Works*, 1:653-54.

[43]For more on Arminius's view of God's foreknowledge of the elect, not only as prescience but as intimate foreknowledge, see Picirilli, *Grace, Faith, Free Will*, 56.

[44]Arminius, *Works*, 1:755. "Apology against Thirty-One Defamatory Articles."

[45]See esp. Articles 5 and 6 of Arminius's "Apology against Thirty-One Defamatory Articles," ibid., 750-60.

[46]The reason for the redundancy of the phrase "libertarian freedom" is probably to distinguish it from the soft-deterministic notion called "compatibilism." Compatibilism holds that divine determinism and human freedom are compatible. Yet, libertarians insist, the only way

compatibilists can make divine determinism and human freedom compatible is to redefine free will to mean, not *the ability to have chosen otherwise*, but rather *the ability to do what one wants to do*. In other words, Arminians believe that freedom is, by definition, the ability to have done something other than what one did in fact do. Compatibilists do not believe individuals have such freedom. So they have to redefine freedom as the quality of not being coerced (or at least, the Arminian would respond, not *feeling as though* one has been coerced)—the ability to do what one wants to do. So compatibilists simply believe that God, through regeneration prior to faith, determines that the will of the elect will *want to* desire God.

[47]Arminius, *Works*, 3:179-80. "Friendly Conference with Francis Junius."

[48]For more on this, see Picirilli, *Grace, Faith, Free Will*, 35-63; and Picirilli, "Foreknowledge, Freedom, and the Future," *Journal of the Evangelical Theological Society* 43 (2000), 259-71.

[49]Arminius, *Works*, 2:368. Private Disputation 18, "On the Providence of God."

[50]See, e.g., Craig, *The Only Wise God: The Compatibility of Divine Foreknowledge and Human Freedom* (Eugene: Wipf and Stock, 2000) and Kenneth Keathley, *Salvation and Sovereignty: A Molinist Approach* (Nashville: B&H Academic, 2010).

[51]Scholars such as Picirilli, Olson, Clarke, Witt, and more recently Hendrik Frandsen properly interpret Arminius on this point, while scholars such as Eef Dekker, Muller, Stanglin, and (to a lesser degree) den Boer read too much Molinism into Arminius. The most that can be said is that Arminius toyed with the concept of middle knowledge but was ambiguous on it and did not actually articulate a Molinist doctrine of predestination. See Dekker, "Was Arminius a Molinist?" *Sixteenth Century Journal* 27 (1996), 337-52; Hendrik Frandsen, *Hemmingius in the Same World as Perkinsius and Arminius* (Praestoe, Denmark: Grafik Werk, 2013), cited by Olson (*http://www.patheos.com/blogs/rogereolson/2014/05/something-for-arminius-geeks/#ixzz32q65yuR6*). Cf. Olson's insightful comments in his blog post, "Are Arminianism and Middle Knowledge Compatible?" (*http://www.patheos.com/blogs/rogereolson/2013/09/are-arminian-theology-and-middle-knowledge-compatible/*).

[52]Arminius, *Works*, 3:178. "Friendly Conference with Francis Junius."

[53]Ashby, "Introduction" to Arminius's *Works*, xix.

[54]Ibid., xix-xx. For a contemporary Arminian treatment of Romans 9 that builds and improves on Arminius, see Forlines, *Classical Arminianism: A Theology of Salvation* (Nashville: Randall House, 2011), Chapter Three.

[55]Arminius, *Works*, 3:490. "Analysis of the Ninth Chapter of St. Paul's Epistle to the Romans."

[56]Ibid., 3:491.

[57]Ashby, xxi, quoting Arminius, *Works*, 3:497.

[58]Arminius, *Works*, 3:502.

[59]Ibid., 3:513.

[60]Ibid., 3:514.

[61]*The Constitution of the Presbyterian Church (U.S.A.), Part I: Book of Confessions* (New York: The General Assembly of the Presbyterian Church [U.S.A.], 1983), 4.005-.012.

[62]*Ecumenical Creeds and Reformed Confessions* (Grand Rapids: CRC Publications, 1987), 91.

[63]Arminius, *Works*, 2:10.

[64]Ibid., 2:11.

[65]Ibid., 2:12.

[66]Ibid., 2:14.

[67]Ibid., 2:156. Public Disputation 7, "On the First Sin of the First Man."

[68]Ibid. It may be inferred from this statement that Arminius would accept (in the terminology of later Protestant Scholastic theology) a "natural headship" view of the transmission of sin, rather than a "federal headship" view. Rather than Adam being "federally" appointed as head of the race, he was naturally the head of the race, and individuals are sinful as a natural consequence of their being "in Adam" or in the race.

[69]Ibid., 2:375. Private Disputation 31, "On the Effects of the Sin of Our First Parents."

[70]See James W. Meeuwsen, "Original Arminianism and Methodistic Arminianism Compared," *Reformed Review* 14 (1960), 22. Meeuwsen relied heavily on Presbyterian theologian William G. T. Shedd (*A History of Christian Doctrine* [New York: Scribner's, 1867], who wrongly read Arminius through the lens of the works of Episcopius and other Remonstrant theologians, whose theology differed significantly from that of Arminius. At one point, Meeuwsen said: "Arminius and his followers held that the imputation of actual guilt was entirely contrary to the justice and equity of God. Shedd fully agreed with such an interpretation when he paraphrased their beliefs in this way: 'Imputation is contrary to divine benevolence, right reason, in fact it is absurd and cruel'" (23). Meeuwsen then went on to quote Episcopius for about half a page.

[71]Arminius, *Works*, 2:374. Private Disputation 31, "On the Effects of the Sin of Our First Parents."

[72]Meeuwsen, 23.

[73]Arminius, *Works*, 2:65, "Nine Questions."

[74]Ibid., 3:224. "Friendly Conference with Junius."

[75]Bangs, *Arminius*, 341.

[76]Arminius, *Works*, 2:192. Public Disputation 11, "On the Free Will of Man and Its Powers."

[77]Ibid., 2:193.

[78]Ibid., 2:192.

[79]Ibid., 2:193.

[80]Ibid., 2:193-94.

[81]Ibid., 2:194. Cf. 2:700, "Letter to Hippolytus à Collibus."

[82]Moses Stuart, "The Creed of Arminius," *Biblical Repository* 1 (1831), 271. Stuart said Arminius went even further than most of the "orthodox" theologians of Stuart's own day. Cf. Hicks, "Theology of Grace," 22. Charles Hodge said similar things; see his *Systematic Theology* (New York: Charles Scribner's Sons, 1888), 3:187.

[83]Bangs boldly states, "Arminius was a monergist" ("Arminius and Reformed Theology," 166). Some scholars, such as Stanglin, McCall, and Olson, prefer to think of Arminius as a synergist, whereas scholars such as Bangs, Picirilli, den Boer, Ellis, and Arthur Skevington Wood do not. I agree with the latter approach. Arminius would not have been comfortable with the term "synergist" or the idea of humans cooperating or working together with God in any way

in their salvation. I would say of Arminius what Gregory Graybill says of Martin Luther's associate Phillip Melanchthon in his recent monograph, *Evangelical Free Will* (Oxford: Oxford University Press, 2010). Conversion for Melanchthon, Graybill insists, "was a passive *reception* of merit rather than an active cooperative work that earned merit. It was *not* synergism!" Graybill distinguishes Melanchthon's view from that of Peter Lombard, which "required God and the human working together in synergism" (297). Just as it is unfair for Lutheran theologians to attribute a term to Melanchthon that was readily associated with his later followers, it is unfair to saddle Arminius with a term that he did not employ and that was foreign to his theological context. This perspective concurs with what Muller said in an earlier work: "It is difficult to label [Arminius's approach] synergism" (Muller, "The Priority of the Intellect in the Soteriology of Jacobus Arminius," *Westminster Theological Journal* 55 [1993], 70. In a more recent article, however, Muller characterizes Arminius as a synergist: "Arminius and the Reformed Tradition," 29). See Stanglin and McCall, *Jacob Arminius*, 152; Olson, "Was Arminius an Arminian?" (http://www.patheos.com/blogs/rogereolson/2013/11/was-arminius-an-arminian-report-on-a-vigorous-discussion/); Picirilli, *Grace, Faith, Free Will*; den Boer, *God's Twofold Love,* 191; and den Boer, "Cum delectu," 83-84; Ellis, *Simon Episcopius*, 84; Wood, "The Declaration of Sentiments: The Theological Testament of Arminius," *Evangelical Quarterly* 65 (1993), 111-29.

[84]Arminius, *Works*, 2:194-95. Public Disputation 11, "On the Free Will of Man and Its Powers."

[85]Quoted in Bangs, *Arminius: A Study in the Dutch Reformation,* 343.

[86]Arminius, *Works*, 3:443. "Examination of Perkins's Pamphlet." Cf. Forlines's juxtaposition of "influence and response" and "cause and effect" in *Classical Arminianism*, 49-61.

[87]Ibid., 3:332. "Examination of Perkins's Pamphlet."

[88]Ibid., 3:333.

[89]Ibid., 3:425.

[90]Ibid.

[91]Ibid., 3:426.

[92]Ibid., 2:9-10. "Apology against Thirty-One Defamatory Articles."

[93]Rather than being a synergist, Arminius would have been more in line with recent theologians who prefer terms like "conditional monergism" (Forlines) or "monergism with resistible grace" (e.g., Keathley, Jeremy Evans, and Richard Cross). See Forlines, *Classical Arminianism*, 264, 297; Cross, "Anti-Pelagianism and the Resistibility of Grace," *Faith and Philosophy* 22 (2005), 199-210; Keathley, 88, 103-08; Evans, "Reflections on Determinism and Human Freedom," in *Whosoever Will: A Biblical-Theological Critique of Five-Point Calvinism* (Nashville: B&H Academic, 2010), 253-74; cf. Kevin Timpe, "Grace and Controlling What We Do Not Cause," *Faith and Philosophy* 24 (2007), 284-99.

[94]See, e.g., Meeuwsen, 27-28. The best treatments of this and the general graciousness of Arminius's theology (and two of the works I most highly recommend be read about Arminius's theology) are John Mark Hicks's dissertation, "Theology of Grace" and article "Righteousness of Saving Faith."

[95]Ibid.

[96]See the above-cited works by Hicks and Ellis.

[97]*Reformed Confessions of the Sixteenth Century*, ed. Arthur C. Cochrane (Philadelphia: Westminster Press, 1966), 204.

[98]*Ibid.,* 307-308, 311-312.

[99]Ibid., 315.

[100]Arminius, *Works*, 2:256. Public Disputation 19, "On the Justification of Man before God."

[101]Ibid., 2:406. Private Disputation 48, "On Justification."

[102]Ibid., 2:702. "Letter to Hippolytus à Collibus."

[103]Gunter, *Declaration of Sentiments*, Kindle location 3433-3435; cf. Arminius, *Works*, 1:700.

[104]Arminius, *Works*, 2:253. Public Disputation 19, "On the Justification of Man Before God."

[105]Ibid., 1:419. Oration IV, "The Priesthood of Christ." For more on Arminius's doctrine of the nature of atonement, see Chapter Two.

[106]Ibid., 2:403-404. Private Disputation 41, "On the Communion of Believers with Christ, and Particularly with His Death."

[107]Ibid., 2:256-57, Public Disputation 19, "On the Justification of Man before God," and 2:406, Private Disputation 48, "On Justification." A few scholars have attempted to make the case that Arminius's doctrine of imputation focused exclusively on the passive obedience of Christ. This is an overstatement. The reality is that the doctrine of the imputation of the active and passive obedience of Christ did not become the consensus of the Reformed community until long after Arminius's death. Arminius never denied the doctrine of the imputation of the active obedience of Christ, which is implied by other statements he made. The seventeenth-century English General Baptist Thomas Grantham (like later Free Will Baptist scholars such as Forlines and Picirilli) was unequivocal in his confession of the imputation of the active obedience of Christ. Calvinists and Reformed Arminians alike might wish there was more of a consensus among the early Reformed divines on the imputation of the active obedience of Christ. But, alas, there was not. Though Arminius believed that Christ's fulfillment of the law in his life of obedience is one of the benefits received by the believer via union with Christ, he wanted to stay out of the controversy in the French Reformed Church surrounding Piscator, who denied outright the active obedience of Christ. Arminius said, "I never durst mingle myself with the dispute, or undertake to decide it; for I thought it possible for the Professors of the same religion to hold different opinions on this point from others of their brethren, without any breach of Christian peace or the unity of faith." This is essentially the same position taken by the Westminster Assembly and the Synod of Dort, as well as the framers of the Belgic Confession, Heidelberg Catechism, and Thirty-Nine Articles of the Church of England. All these people and confessional documents did not "undertake to decide" this controversy, because so many early Reformers did not articulate the imputation of the active obedience of Christ with the clarity of the later Reformed consensus. See Alex F. Mitchell, *The Westminster Assembly: Its History and Standards* (London: James Nisbet & Co., 1883); William Barker, *Puritan Profiles: 54 Contemporaries at the Westminster Assembly* (Christian Focus, 2000); R. W. Landis, "What Were the Views Entertained by the Early Reformers, on the Doctrines of Justification, Faith, and the Active Obedience of Christ?" *The American Biblical Repository* 11 (1838): 31:179-97, 32:420-57; and Robert A. Letham, *The Westminster Assembly: Reading Its Theology in Historical Context* (Phillipsburg: P&R, 2009). Interestingly, the Reformed theologian J. V. Fesko argues that

Arminius's theology entails the imputation of both the active and passive obedience of Christ; see his *Beyond Calvin: Union with Christ and Justification in Early Modern Reformed Theology (1517-1700)* (Göttingen: Vandenhoek and Ruprecht, 2012), 277, 282.

[108] Arminius, *Works*, 2:42. "Nine Articles."

[109] Ibid., 2:43-45.

[110] Ibid., 2:49-51.

[111] *Institutes*, 3.11.23.

[112] With regard to perfectionism, Arminius said in his *Declaration of Sentiments* that he "never actually stated that a believer could perfectly keep the precepts of Christ in this life." Nor did he deny it. He left it as an open question, contenting himself with the sentiments of Augustine. In short, Arminius believed that, through grace, perfection was a logical possibility but that an individual who had attained it had never yet been found! (Gunter, *Declaration of Sentiments*, Kindle locations 3313-3314; cf. Arminius, *Works*, 1:677-78).

[113] I am grateful to the editors of *Integrity: A Journal of Christian Thought* for their permission to adapt, for this chapter, portions of a previous article entitled "Will The Real Arminius Please Stand Up? A Study of the Theology of Jacobus Arminius in Light of His Interpreters," *Integrity: A Journal of Christian Thought* 2 (2003), 121-39.

2

THE NATURE OF ATONEMENT IN THE THEOLOGY OF JACOBUS ARMINIUS

Jacobus Arminius is one of the best known and least studied theologians in the history of Christianity. His writings have been neglected by Calvinists and Arminians alike. Calvinists have disliked him because of his opposition to scholastic predestinarian theology. Most Arminians have neglected him because what little they have read of him reminds them more of Calvinism than they like. Arminius scholar Carl Bangs is correct when he says that most modern treatments of Arminius assume a definition of Arminianism that does not come from Arminius. Bangs states that most interpreters of Arminianism "begin with a preconception of what Arminius should be expected to say, then look in his published works, and do not find exactly what they are looking for. They show impatience and disappointment with his Calvinism, and shift the inquiry into some later period when Arminianism turns out to be what they are looking for—a non-Calvinistic, synergistic, and perhaps semi-Pelagian system."[1]

This is the approach many scholars have taken toward Arminius regarding his doctrine of atonement. For example, the Calvinist scholar Robert L. Reymond has said that the Arminian theory of atonement is the governmental

37

theory, which "denies that Christ's death was intended to pay the penalty for sin." He claims that the roots of the governmental theory lie in Arminius, who Reymond implies did not believe that Christ's death paid the penalty for sin.[2] Similarly, well-known Wesleyan-Arminian scholar James K. Grider states: "A spillover from Calvinism into Arminianism has occurred in recent decades. Thus many Arminians whose theology is not very precise say that Christ paid the penalty for our sins. Yet such a view is foreign to Arminianism."[3]

Recent scholars have taken one of two positions on the soteriology of Jacobus Arminius. One group says his theology was a development of the Dutch Reformed theology of his day, while the other says it was a departure from those Reformed categories. Scholars such as Carl Bangs fall into the first category, while scholars such as Richard Muller fit the second.[4]

This chapter is representative of the first perspective.[5] It argues that Arminius's concept of the nature of atonement was consistent with the theology of atonement that characterized Reformed theology in the seventeenth century.[6] This conclusion is not surprising, given Arminius's description of himself as a Reformed theologian and his repeated affirmation of the Belgic Confession of Faith and Heidelberg Catechism. He made this clear in a letter to the Palatine Ambassador, Hippolytus à Collibus, in 1608: "I confidently declare that I have never taught anything, either in the church or in the university, which contravenes the sacred writings that ought to be with us the sole rule of thinking and of speaking, or which is opposed to the Belgic Confession or to the Heidelberg Catechism, that are our stricter formularies of consent."[7] Given the dearth of scholarship on Arminius's theology of atonement[8] and the current debates on the nature of atonement in the evangelical community,[9] an understanding of Arminius's doctrine of atonement provides fresh and valuable insight.[10]

THE THREEFOLD OFFICE OF CHRIST

Arminius rooted his doctrine of atonement in the priesthood of Christ. The threefold office of Christ as prophet, priest, and king was a popular motif in Reformed theology both on the continent and in the British Isles. A classic expression of the threefold office is found in the Westminster Shorter Catechism, which reads:

Q. 23. *What offices doth Christ execute as our Redeemer?*
A. Christ, as our Redeemer, executeth the offices of a prophet, of a priest, and of a king, both in his estate of humiliation and exaltation.

Q. 24. *How doth Christ execute the office of a prophet?*
A. Christ executeth the office of a prophet in revealing to us, by his Word and Spirit, the will of God for our salvation.

Q. 25. *How doth Christ execute the office of a priest?*
A. Christ executeth the office of a priest in his once offering up of himself as a sacrifice to satisfy divine justice, and reconcile us to God, and in making continual intercession for us.

Q. 26. *How doth Christ execute the office of a king?*
A. Christ executeth the office of a king in subduing us to himself, in ruling and defending us, and in restraining and conquering all his and our enemies.[11]

The Belgic Confession of Faith, to which Arminius himself subscribed, goes into greater detail on the priestly office of Christ in Article 21, "The Satisfaction of Christ, Our Only High Priest, for Us":

We believe that Jesus Christ is ordained with an oath to be an everlasting High Priest, after the order of Melchizedek; and that He has presented Himself in our behalf before the Father, to appease His wrath by His full satisfaction, by offering Himself on the tree of the cross, and pouring out His precious blood to purge away our sins, as the prophets had foretold. For it is written: *He was wounded for our transgressions, he was bruised for our iniquities; the chastisement*

39

of our peace was upon him; and with his stripes we are healed. He was led as a lamb to the slaughter, and numbered with the transgressors; and condemned by Pontius Pilate as a malefactor, though he had first declared Him innocent. Therefore, *He restored that which he took not away, and suffered, the righteous for the unrighteous*, as well in His body as in His soul, feeling the terrible punishment which our sins had merited; insomuch that *his sweat became as it were great drops of blood falling down upon the ground*. He called out: *My God, my God, why hast thou forsaken me?* and has suffered all this for the remission of our sins.[12]

These two Reformed confessional statements summarize Arminius's essential views on the threefold office of Christ as prophet, priest, and king. The priestly office of Christ provides the theological framework for Arminius's doctrine of atonement.

THE PRIESTHOOD OF CHRIST

Arminius, like all Reformed theologians of his time, believed that sin demands atonement for individuals to be reconciled to God.[13] He argued from the Letter to the Hebrews that Christ is the only possible priest or mediator between sinful humanity and a holy God. In his priestly office, Christ exercises two "sacerdotal functions."[14] The first of these functions is "oblation"—the offering or sacrifice of Himself to God as the perfect "expiation" or "propitiation" for the sins of humanity, and the acquisition of righteousness and eternal life for the faithful.[15] The second of these functions is intercession, whereby Christ intercedes presently to the Father in heaven for the sins of His people.[16]

In His exercise of these priestly functions, Christ the Messiah is both priest and victim. "For 'He offered himself,' (Heb. ix, 14) and 'by his own blood has entered into heaven,'" (ix, 12,) and all this as it is an expiatory Priesthood."[17] Christ as priest exercises His office by fulfilling the law in complete obedience to His Father in His life and death. Christ "could not perform" His priestly duties "except through true and (*solidam*) substantial obedience towards God who imposed the office on Him."[18] Christ the Priest "was prepared by vocation or the imposition of the office, by the sanctification and consecration of his person through the Holy Spirit, and through his obedience and sufferings, and even in some respects by his resuscitation from the dead."[19] Christ the victim "was also prepared by separation, by obedience (for it was necessary that the victim should likewise be holy,) and by being slain."[20]

One of Arminius's chief concerns in discussing the priesthood of Christ was who qualifies as the priest to offer this expiatory sacrifice. In a manner reminiscent of Anselm in *Cur Deus Homo*, Arminius asked the question who is qualified to fulfill this sacerdotal function. He argued that this person must be both priest and sacrifice, but "in the different orders of creatures neither sacrifice nor priest could be found."[21] An angel could not qualify as a priest, because priests were to be representatives of humanity (Heb. 5:1), and the death of an angel could never serve as expiation for human sin. A human being "could not be found" to fulfill the priestly office, because human beings were sinners held captive under the "tyranny of sin and Satan."[22] Because of this sinfulness, Arminius held, humans cannot approach God, "who is pure light," to make a sacrifice.[23] Still, however, "the priest was to be taken from among men, and the oblation to God was to consist of a human victim."[24] The divine wisdom determined that a human was required who had humanity in common with "his brethren," being "in all things tempted as they were" and thus "able to sympathize" with them in their sufferings.[25] Yet this individual could not be under sin's dominion. Arminius cited Hebrews 7:26, which speaks of Jesus's being "born in the likeness of sinful flesh, and yet without sin. For such a high priest became us, who is holy, harmless, undefiled, and separate from sinners."[26] For such a state of affairs to obtain, such a person must be conceived by the Holy Spirit. Moral purity, Arminius maintained, is only one qualification of this cosmic priest. The priest must be divine: "Therefore the Word of God, who from the beginning was with God, and by whom the worlds, and all things visible and invisible, were created, ought himself to be made flesh, to undertake the office of the priesthood, and to offer his own flesh to God as a sacrifice for the life of the world."[27]

41

In this same oration, *On the Priesthood of Christ*, Arminius explained what he meant by "expiatory sacrifice" in his discussion of Christ's priestly oblation of an expiatory or propitiatory sacrifice. The "immolation or sacrifice of the body of Christ" consists of the shedding of His blood on the priestly "altar of the cross" and subsequently dying.[28] In this sacrifice, Arminius explained, Christ "pa[id] the price of redemption for sins by suffering the punishment due to them."[29]

JUSTICE

To understand Arminius's doctrine of atonement as it relates to the priesthood of Christ, one must delve more deeply into his view of divine justice. Only then can one grasp the need for the mediation of Christ as priest and the nature of that priesthood. In his oration *On the Priesthood of Christ*, Arminius personified justice, mercy, and wisdom, explaining the role of each in the divine decision to impose the office of priest. On one hand, "Justice," he explained, "demanded, on her part, the punishment due to her from a sinful creature," and rigidly enforced this judgment.[30] Mercy, on the other hand, "like a pious mother, moving with bowels of commiseration," wanted to turn aside the punishment that Justice demanded.[31] Yet Justice, "tenacious to her purpose," countered that "she could not bear with patient indifference that no regard should be paid to her" and that "the authority of managing the whole affair was to be transferred to mercy."[32] Yet she agreed that, if there could be a way in which her "inflexibility" and "the excess of her hatred of sin" could be acknowledged, she would yield to Mercy.[33]

Arminius explained that ascertaining such a method was not the province of Mercy but of Wisdom, who devised a plan that would please both Justice and Mercy. This method was "expiatory sacrifice" or "voluntary suffering of death."[34] Such a sacrifice, Wisdom concluded, would "appease Justice" yet "open such a way for Mercy as she has desired."[35] Thus, according to Arminius's anecdote, both Justice and Mercy assented to Wisdom's terms.

Arminius repeated this juxtaposition of justice and mercy throughout his writings, explaining how divine salvific grace is an exhibition of both without sacrificing the demands of either. In his disputation, "On the Offices of Our Lord Jesus Christ," he argued that God's love is "two-fold": a love for the creature and a love for justice.[36] God's love for the creature expresses itself in His desire to save sinners. His love for justice expresses itself in "a hatred against sin."[37] Similar to his discussion of divine wisdom finding a way to meet the demands of both justice and mercy, Arminius stated that it "was the will of God that each of these kinds of love should be satisfied."[38] Thus, God

> gave satisfaction to his Love for the creature who was a sinner, when He gave up his Son who might act the part of Mediator. But He rendered satisfaction to his Love for Justice and to his Hatred against sin, when He imposed on his Son the office of Mediator by the shedding of his blood and by the suffering of death; (Heb. ii. 10; v, 8, 9;) and He was unwilling to admit Him as the Intercessor for sinners except when sprinkled with his own blood, in which He might be made the propitiation for sins. (ix, 12.).[39]

Thus, God satisfies His love for the creature by forgiving sins, while at the same time satisfying His love for justice by inflicting the punishment for sin ("inflicting stripes") on His Son.[40] Arminius stated: "It was not the effect of those stripes, that God might love his creature, but that, while his Love for Justice presented no hindrance, through his Love for the creature He could remit sins and bestow life eternal."[41] In this satisfaction of God's love for the creature and for His own justice, Arminius explained, God "rendered satisfaction to himself, and appeased himself 'in the Son of his love.'"[42]

In his Private Disputation 33, "On the Restoration of Man," Arminius underscored the importance of the divine justice being satisfied in the salvation of sinners: "But it has pleased God not to exercise this mercy in restoring man, without the declaration of his justice, by which He loves righteousness and hates sin." Thus, Arminius said, God has appointed a mediator to intervene between Himself and sinful humanity. This mediation "should be so performed as to make it certain and evident, that God hates sin and loves righteousness, and that it is his will to remit nothing of his own right except after his justice has been satisfied."[43]

In his "Reply" to the Calvinist Francis Junius, Arminius argues that God's justice can be upheld only if either the sinner is punished or a divine-human mediator is punished in the sinner's place. The latter is the more noble way, the way of the gospel rather than of the law.

> God's justice can be declared by the exaction of punishment from those who have sinned: the same justice can also be declared by the exaction of the same punishment from Him who has offered Himself according to God's will as bail and surety for sinners. [He cites 2 Cor. 5:21, "He hath made Him (to be) sin for us, who knew no sin."] This way is more excellent and more noble than the other: for thereby it is more clearly manifested how greatly God abhors sin. . . .[44]

God's justice, as exhibited in either the legal way of punishing the sinner, or the evangelical way of punishing Christ in the sinner's place, is inflexible and rigorous. Thus, individuals can receive eternal life only when God "impose[s] upon His son the punishment due from sinners, and taken away from them, to be borne and paid in full by Him."[45] In this way, Arminius explained, "the rigour of inflexible justice was declared, which could not pardon sin, even to the interceding Son, except the penalty were fully paid. . . ."[46]

Arminius's emphasis on the importance of God's maintaining His love for His own justice is borne out strongly in an interesting passage from his *Declaration of Sentiments*. Arminius was arguing against the Calvinistic idea of election to faith rather than in view of faith or in view of one's union with Christ. He believed this concept involves God's setting His elective love on people without regard to Christ's work or one's participation in it. He argued that this schema was inconsistent with God's justice "because it affirms that God has absolutely willed to save certain individual persons and has decreed their salvation with no regard for their righteousness or obedience. From this it may be properly concluded that God loves such creatures far more than God loves his own justice."[47]

For Arminius, divine justice is at the essence of the divine nature. In his *Examination of Perkins's Pamphlet*, Arminius argued against the Calvinistic doctrine of divine reprobation by saying that it impugns the justice of God. In making that argument, Arminius emphasized that divine justice is not something outside of God but arises from His own holy nature.

> "God," indeed, "is not bound by created laws," but He is a law to Himself; for He is Justice itself. And that law according to which it is not allowable to inflict punishment on any one who is not deserving of it, is not created, nor made by men, nor does it hold any such place amongst men; but it is the eternal law, and unmoveable Divine justice, to which God is bound by the immutability of His own nature and justice.[48]

DIVINE WRATH

For Arminius, divine justice intertwines with three central concepts: divine wrath, satisfaction, and payment. Wrath is an expression of divine justice against humanity's violation of divine law and gospel. Sinners' violation of the law provokes God's wrath and brings punishment. Sinners' rejection of the gospel causes God's wrath to abide on them, "preventing the remission of punishment."[49] This wrath abides on all people, owing to the imputation of Adam's sin to the human race.[50] The effect of God's wrath on sinful humanity is divine punishment: "Punishment was consequent on guilt and the divine wrath; the equity of this punishment is from guilt, the infliction of it is by wrath."[51]

In his Private Disputation 20, "On the Attributes of God Which Come to Be Considered under His Will," Arminius stated that love "is an affection of union in God, whose objects are not only God himself and the good of justice, but also the creature, imitating or related to God. . . . "[52] Hatred, on the contrary, "is an affection of separation in God," whose object is "injustice or unrighteousness."[53] God loves His own nature and thus His justice and so is naturally repulsed by injustice or human sin. In this disputation, Arminius made a distinction he did not explicitly make in his other writings. He describes God's love for the creature and the creature's blessedness as secondary to His love of His essential nature and justice. Still, since He hates the misery wrought in the creature by sin, God desires to find a way to remove it. Yet for the creature that persists in unrighteousness, God hates the creature and loves his misery. However, this hatred does not arise from God's free will but from "natural necessity."[54] In other words, God's love for human beings provides a way for them to escape the hatred for their sin that arises necessarily from His holy nature. God's act of love toward human beings in their sin is one of "deliverance from sin through the remission and the mortification of sin. And this progress of goodness is denominated mercy, which is an affection for giving succour to a man in misery, sin presenting no obstacle."[55]

SATISFACTION

The concept of satisfaction plays a vital role in Arminius's view of divine justice. He portrayed God as a judge who must sentence individuals to eternal death if they do not meet His requirements. Arminius employed the analogy of "a judge making an estimate in his own mind of the deed and of the author of it, and according to that estimate forming a judgment and pronouncing sentence."[56] In his Disputation 48, "On Justification," Arminius declared that God as judge demands satisfaction:

> We say, that "it is the act of God as a Judge," who though as the Supreme Legislator he could have issued regulations concerning this law, and actually did issue them, yet has not administered this direction through the absolute plenitude of infinite power, but contained himself within the bounds of Justice which He demonstrated

by two methods: First. Because God would not justify, except as justification was preceded by reconciliation and satisfaction made through Christ in his blood. Secondly. Because he would not justify any except those who acknowledged their sins and believed in Christ.[57]

However, the satisfaction demanded by the divine judge does not mitigate divine mercy. Arminius responds to opponents of penal satisfaction who held that God's acceptation of sinners according to the rigor of His justice would mitigate the mercifulness of His salvific action. Arminius replied that, when he says Christ's reconciliatory work is gracious and merciful, he says it

> not with respect to Christ, as if the Father, through grace as distinguished from strict and rigid justice, had accepted the obedience of Christ for righteousness;—but with respect to us, both because God, through his gracious mercy towards us, has made Christ to be sin for us, and righteousness to us, that we might be the righteousness of God in Him; and because He has placed communion with Christ in the faith of the gospel, and has set forth Christ as a propitiation through faith.[58]

This divine justice must be satisfied. As cited above, God "rendered satisfaction to his Love for Justice and to his Hatred against sin, when He imposed on his Son the office of Mediator by the shedding of his blood and by the suffering of death."[59] There is no satisfaction, Arminius explained, except through "the obedience of the passion of our Lord Jesus Christ, by which the Justice of God can be satisfied either for sin or for its punishment, even for the very least of either."[60] Arminius spoke of God as having the "right" to demand satisfaction from sinners "for the injuries which He has sustained" because of their sin. God is the "Divine Person in whose hands rests the right" to receive satisfaction for His justice. It is not fitting, Arminius argued, that God should "recede . . . or resign any part of it," because of "the rigid inflexibility of his justice, according to which he hates iniquity and does not permit a wicked person to dwell in his presence."[61]

Arminius also argued that the satisfaction made by Christ in His reconciling work was a satisfaction of the divine law. This was another way Arminius employed to say that the work of Christ satisfies the divine justice. In his Public Disputation 12, "The Law of God," Arminius argued that the primary use of the law is that human beings "might perform it, and by its performance might be justified, and might 'of debt' receive the reward which was promised through it. (Rom. ii. 13; x, 5; iv, 4.)."[62] Of course, since they cannot perform it, Arminius stressed, Christ the mediator must perform it on their behalf. God's law, Arminius explained, is two-fold, consisting of obedience and punishment. "That of obedience is first and absolute: that of punishment is the later, and does not take place except when obedience has not been rendered."[63] Thus, he averred, there is a "twofold satisfaction of the law: one, by which the obedience prescribed by the law is rendered; the other, by which the punishment imposed by the law on disobedience is suffered. He who fulfills [satisfies] the one is free from the other requirement of the law. He, therefore, who undergoes the punishment [pays the penalty] enacted by the law is thereupon freed from the obligation of rendering obedience. This is true in general of every sort of punishment."[64]

PAYMENT

In various writings, Arminius used motifs common in Reformed circles to describe this satisfaction of the divine justice. The most common among these are "paying the debt," "paying the penalty" and "paying the price" of sin. We have already mentioned Arminius's discussion, in his oration "On the Priesthood of Christ," of God's right to demand satisfaction for injuries against Himself (that is, His justice). In that same passage, he describes these injuries as "debt" that sinners must pay if God is to reconcile them to Himself.[65]

> The first of those relations which subsist between God and men, has respect to something given and something received. The latter

requires another relation supplementary to itself—a relation which taking its commencement from men, may terminate in God; and that is, an acknowledgment of a benefit received, to the honour of the munificent Donor. It is also a debt, due on account of a benefit already conferred, but which is not to be paid except on the demand and according to the regulation of the Giver; whose intention it has always been, that the will of a creature should not be the measure of his honour.[66]

In the passage cited above from his *Examination of Perkins's Pamphlet*, Arminius employed the imagery of "paying the penalty," that is, suffering the punishment that is due for sins.[67] Of course, Arminius argues, no human being can pay this penalty. It must be paid by another—a sinless priest.[68]

However, the most common imagery Arminius used in describing the satisfaction of divine justice made in the work of Christ is the payment of the price of redemption. He described Christ as "paying the price of redemption for sins by suffering the punishment due to them."[69] He spoke of "the price of our redemption paid by Christ," God being the one "who receives that price."[70] While Arminius occasionally used the word "ransom" and utilized ransom imagery in his doctrine of the work of Christ, he usually used it without comment. He never spoke, for example, of a price paid to the devil. Rather, God the Father is the person who receives the price of redemption from the divine Son.[71] In his oration *On the Priesthood of Christ*, Arminius utilized his paying the price imagery in a passage that encapsulates his approach to the work of Christ. He explained that God required of Christ "that he should lay down his soul as a victim in sacrifice for sin, (Isa. liii. 11,) that he should give his flesh for the light of the world, (John vi. 51) and that he should pay the price of redemption for the sins and the captivity of the human race."[72]

SUMMARY AND CONCLUSION

Arminius asserted that God's wisdom allowed His justice and mercy both to maintain their interests in the imposition of Christ's priesthood. The only individual who could fulfill the duties of this priesthood was a sinless person who was fully human and fully divine. Arminius's understanding of priestly sacrifice is intimately entwined with his emphasis on the sinfulness of humanity and the inflexible justice of God. The inexorable demands of divine justice cannot be set aside without doing damage to the divine essence. However, mercy requires a way for people to be released from the sufferings of divine punishment that results from human sin. Thus, in His wisdom, God the Son offers Himself as divine-human priest-sacrifice to offer a way out of the divine wrath while not requiring a relaxation of the divine justice. He offers an expiatory or propitiatory sacrifice. Such a voluntary propitiation, Arminius contends, is necessary to appease the divine justice. Furthermore, Arminius stresses that the oblation—the offering—that Christ as priest makes to God must be a "human victim." Yet the priest-sacrifice must be a divine being to be qualified as priest.

Christ, in His execution of the role of priesthood, becomes the human victim that is offered up to God to appease God's justice. Indeed, as the priest-sacrifice, Christ offers Himself up as an oblation to God. This oblation, this offering, consists of the sacrifice of His body—His shedding of blood and subsequent death. Arminius describes this oblation as a payment that Christ renders to God as the price of redemption for human sin. In Christ's oblation, Arminius argues, Christ as priest and sacrifice suffers the divine punishment that is due for human sin. This suffering constitutes the satisfaction or payment to the divine justice for redemption of humans from sin, guilt, and wrath. Thus, Arminius presents an understanding of atonement, in the context of his view of the priestly office of Jesus Christ, which is consistent with the penal substitution motifs regnant in sixteenth-and early seventeenth-century Reformed theology.

[1]Carl Bangs, "Arminius and Reformed Theology," Ph.D. diss., University of Chicago, 1958, 14.

[2]Robert L. Reymond, *A New Systematic Theology of the Christian Religion* (Nashville: Nelson, 1998) 474.

[3]J. K. Grider, "Arminianism," in *Evangelical Dictionary of Theology*, Walter A. Elwell, ed. (Grand Rapids: Baker, 1984) 80.

[4]Following Carl Bangs, scholars such as John Mark Hicks, Robert E. Picirilli, Roger E. Olson, F. Stuart Clarke, William G. Witt, William den Boer, G. J. Hoerdendaal, Mark A. Ellis, and Sarah Mortimer fall into the first category. Richard Muller and his students Keith Stanglin and Thomas McCall fall into the second. See Bangs, *Arminius: A Study in the Dutch Reformation* (Nashville: Abingdon, 1971); Bangs, "Arminius and the Reformation," *Church History* 30 (1961) 155-70; Bangs, "Arminius and Reformed Theology"; John Mark Hicks, "The Theology of Grace in the Thought of Jacobus Arminius and Philip Van Limborch: A Study in the Development of Seventeenth-Century Dutch Arminianism," Ph.D. diss., Westminster Theological Seminary, 1985; Robert E. Picirilli, *Grace, Faith, Free Will: Contrasting Views of Salvation—Calvinism and Arminianism* (Nashville: Randall House, 2002); Roger E. Olson, *Arminian Theology: Myths and Realities* (Downers Grove: InterVarsity, 2006); William G. Witt, "Creation, Redemption, and Grace in the Theology of Jacobus Arminius," Ph.D. diss., University of Notre Dame, 1993; William den Boer, *God's Twofold Love: The Theology of Jacob Arminius (1559-1609)* (Gottingen: Vandenhoeck and Ruprecht, 2010); G. J. Hoerdendaal, "The Debate about Arminius outside the Netherlands," in *Leiden University in the 17th Century* (Leiden: Brill, 1975), 137-59; Mark A. Ellis, *Simon Episcopius*; Sarah Mortimer, *Reason and Religion in the English Revolution* (Cambridge: Cambridge University Press, 2010); Muller, *God, Creation, and Providence in the Thought of Jacob Arminius* (Grand Rapids: Baker, 1991); Keith D. Stanglin, *Arminius and the Assurance of Salvation* (Leiden: Brill, 2007); Keith D. Stanglin and Thomas H. McCall, *Jacob Arminius: Theologian of Grace* (New York: Oxford University Press, 2012).

[5]As I say elsewhere, while Arminius "veered from Calvinism on the question of how one *comes to be* in a state of grace (predestination, free will, and grace) he retained Reformed categories on the *meaning* of sin and redemption. (J. Matthew Pinson, "Introduction," in J. Matthew Pinson, ed., *Four Views on Eternal Security* [Grand Rapids: Zondervan, 2002], 14-15).

[6]For examples of Reformed theologians before and after Arminius to whom he bears striking resemblance in his doctrine of atonement and the priesthood of Christ, see John Calvin, *Institutes of the Christian Religion*, ed. John T. McNeill (Philadelphia: Westminster, 1960) 501-03, 504-12 (2.25.6, 2.26.2-2.26.7) and Francis Turretin, "The Necessity of Atonement," available online at *http://www.fivesolas.com/ftnecatone.htm*.

[7]Jacobus Arminius, *The Works of James Arminius*, trans. James Nichols and William Nichols (Nashville: Randall House, 2007) 2:690. (Hereafter referred to as "Arminius, *Works.*")

[8]There has been almost no scholarly research conducted on Arminius's doctrine of the nature of atonement. Scholars tend to rely on secondary sources for their information on his views on this subject, making brief assertions of only a few sentences without supporting them with primary research. Four exceptions to this rule are Olson, *Arminian Theology*; Hicks; Witt; and den Boer. However, the general nature of these works allows their authors only a few pages to discuss Arminius's thought on the nature of atonement. These authors seem to be in agreement with the basic thesis of this chapter.

[9]See e.g., Joel B. Green and Mark D. Baker, eds., *Recovering the Scandal of the Cross: Atonement in New Testament & Contemporary Contexts* (Downers Grove: InterVarsity, 2000); Charles

ARMINIAN AND BAPTIST

E. Hill and Frank A. James, III, eds., *The Glory of the Atonement: Biblical, Historical & Practical Perspectives : Essays in Honor of Roger R. Nicole* (Downers Grove: InterVarsity, 2004); James K. Beilby and Paul R. Eddy, eds., *The Nature of the Atonement: Four Views* (Downers Grove: Inter-Varsity, 2006); Garry J. Williams, "Penal Substitution: A Response to Recent Criticisms," *Journal of the Evangelical Theological Society* 50 (2007), 71-86; and other debate over the views of atonement in movements such as the New Perspective on Paul, the Emerging church, and Federal Vision theology.

[10]I give a much fuller description of the ways in which Arminius defies both modern Calvinistic and Arminian interpretations in Chapter One. See also J. Matthew Pinson, "Introduction," in Pinson, ed., *Four Views on Eternal Security.*

[11]The Westminster Shorter Catechism, in *The Constitution of the Presbyterian Church (U.S.A.) Part I: Book of Confessions* (New York: Office of the General Assembly, 1983) 7.023-7.026.

[12]The Belgic Confession of Faith, Article 21, in Philip Schaff, *The Creeds of Christendom*, vol. 1 (Grand Rapids: Baker, 1983).

[13]Though Arminius does not use the word "atonement."

[14]Arminius, *Works*, 2:220, Public Disputation 14, "On the Offices of Our Lord Jesus Christ."

[15]Ibid., 2:219-21.

[16]Ibid.

[17]Ibid., 2:217.

[18]Ibid. Cf. Private Disputation 35, "On the Priestly Office of Christ," 2:380-81.

[19]Ibid., 2:381, Private Disputation 35, "On the Priestly Office of Christ."

[20]Ibid.

[21]Ibid., 1:414, Oration IV, "The Priesthood of Christ."

[22]Ibid.

[23]Ibid.

[24]Ibid.

[25]Ibid., 1:415.

[26]Ibid.

[27]Ibid.

[28]Ibid., 1:419; 2:256; 2:381.

[29]Ibid., 1:419

[30]Ibid., 1:413.

[31]Ibid.

[32]Ibid.

[33]Ibid.

[34]Ibid., 1:413-14.

[35]Ibid., 1:414.

[36]Ibid., 2:221, Public Disputation 14, "On the Offices of Our Lord Jesus Christ."

[37]Ibid.

[38]Ibid.

[39]Ibid.

[40]Ibid.

[41]Ibid.

[42]Ibid. See also the *Declaration of Sentiments*: "The third divine decree: God decided to administer in a sufficient and efficacious manner the means necessary for repentance and faith—this being accomplished according to divine wisdom, by which God knows what is proper and becoming both to his mercy and his severity. And this all proceeds according to divine justice, by which God is prepared to adopt whatever his wisdom may prescribe and carry out" (W. Stephen Gunter, *Arminius and His Declaration of Sentiments: An Annotated Translation with Introduction and Theological Commentary* [Waco: Baylor University Press, 2012], Kindle locations 3163-3166); cf. Arminius, 1:653.

[43]Arminius, *Works,* 2:378-79, Private Disputation 34, "On the Restoration of Man." See also Public Disputation 1, "On the Authority and Certainty of the Sacred Scriptures": " . . . the admirable attempering of the Justice of God by which He loves righteousness and hates iniquity, and his Equity by which he administers all things, with his Mercy in Christ our Propitiation" (2:86).

[44]Ibid., 3:195, "Friendly Conference with Francis Junius."

[45]Ibid., 3:195.

[46]Ibid. With regard to rigor and inflexibility, see also Oration IV, "On the Priesthood of Christ" (1:409), where Arminius spoke of "the invariable rule of Divine Justice." It is remarkable, after having read the statements above, how theologians for centuries have misread (or, more likely, not read) Arminius in ways similar to the following views of the eminent historical theologian H. D. McDonald, who repeated the oft-stated maxim that certain "latent" ideas in Arminius's doctrine of atonement are "made fundamental in later Arminian statements. There is, first, the view that Christ's expiatory sacrifice was not an equivalent for the punishment due to sin. The sacrifice was not the payment of a debt, nor was it a complete satisfaction for sin." McDonald continues to discuss these ideas "latent" in Arminius: "What Christ did on the cross was not to bear the penalty for sin." His sufferings are "a substitute for a penalty." "Christ did not endure the full penalty due to sin . . . he did not make a complete atonement for sin by bearing the full penalty" (H. D. McDonald, *The Atonement of the Death of Christ* [Grand Rapids: Baker, 1985] 200-01). Unfortunately, secondary sources for four centuries, both Calvinist and Arminian, have been replete with such lack of attention to Arminius's actual statements on atonement and a host of other doctrines (for examples, see Chapter One).

[47]Gunter, *Declaration of Sentiments,* "On Predestination," Kindle locations 2734-2737; cf. Arminius, 1.624.

[48]Arminius, *Works,* 3:357, "Examination of William Perkins's Pamphlet on the Mode and Order of Predestination."

[49]Ibid., 2:157, Public Disputation 8, "On Actual Sins"; see also Public Disputation 7, "On the First Sin of the First Man."

[50]Ibid., Public Disputation 8, "On Actual Sins"; see also Public Disputation 7, "On the First Sin of the First Man."

[51]Ibid., 2:374; Private Disputation 31, "On the Effects of the Sin of Our First Parents." On punishment, see also Private Disputation 19, "On the Various Distinctions of the Will

of God": "Thus He wills the evils of punishment; because he chooses that the order of justice be preserved in punishment, rather than that a sinning creature should escape punishment, though this impunity might be for the good of the creature" (2:346).

[52]Ibid., 2:347, Private Disputation 20, "On the Attributes of God Which Come to Be Considered Under His Will. And, First, on Those Which Have an Analogy to the Affections or Passions in Rational Creatures."

[53]Ibid., 2:348.

[54]Ibid.

[55]Ibid.

[56]Ibid., 2:256, Public Disputation 19, "On the Justification of Man before God."

[57]Ibid., 2:406, Private Disputation 48, "On Justification."

[58]Ibid.

[59]Ibid., 2:221, Public Disputation 14, "On the Office of Our Lord Jesus Christ."

[60]Ibid., 2:241, Public Disputation 17, "On Repentance."

[61]Ibid., 1:412-13, Oration IV, "On the Priesthood of Christ."

[62]Ibid., 2:198, Public Disputation 12, "On the Law of God."

[63]Ibid., 3:477, "Examination of William Perkins's Pamphlet on the Mode and Order of Predestination."

[64]Ibid. The bracketed words are alternate translations from William Bagnall's translation in the Boston edition of Arminius's *Works*.

[65]Ibid., 1:406, Oration IV, "On the Priesthood of Christ." See also Public Disputation 12, "On the Law of God" (2:198).

[66]Ibid., 1:406.

[67]Ibid., 3:477, "Examination of William Perkins's Pamphlet on the Mode and Order of Predestination."

[68]Ibid., 1:415, Oration IV, "On the Priesthood of Christ."

[69]Ibid., 1:419. Arminius's use of the imagery of paying a price is consistent with Francis Turretin's approach in Topic 14, question 10 of *Institutes of Elenctic Theology*, trans. George Musgrave Giger, ed. James T. Dennison, Jr. (Phillipsburg: P&R, 1994) 2.417-26.

[70]Arminius,*Works*, 3:74, "Sixth Proposition of Arminius: Arminius's Reply, or Consideration of [Junius's] Answer to the Sixth Proposition."

[71]Ibid.

[72]Ibid., 1:416, Oration IV, "On the Priesthood of Christ." Elsewhere, Arminius favorably quotes Prosper of Aquitaine to the effect that "the blood of Jesus Christ is the price paid for the whole world" (Article 12). See also Public Disputation 20, "On Christian Liberty": "The external cause [of Christian liberty] is the ransom, or the price of redemption, and the satisfaction, which Christ has paid. (Rom. v. 6-21; vii, 2, 3.)"; Private Disputation 79, "On the Sixth Precept," where Arminius says that Christians "have been redeemed by Christ with a price"; his "Letter to John Uytenbogard": " . . . that blood by which God hath redeemed the church unto himself, which is the price of redemption. . . . "; Public Disputation 14, "On the Offices of Our Lord Jesus Christ": "All these blessings really flow from the sacerdotal functions of Christ; because he hath offered to God the true price of redemption for us, by which He has

satisfied Divine justice, and interposed himself between us and the Father, who was justly angry on account of our sins; and has rendered Him placable to us (1 Tim. Ii. 6; Matt. Xx. 28.)."

3

SIN AND REDEMPTION IN THE THEOLOGY OF JOHN SMYTH AND THOMAS HELWYS

INTRODUCTION

John Smyth and Thomas Helwys, the direct forebears of the modern Baptist movement, are normally studied in the context of English Separatism or Baptist origins. Scholars have scrutinized their concepts of the gathered church, believer's baptism, separation of church and state, and freedom of conscience. Yet they have largely neglected their soteriology, thereby ignoring the fact that the General Baptist movement to which Smyth and Helwys gave birth was as significantly a soteriological program as it was an ecclesiological one.

Most scholars have recognized the Arminianism of this movement, and hence of Smyth and Helwys. Yet they have assumed that General Baptist views on salvation were like the Arminian tenets that were gaining popularity in the Church of England in the early seventeenth century. However, the Anti-Calvinism of the General Baptists was much more like that of Arminius and conspicuously different from Arminianism in the Church of England. In dialogue with his mentor Smyth, Helwys fashioned a soteriology that avoided the semi-

Pelagian excesses of Dutch Mennonite theology and thus sharply contrasted with Anglican Arminianism. Though we cannot conclusively demonstrate Helwys's reliance on Arminius, a striking similarity between their soteriological systems is evident. This evangelical Arminianism, shaped by the Reformed categories of Helwys's Puritan past, was closer to Calvinism than most English Arminianism. Mediated through seventeenth-century General Baptist confessions of faith and preacher-theologians such as John Griffith, Joseph Wright, and Thomas Grantham, Helwys's "Reformed Arminianism" became a significant factor in seventeenth-century English polemics.

SMYTH AND HELWYS: A HISTORICAL SKETCH

In 1590 Smyth graduated from Christ's College, Cambridge, a seedbed of Puritan thought.[1] At Cambridge, he was profoundly influenced by his tutor Francis Johnson, a Separatist who would later lead his congregation to exile in Amsterdam. Despite this influence, Smyth was ordained by the Bishop of London in 1594 and remained a moderate Puritan throughout his fellowship at Christ's College (1594-1598).[2] During his appointment as lecturer to the Corporation of Lincoln, however, Smyth began to evince a more strident Puritan posture. His opinions were questionable enough to cause the corporation to terminate his lectureship in October 1602 for being "a factious man," guilty of "personal preaching, and that untruly, against divers men of good place."[3] Although his book *The Bright Morning Starre* (1603) showed evidence of his awareness of Separatist thought, he maintained his loyalty to the Church of England.[4]

Soon, however, Smyth began more keenly to sense that the mainstream of the Puritan movement had failed in its efforts to accomplish ecclesiastical reform in the Church of England. During the next few years, Smyth maintained a middle course between moderate Puritanism and Separatist Radical Puritanism. Though he began working as a physician at Gainsborough in the Lower Trent Valley, he was censured by Bishop Richard Bancroft for preaching in the parish church in 1606. In reaction to the vicar, whom Smyth believed was absent from his parish far too often, Smyth assumed the preaching duties, styling himself "Pastor of the Church of Ganesburgh."[5]

Smyth had embraced full-blown Separatism by the autumn of 1607.[6] He became leader of the Separatist congregation in Gainsborough, which included the "Pilgrim Fathers," William Brewster, John Robinson, and William Bradford. This church later amicably split into two congregations, the one in Gainsborough and the other in Scrooby under the leadership of Bradford. They modeled themselves after Francis Johnson's church which had left London for exile in Amsterdam.

Because of intense persecution in England, the Gainsborough and Scrooby congregations moved to Amsterdam by early 1608. Soon after their arrival in the Netherlands, Smyth and several followers broke with the other Gainsborough-Scrooby Separatists and the Francis Johnson congregation. Smyth explained some of the reasons for this schism in his *Differences of the Churches of the Separation,* published in 1608. That book discussed three of the Smyth group's censures, which centered on the worship, ministry, and financing of Johnson's church. However, the principal reason for the split was the Smyth group's new conviction that infant baptism is invalid and that believer's baptism is the only foundation for a true Christian church. Earlier, in his work *Principles and Inferences Concerning the Visible Church* (1607), Smyth had articulated the Separatist understanding of the church as "two, three, or more saints joined together by covenant with God and themselves . . . for their mutual edification, and God's glory."[7] Smyth supplemented this covenantal understanding of the church with a notion gleaned from his reading of the New Testament, namely, that believers must be baptized to covenant with one another in a "visible communion of saints."[8] Smyth also viewed his new understanding of baptismal theology as a natural outgrowth of Separatist ecclesiology. In his book *The Character of the Beast* (1609), Smyth maintained, "All that shall in time to come separate from England must separate from the baptism of England, and if they will not separate from baptism there is no reason why they should separate from England as from a false church."[9]

Sometime in late 1608 or early 1609, Smyth baptized himself and the other members of his newly formed fellowship, having been unable to find anyone to baptize him and deeming the Dutch Mennonites heretical because of their views on the person of Christ.[10] This sensational "se-baptism" scandalized not only the Separatists but also many others throughout the English Church. Typical of this outrage was that of Henry Ainsworth, the teaching elder of Francis Johnson's congregation:

> Mr. Sm[yth] anabaptised himself with water: but a child could have done the like unto himself, who cannot performe any part of spirituall worship: therefore, Mr. Sm[yth] anabaptising himself with water, did no part of spirituall worship: and consequently it was carnal worship, and service of the Divil. . . . The babes and sucklings whose soules he would murder by depriving them of the covenant promise and visible seal of salvation in the Church; shal rise up in judgment & shall condemn him in the day of Christ.[11]

By late 1609 Smyth had made the remarkable pilgrimage from mainstream Puritan to Separatist/Radical Puritan to Baptist.

While Smyth was the guiding influence in the new Baptist congregation, his chief disciple was Thomas Helwys. A resident of Broxtowe Hall near Basford, Helwys was a son of minor gentry and had been educated at Gray's Inn, London. Prior to his espousal of Separatist principles, Helwys had also been a mainstream Puritan.[12] Yet in 1606 he associated with the Separatists in the Lower Trent Valley and became a close friend of Smyth. Helwys's thought was deeply influenced at a small meeting of Separatist leaders at the home of Sir William Bowes. His indebtedness to Lady Isabel Bowes is reflected in *A Short and Plaine Proofe*, a small book he dedicated to her in 1611. Helwys helped arrange and finance the migration of the Gainsborough and Scrooby Congregations to Amsterdam.[13]

The movement away from Separatist ecclesiology was not enough for Smyth, Helwys, and their congregation. At some point in 1609-1610, they made another theological shift that drove them even further from the Calvinist-minded Separatists: they adopted anti-Calvinist views. Owing to this development, the group would later be called "General Baptists" because of their belief that Christ's atonement was *general*—that is, it extended to all humanity rather than just the elect. In a period of three or four years, Smyth and Helwys, through their reading of Scripture, had moved on a straight and almost systematic course from being staunch Calvinist Puritans within the Church of England to anti-Calvinist, antipaedobaptist Separatists.[14]

Thomas Helwys was Smyth's most loyal confidant, but his devotion was more to Smyth's principles than to his person. Thus, when Smyth began to retreat from some of the views he had come to hold, Helwys reacted negatively. Tension between Helwys and Smyth surfaced after the congregation had come into contact with the Dutch Waterlander Mennonites. Sensing that these Anabaptists were kindred spirits, Smyth began to question the propriety of his earlier se-baptism and expressed the desire to join the Waterlanders so that he and his congregation could receive true baptism from them. Smyth had become convinced of a form of apostolic succession or "succession of baptisms." Helwys vigorously protested this move, insisting that this kind of succession violated the principle of "two or three" covenanted together through faith and baptism—Smyth's earlier definition of a true church. On March 12, 1610, Helwys and his compatriots William Pigott, Thomas Seamer, and John Murton, in a letter to the Waterlanders, explained the essence of the controversy between Smyth and themselves. They stated their "warrant by ye word of truth": "Iohn Baptist being vnbaptized preached the baptisme of repentance and they that beleeued and confessed their sinnes, he baptized. And whosoeuer shall now be stirred vp by the same spiritt, to preach the same word, and men thereby being converted, may according to Iohn his example, wash them with water and who can forbid."[15]

In addition to the question of succession, Helwys also opposed union with the Mennonites because they did not allow magistrates church membership. Helwys repudiated the typical Anabaptist beliefs of passive non-resistance and quietism. These and other theological divergences led Helwys, Pigott, Seamer, Murton, and their followers to break with Smyth and his adherents. In 1611 Helwys and his congregation issued a confession of faith, *A Declaration of Faith of English People Remaining at Amsterdam*. In this work Helwys outlined the major reasons for his separation from Smyth. In addition to soteriological differences, which will be the focus of this chapter, the confession delineated objections to Smyth's Hoffmanite Christology—which taught that Christ's flesh was celestial or heavenly rather than derived from the Virgin Mary. The confession also differed with Smyth's opinions on succession and the role of the magistracy.[16]

Smyth died of tuberculosis in August 1612, having never secured membership in the Waterlander congregation in Amsterdam. Not until 1615 did his followers gain admission to Mennonite fellowship. The antipaedobaptist wing of English Separatism would have disappeared had it not been for the endeavors of Helwys and his congregation. They moved back to England in 1612 and established the first English Baptist church at Spitalfields near London. Here Helwys produced his greatest work, *A Short Declaration of the Mistery of Iniquity* (1612), which preserved for Helwys the legacy of having been among the first outspoken proponents of full religious liberty in history. Helwys sent a copy of the book to James I, to which was attached a letter asserting that the king had no right to govern souls: "Heare O king, and dispise not ye cousell of ye poore, and let their complaints come before thee. The king is a mortall man, and not God therefore hath no power over ye immortall soules of his subiects, to make lawes and ordinances for them, and to set spirituall Lords over them."[17]

Helwys predicted that he and his followers would suffer persecution upon their return to England, but he believed they had been mistaken in their initial decision to flee the country. As he had expected, he was imprisoned in Newgate jail. He was dead by 1616.

The mantle of leadership fell to John Murton, who in some ways was more like Smyth than Helwys. Murton died at some point between June 1624 and November 1626. By the time of his death, at least five General Baptist churches existed in the London area. There were probably other General Baptists in the counties, but no record of them survives. On November 12, 1626, the five London General Baptist churches petitioned the Waterlanders for union, but this was never achieved owing to unresolvable theological differences. Though Murton and these five General Baptist churches were not as precise in their agreement with Helwys, the latter's thought would form the basis for the mainstream of General Baptist theology in the seventeenth century.

Smyth and Helwys laid the foundation for the most vigorous movement of dissent in seventeenth-century England: the Baptists. The General Baptists and their Calvinist contemporaries, the Particular Baptists, who arose a generation later, comprised the largest group of religious radicals in the middle and late 1600s.[18] Thus it is ironic that these early General Baptist radicals have often been lumped with the Laudian Arminians because of their soteriology.

INTELLECTUAL INFLUENCE ON THE SOTERIOLOGY OF SMYTH AND HELWYS

The soteriology of Smyth and Helwys cannot be adequately understood apart from a discussion of their intellectual influences. The latter question looms large in studies of Baptist history written over nearly four centuries. Many early scholars avoided the question by postulating that Smyth and Helwys gleaned their religious views directly from Holy Scripture. Others traced Baptist origins through a succession of Anabaptist principles from the apostles through medieval sects such as the Albigenses and Waldenses through the Continental Anabaptists of the sixteenth century right up to Smyth and Helwys.[19] Another traditional view of Baptist origins emphasized the influence of the Waterlander Mennonites. While the first two views have been articulated by some twentieth-century historians, the majority of modern scholars have rejected these interpretations. The modern debate centers on whether Smyth and Helwys were primarily influenced by Continental Anabaptists through the Dutch Waterlanders or whether their thought was essentially a natural development from their English Separatist background. W. T. Whitley and more recently Lonnie Kliever, B. R. White, and Stephen Brachlow have been the main advocates of the latter view,[20] while James R. Coggins and Jason K. Lee represent the former.[21]

The question of theological influence on Smyth's and Helwys's soteriology is immediately connected to the more general debate. Scholars who stress Mennonite influence on the origin of Baptist thought claim that Smyth and Helwys acquired their anti-Calvinism from the Mennonites, whereas those who highlight their English Separatist milieu ascribe the soteriological change either to influence from Dutch Arminianism or to their reading of the Bible. Other scholars offer slight variations on these themes. Some recent historians, however, insist that the question of intellectual influence is too complicated to answer. They assert that Smyth's and Helwys's theology is the result of the many perspectives they encountered as well as their interpretation of Scripture.[22] While this is true, it is possible to isolate certain themes in the soteriology of Smyth and Helwys that are similar to or different from the theological currents of their day—currents with which they could not have avoided contact, given their theological acumen.

Much of the research on the intellectual influences on Smyth and Helwys deals superficially with their ideas, failing to reckon with the subtleties and diversity of seventeenth-century theology. Thomas Gulley, for instance, sums up Smyth and Helwys's anti-Calvinism as a "rejection of predestination," failing to understand that both men advanced detailed doctrines of predestination, though both differed greatly from Calvinistic views. He also misunderstands the profound degree to which Smyth and Helwys differed from each other in their soteriological views.[23] Such over-simplifications obfuscate the question of intellectual influence by glossing over the important disagreements between various strands of anti-Calvinism.

Four major interpretations of the soteriological influences on Smyth and Helwys have been advanced. The first view, held by the majority of scholars who have commented on this question, is that Smyth's and Helwys's initial departure from Calvinism resulted from their appropriation of Dutch Arminian ideas. The views of of B. R. White, who implies that Smyth and Helwys were influenced by the theology of Arminius, are typical of this approach. [24] The rationale for this view is that Smyth and Helwys held anti-Calvinist sentiments in common with the Dutch Arminians, and that the latter must have been the primary influence on Smyth and Helwys owing to the Arminian controversy in the Netherlands. On closer examination, this view is incorrect primarily because it does not recognize the divergences of Helwys's developing soteriology from that of Smyth, whose doctrine of grace bears greater resemblance to Anabaptism than to Dutch Arminianism. Thus, as will be demonstrated, Helwys's theology, as expressed after 1610, was influenced by Dutch Arminianism, but Smyth's view of salvation reflects no such influence.

The second view, held by historians such as Lonnie Kliever, Goki Saito, R. T. Kendall, and Jason K. Lee, correctly argues that Helwys's post-1610 soteriology diverged from Smyth's. These scholars ascribe this difference to Dutch Arminian influence on Helwys, but this is more an inference than an argument supported by evidence. The advocates of this view fail to interact deeply with the soteriological content of the writings of Arminius, the Remonstrants, or Helwys, and they tend to muddle the distinctions between Arminius and the Remonstrants.[25]

A third view, advanced by Stephen Brachlow, argues that Smyth's shift away from Calvinist soteriology was actually a logical development of the trajectory of his Radical Puritan thought. However, Brachlow does not discuss theological differences between Smyth and Helwys.[26]

A fourth position, advanced by Stephen M. Johnson and James R. Coggins, applies the interpretive framework of scholars who have emphasized Waterlander influence on the thought of Smyth and Helwys to the question of their soteriology.[27] In his stress on the early General Baptist dependence on Mennonite theology, Johnson ignores any evidence of Arminian influence on Helwys. Though he correctly argues that scholars such as Kliever, Saito, and Kendall base their assumption of Arminian influence on an "argument from silence," Johnson goes to extremes in denying any evidence that supports that interpretation. He argues, for example, that Smyth and Helwys naturally eschewed Dutch Arminian soteriology because they were opposed to Arminius's ecclesiology. Furthermore, he goes to great lengths to try to establish why it is unlikely that Smyth and Helwys would have been influenced by Arminianism: "To be sure, the topic was discussed in all Dutch communities during the period Smyth, Helwys, and Murton resided in Amsterdam; but it is quite conceivable that English refugees, who spoke no Dutch and knew very little Latin . . . could be only superficially aware of the theological issues of the Arminian-Remonstrant debate."[28] On the contrary, it is inconceivable—if only because of their theological proficiency and intense interest in soteriological questions—that Smyth's and Helwys's knowledge of Dutch Arminianism would have been superficial. This question can be settled only by showing how radically different Smyth's soteriology was from Arminius's and how remarkably similar Helwys's was to Arminius's, which will be done in the remainder of this chapter.

Johnson acknowledges Helwys's tacit approval of Dutch Arminianism in *A Short and Plaine Proofe,* in which Helwys tells Lady Isabel Bowes of the new light of general redemption that was "daily break[ing] forth" in the Dutch Reformed churches, which even the strictest English Calvinists would consider "the best reformed churches."[29] Yet he explains this away by saying that "Helwys, as an apologist, used the Dutch controversy as leverage to persuade English Calvinists who admired the Dutch Reformed Church."[30] This statement might be more understandable if the content of Helwys's soteriology were not so strikingly similar to that of Arminius.

To establish intellectual influence on thinkers such as Smyth and Helwys, who almost never acknowledged their sources, we must examine the doctrinal substance of their writings. We can understand the complexity of their anti-Calvinist soteriology only by comparing and contrasting their respective theologies with those of the Dutch Arminians, as represented by Arminius himself, and the Waterlander Mennonites as exemplified by Hans de Ries and the Waterlander confessions of faith.

THE SOTERIOLOGY OF SMYTH AND HELWYS

At first glance Smyth's and Helwys's doctrinal systems seem similar. Because of their agreement on the basic principles of anti-Calvinism, historians have mistakenly assumed they were articulating basically comparable systems.

Although this was true at first, Helwys's Arminianism evolved in the year 1610, probably owing to contact with the writings of Arminius. While Smyth continued to expound a soteriology shaped by his contact with the Waterlander Mennonites, Helwys launched out into new directions.

Nevertheless, Smyth and Helwys agreed on several fundamental points. They asserted, like all Arminians, that the benefits of Christ's atonement extend to the entire human race so that all human beings potentially can be saved. In opposition to the Calvinistic doctrine of irresistible grace, they believed that the divine grace that draws individuals toward God can be freely thwarted by the human will. These doctrines resulted in the corollary Arminian tenet of conditional predestination. Election to salvation, they believed, is conditioned on God's intimate foreknowledge of the believer because of the individual's union with Christ through faith. Reprobation to damnation is contingent on the foreseen sinfulness of the unbeliever. This teaching deviated from the widespread Reformed view that God, in eternity past, unconditionally predestined some individuals to salvation and others to reprobation irrespective of personal belief or unbelief.

Despite their essential agreement on a number of fundamental points, Smyth and Helwys parted ways on many others. The degree to which their theologies diverged is related to the extent to which they deviated from traditional Reformed understandings of sin and redemption. Like the Waterlanders, Smyth not only abandoned the more objectionable, arbitrary features of Reformed predestinarianism, but he also jettisoned the entire Augustinian-Calvinist edifice, including original sin and justification, *sola fide* and *Solo Christo*. Helwys, like Arminius, attempted to salvage as much as he could from Reformed theology, clinging to a strictly Augustinian approach to the nature and extent of human depravity and redemption. To put it another way, Smyth and Helwys agreed on the nature of predestination and the extent of God's grace in Christ, but they fundamentally disagreed on sin and redemption, faith and works. To understand this, one must compare and contrast Smyth and Helwys's doctrines of sin and justification.

Original Sin, Depravity, Human Ability, and Free Will

As early as 1609, Smyth rejected the Calvinistic view of original sin he formerly held. In Article 5 of his *Corde Credimus*, or Short Confession of Faith, Smyth brazenly stated that "there is no original sin . . . but all sin is actual and voluntary."[31] In his confessions he advanced several reasons for this view. The Smyth group's publication, *Propositions and Conclusions Concerning True Christian Religion* (1612), gave Smyth's rationale for his conviction that "original sin is an idle term, and that there is no such thing as men intend by the word."[32] The first argument is exegetical: Smyth believed that God's sentence of death threatened in Genesis 2:17 applied only to Adam and Eve and not to their posterity.[33]

Smyth's second reason for rejecting original sin was more theological and somewhat more complex: "because God created the soul."[34] Smyth held a Creationist position on the origin of the soul in the individual, as opposed to a Traducianist view. The debate between these two views originated with the Augustinian-Pelagian controversy. Pelagius advanced the Creationist position, arguing that God forms the soul at a distinct moment in the creation of each human being. Therefore, he argued, it is impossible for human beings to be hereditarily tainted with sin or guilt. Most Augustinians countered with the Traducianist view, asserting that the human soul originates naturally by heredity from parent to child. By extension, Augustine maintained that sin and guilt are transmitted naturally from Adam, the head of the race, to all humanity. This has traditionally been termed the Augustinian or "natural headship" view of the transmission of sin.[35]

Despite the Pelagian associations with Creationism, it is ironic that most English Calvinists in this period were Creationists as a result of their "federal headship" view of the origin of sin. Rather than seeing Adam and Eve as *natural* heads of the human race, and sinfulness as a natural part of being human, the federalists viewed Adam as the *federal* head of the race and thus asserted that God appointed Adam as a representative of humanity. According to this view, sin is not transmitted naturally through human heredity, but the human soul is created in a sinful state in each individual, based on the transgression of Adam as the divinely appointed head of the race. Quite unlike his Reformed federalist contemporaries, Smyth used Creationism to refute the doctrine of original sin. The federalist scheme, according to which God created each soul as sinful and depraved, was abhorrent to Smyth. Thus to assert a Creationist position on the origin of the soul was sufficient warrant for Smyth to repudiate original sin. Smyth's argument was clear-cut. His major premise was that God distinctly creates every soul. His minor premise was that God could not create a sinful soul. Therefore, he concluded, there is no original sin.

Smyth anticipated the objection of his opponents who held the view that original sin passed naturally from Adam and Eve to their posterity. Thus his third argument was that the atonement of Christ "stopped the issue and passage" of original sin.[36] He did not refute the natural headship view but simply insists that Christ's atonement interrupted the transmission of original sin. Ironically, the implication of this reasoning is that natural transmission of sin would have occurred had it not been for Christ's atonement. This notion was at odds with his Creationist position. While Smyth's first two arguments are not found in Waterlander confessions, this third reason appears in "A Short Confession," which was written by the Waterlander leaders Hans de Ries and Lubbert Gerritsz in 1580, revised and translated into English in 1610, and signed by Smyth and the remainder of his congregation after the break with Helwys.[37] Article 4 of the 1610 confession reads: "The first man was fallen into sin and wrath and was again by God, through a sweet and comfortable promise, restored and affirmed to everlasting life, with all those that were guilty through him so that none of his posterity (by reason of this institution) are guilty, sinful, or born in original sin."[38]

The implications Smyth drew from this formulation are striking in their departure from Reformed norms. Because of God's provision of Christ to Adam and his descendants, Smyth contended that human beings "bear the image of the first Adam, in his innocency, fall, and restitution in the offer of grace (1 Cor. 15:49), and so pass under these three conditions, or threefold estate."[39] Thus human beings are just as free as Adam was before the fall. This doctrine inspires Smyth's formulation of human free will. He argued "that Adam being fallen did not lose any natural power or faculty, which God created in his soul, for the work of the devil, which is (sin), cannot abolish God's work or creatures: and therefore being fallen he still retained freedom of will."[40] This optimistic portrait of human ability is reflected in the 1610 version of the Waterlander Confession prepared by de Ries and Gerritsz:

> Man being created good, and continuing in goodness, had the ability, the spirit of wickedness tempting him, freely to obey, assent, or reject the propounded evil: man being fallen and consisting (*sic*) in evil, had the ability, the T—[unreadable] himself moving freely to obey, assent, or reject the propounded good; for as he through free power to the choice of evil, obeyed and affirmed that evil; so did he through free power to the choice of good, obey and reassent that propounded good. *This last power or ability remaineth in all his posterity.*[41]

Smyth agreed wholeheartedly with the Waterlanders that human beings after the fall have the same level of free will and ability that Adam had prior to it.

Smyth's Creationism, combined with the seemingly contradictory understanding of Christ's atonement interrupting the natural transmission of original sin, which Smyth gleaned from the Waterlanders, drove him to an essentially semi-Pelagian position on original sin, depravity, human ability, and free will that is at odds with the core of the Augustinian-Reformed understanding of original sin and human depravity.

Helwys's mature understanding of these doctrines diverged radically from that of Smyth, reflecting Helwys's attempt to maintain fidelity to the Augustinian view of sin and redemption that characterized his former Calvinism, while avoiding its more objectionable predestinarian features. Helwys went through a phase of agreement with Smyth and the Waterlanders on the doctrine of original sin that is reflected in his brief Latin confession, *Synopsis Fidei,* published in February or March of 1610. In that document Helwys simply stated, "There is no sin from our parents through generation,"[42] thus agreeing with the Waterlander-Smyth position in opposition to the natural headship view of the transmission of original sin. Yet in 1611, Helwys reflected a change to a more Reformed understanding of original sin much like that of Arminius. The fullest statement of the mature theology of the Helwys group is found in the *Declaration of Faith of English People Remaining at Amsterdam,* which Helwys wrote in 1611. This confession consists of twenty-seven articles followed by a long letter against Smyth beginning with a list of the latter's six most substantive errors. In paragraph three of this section, Helwys castigated Smyth for holding three erroneous views: first, that Adam's sin was not imputed to his posterity; second, that all people are "in the estate of Adam in his innocency"; and third, that infants "were not redeemed by Christ, but as the Angels and all other Creatures."[43]

Helwys had come to the firm conviction that the traditional Augustinian-Reformed position on original sin was correct. Thus he concluded in Article 2 of the *Declaration* that all human beings sinned in Adam and that Adam's sin was "imputed unto all."[44] Helwys's Traducianism and Augustinian view of headship is evident in this article, and it is also borne out in his *Short and Plaine Proofe,* in which he argued that Adam's posterity was "yet all in his loynes."[45] This is a standard argument from the vantage point of the Traducian and Augustinian position. Humanity's natural connection with Adam—that all humanity was in Adam's loins—is significant for the transmission of original sin, not God's appointment of Adam as humanity's representative, as federal theology held. Thus Adam's sin is imputed to his posterity in the sense that each human being naturally inherits original sin. Helwys's view is reminiscent of that of Arminius, who argued that original sin "is not peculiar to our first parents, but is common to the entire race and to all their posterity, who, at the time this sin was committed, were in their loins, and who have since descended from them by the natural mode of propagation."[46] It cannot be known precisely to what extent Arminius's influence caused Helwys to modify his views on original sin and change from Creationism to Traducianism, but Helwys's conception of the transmission of original sin in the human family is identical to Arminius's.

71

Helwys argued in Article 3 that "by the promised seed off the woman, Jesus Christ, [and by] his obedience, all are made righteous."[47] At first glance it might seem that Helwys was embracing a view similar to that of Smyth and the Waterlanders, who argued that Christ's atonement reversed the effects of original sin for everyone. Yet he repudiates Smyth and the Waterlanders in Article 4, in which he contended that the consequences of the fall consist in humanity's total depravity. As a result of the fall, human beings have "all disposition unto evill, and no disposition or will unto anie good."[48]

Helwys's conception of the fall and its ramifications for humanity shape his understanding of free will. In two of his works, *A Short and Plaine Proofe* (1611) and *An Advertisement or Admonition unto the Congregation, Which Men Call the New Fryelers* (1611), Helwys issued a disclaimer concerning free will. He resented the recurring accusation that his doctrine of God's universal provision of salvific grace (which he called "universal redemption") implied Pelagian understandings of free will. He vehemently insisted in both these works that the common conception of freedom of the will was erroneous. Furthermore, such a view was not only logically unnecessary to the doctrine of God's general provision of salvific grace, but was also inconsistent with it. This idea is strongly reflected in Helwys's appendix to his *Advertisement or Admonition,* which was addressed to the Waterlanders:

> Whereas it is suspected that they which hold universal Redemption, do, or must hold freewill, wee desire to testifie unto all, for the cleering of ourselves from the suspect of that most damnable heresie, that god in mercie hath thus farr given us grace to see That whosoever holds uniuersall redemption by Christ, they cannot hold freewill, if they have any understanding: for freewill doth utterly abolish Christ, and destroy faith and set vp workes: for freewill is to have absolute power in a mans self to worke righteousness and obey god in perfect obedience; And such men need no Christ.[49]

Helwys was not falling back into a Reformed predestinarianism that would deny any meaningful free choice, but was rather combatting the semi-Pelagian notion of free will that characterized Smyth and the Waterlanders. Helwys, again like Arminius, believed individuals have free will in the sense that they are free from necessity and are able freely to resist and reject divine grace. Yet he denied they have the ability to choose the good without divine grace, thus retaining the same free will that Adam and Eve possessed before the fall.[50]

Helwys argued that even the image of God in human beings does not make them able to do good, much less attain salvation, without the aid of divine grace.[51] He concurred with the opinion of Arminius, that, while people remain free from necessity, they are not liberated from sin and its dominion. Arminius had stated: "the free will of man towards the true good is not only wounded, maimed, infirm, bent, and weakened; but it is also imprisoned, destroyed, and lost: And its powers are not only debilitated and useless unless they be assisted by grace, but it has no powers whatever except such are excited by divine grace."[52] In the same passage in *An Advertisement or Admonition,* Helwys directed his attention to Smyth and the Waterlanders' view that human beings, after the fall, are as innocent as Adam before it. If anyone is so blind as to think "that Christ restored man into his former estate of Innocencie," Helwys argued, then there must be another tree of knowledge of good and evil, for the only way for a perfect man to sin is by eating the fruit of that tree.[53]

Helwys's theology of sin, depravity, and human inability changed radically in the year 1610, helping to precipitate the break with Smyth. Whereas Smyth shared the more semi-Pelagian views of the Waterlanders, Helwys, like Arminius, reached back into his Reformed categories and salvaged the Augustinian doctrines of original sin, the imputation and natural transmission of Adam's sin, and the resultant inability of humanity to do any good thing or attain salvation without divine grace.

Justification

Smyth's and Helwys's differences on justification were as pronounced as their disagreements on original sin, depravity, and freedom of the will. In accord with the Waterlanders, Smyth departed sharply from his former Calvinistic theology by renouncing the Reformed doctrine of justification by the imputed righteousness of Christ. The Magisterial Reformers held to a forensic doctrine of justification that was a corollary to their penal satisfaction theory of atonement. According to this view, Christ lived sinlessly and died sacrificially to satisfy or appease the justice of God. Christ fully obeyed the divine law in His life and suffered the penalty for sin in His death. Through faith, the accomplishments of Christ's atonement—His death and righteousness—are imputed or credited to the believer. Thus the believer becomes righteous forensically. The righteousness that makes the believer just in the sight of God the judge is imputed and is to be distinguished from actual or imparted righteousness. The notion that human merit aids in justification is excluded by the fact that the righteousness of Christ alone is credited to believers for their divine acceptance and reconciliation. This understanding was common currency in the Magisterial Reformation in both its Reformed and Lutheran manifestations.

In his *Institutes of the Christian Religion,* Calvin stated that

> it is entirely by the intervention of Christ's righteousness that we obtain justification before God. This is equivalent to saying that man is not just in himself, but that the righteousness of Christ is communicated to him by imputation, while he is strictly deserving of punishment. Thus vanishes the absurd dogma, that man is justified by faith, inasmuch as it brings him under the influence of the Spirit of God by whom he is rendered righteous.[54]

Calvin made clear in this passage that justification involves more than being transformed by the Holy Spirit; it is essentially imputative in nature rather than impartative. In explaining the forensic nature of justification, Luther described imputed righteousness as an "alien holiness," a "righteousness which is in us but is entirely outside us in Christ and yet becomes our very own, as though we ourselves had achieved and earned it."[55] This understanding of justification gave

74

rise to Luther's statement that the Christian is *simul iustus et peccator* (at once justified and yet a sinner). The justifying righteousness that comes through faith in Christ makes the sinner just before the divine tribunal but does not make the sinner holy in actuality.[56]

Before his break with the Church of England, Smyth had thoroughly immersed himself in the Calvinism that had become entrenched during Elizabeth's reign. The Separatists Smyth joined after his defection were as strictly Calvinistic as the Puritans within the Church. Prior to his exile in the Netherlands, Smyth held firmly to a basic Calvinist soteriology, as seen in his *Character of the Beast*. In this work he did not offer details about his doctrine of justification. Yet it is safe to assume that, prior to his move to Amsterdam, he continued to articulate the Reformed understanding of imputed righteousness he had enunciated in his *Bright Morning Starre* and *Paterne of True Prayer*, both of which he wrote prior to embracing Separatist principles.[57] However, Smyth's encounter with the Waterlander Mennonites radically altered his views on the nature of justification and the Christian life.

Smyth exchanged his Reformed understanding of justification for the Waterlander Mennonite view. The Waterlanders melded Reformational understandings of justification with the late medieval view that the righteousness that justifies the sinner is not merely imputed forensically but imparted or infused in the believer. Smyth published his *Short Confession in XX Articles* in April 1609, before seeking admission to fellowship with the Waterlanders. That confession, however, shows the influence of the Waterlanders, not least on Smyth's doctrine of justification. Here he shifted from a purely imputational view to one that incorporates the notions of both imputation and impartation: "The justification of man before the Divine tribunal . . . consists partly of the imputation of the righteousness of Christ apprehended by faith, and partly of inherent righteousness, in the holy themselves, by the operation of the Holy Spirit, which is called regeneration and sanctification."[58] This assertion indicates Smyth's concern to affirm a middle ground between justification as purely imputation and justification solely as impartation.

Smyth's *Short Confession of Faith* of 1610, a slight revision of the Water-lander Mennonite Confession of 1580, exhibits the same bipartite conception of justification, but in less explicit terms. In justification, Smyth confessed, believers receive "true righteousness, forgiveness, absolution from sin through the bloodshed of Jesus Christ."[59] This statement, taken by itself, reflects a weakening but not necessarily a departure from the forensic language of the Magisterial Reformation. Yet this statement is followed by a second one indicating a conscious shift from a purely forensic conceptualization: Justification comes also "through righteousness, which through the Christ Jesus, by the co-operation of the Holy Ghost is plentifully shed and poured into us, so that we truly are made, of evil men, good; of fleshly, spiritual; of covetous, liberal; of proud, humble; and through regeneration are made pure in heart, and the children of God."[60]

Smyth not only emphasized the language of impartation or infusion but also identified justification with regeneration, a move that was considered a grave error in Reformed theology. This same maneuver is seen in the *Short Confession in XX Articles* cited above, in which Smyth blurred the distinction between justification and both regeneration and sanctification.[61] One also notices it in *Propositions and Conclusions*: "This quickening or reviving of Christ, this laver of regeneration, this renewing of the Holy Ghost, is our justification and salvation."[62] Smyth thus confesses what Calvin, in the above-cited passage, branded "the absurd dogma, that man is justified by faith, inasmuch as it brings him under the influence of the Spirit of God by whom he is rendered righteous."[63]

These affirmations about justification are astonishing and ironic in view of the statement on atonement in *A Short Confession* (1610), which could have easily been stated by Calvin and is inconsistent with the Waterlander/Smyth doctrine of justification: "We acknowledge that the obedience of the Son of God, his suffering, dying, bloodshed, bitter passion, death, and only sacrifice upon the cross, is a perfect reconciliation and satisfaction for our sins and the sins of the world; so that men thereby are reconciled to God, are brought into power, and have a sure hope and certainty to the entrance into everlasting life."[64]

Smyth, then, like the Waterlanders, affirmed a notion of justification that attempted to steer a middle course between the forensic formulations of Magisterial Protestantism and the relational conceptions of justification regnant in late medieval Catholic theology, which relied on notions of the impartation or infusion of righteousness.[65]

As a Radical Puritan, Helwys shared Smyth's early Reformed convictions. When Smyth embraced the Waterlanders' more semi-Pelagian views on original sin, depravity, human ability, and free will, Helwys followed suit, as evidenced by statements in his *Synopsis Fidei,* only later to adopt more Reformed sentiments similar to those that had been advanced by Arminius. One would naturally expect that the *Synopsis* would have also confirmed less-than-Reformed ideas about justification, that Helwys would have followed Smyth and the Waterlanders on this doctrine as he had on the other ones. This, however, is not the case. Helwys's views on justification were brief but poignant. Although he did not write as much on this doctrine as he did on others, his views on the subject were important to him. Indeed, his difference with Smyth on justification was one of his stated reasons for breaking with him. Despite his essential agreement with Smyth in *Synopsis Fidei,* Helwys diverged from Smyth in the confession's article on justification. The article reads: "That justification of man in the presence of God only consists in the obedience and righteousness of Christ, apprehended by faith. Yet faith without works is dead."[66] This statement represents a stark contrast to Smyth's views on justification. Unlike Smyth, Helwys apparently never abandoned his Calvinist understanding of justification by imputed righteousness through faith, despite his defection from Calvinism at almost every other crucial point prior to 1611.

In 1611 Helwys published, along with his *Declaration of Faith of English People Remaining at Amsterdam in Holland,* a list of six reasons for the schism between his group and Smyth's party. Helwys disagreed with Smyth over the latter's Hoffmanite Christology,[67] his repudiation of original sin, and his views on ecclesiastical succession, eldership, and magistracy.[68] Justification is second in this list of grievances. Helwys opposed Smyth's teaching "that men are justified partelie by the righteousness off Christ apprehended by faith, partely by their owne inherent righteousness."[69] In the same publication, Helwys affirmed the Magisterial Reformers' doctrine of justification, a view that Arminius had articulated in the Netherlands and around Europe. The wording in the *Declaration* is similar to that in *Synopsis Fidei:* "That man is justified onely by the righteousness off CHRIST, apprehended by faith, Roman. 3.28. Gal. 2.16. yet faith without works is dead. Jam. 2.17."[70]

In this concise statement, Helwys reaffirmed the forensic notion that the alien righteousness of Christ becomes the believer's by imputation through faith. His statement on the relation of faith and works—a quotation from James 2:17—served to reaffirm the traditional Reformed distinction between justification and sanctification while at the same time maintaining that sanctification is a guaranteed result of justification; that is, true faith will necessarily result in good works. It is impossible conclusively to ascertain the most direct influence on Helwys's doctrine of justification outside his reading of the Bible. We must emphasize, however, that the only other thinkers of the late sixteenth- and early seventeenth-century who affirmed a forensic theory of justification in the context of an essentially anti-Calvinistic theological framework were Arminius and some of his earliest followers.

CONCLUSION

When one considers that Helwys affirmed basic understandings of justification, original sin, human depravity, human inability, and freedom of the will that lined up with those of Arminius at a time when no other group promulgated this unique doctrinal synthesis, we can only conclude that Arminius's direct influence on Helwys's thought through some of his more widely circulated writings is possible. When Helwys's theological development is viewed in the context of his relationship with Smyth, his ability to read and write Latin, the theological *lingua franca,* and his residence in the Netherlands, this possibility becomes likely.

It is ironic that Smyth and Helwys, two Englishmen who were baptized and reared in the Church of England, developed distinctly anti-Calvinist theologies at a time when anti-Calvinism was one of the hottest topics in Cambridge and Oxford. With Smyth's Cambridge background, there is no doubt that these men were at least knowledgeable of Peter Baro, Samuel Harsnett, and other English Arminians in the Church of England. Yet when they left England they were convinced of the verity of Calvinist orthodoxy. Even after embracing Anabaptist convictions after exiling themselves in the Netherlands, they were for a time still convinced of Calvinistic predestinarian principles. It is remarkable that the anti-Calvinism fostered by these two men had its roots in theological systems cultivated outside the English context. Even more extraordinarily, they developed radically divergent views from one another, which, while both fervently anti-Calvinist, were also both distinctively unlike the Anglican Arminianism developing across the channel.

[1]H. C. Porter, *Reformation and Reaction in Tudor Cambridge* (Cambridge: Cambridge University Press, 1958), 235-39.

[2]W. T. Whitley, ed, *The Works of John Smyth, Fellow of Christ's College, 1594-1598*, 2 vols. (Cambridge: Cambridge University Press, 1915), 2:493.

[3]Quoted in B. R. White, *The English Separatist Tradition: From the Marian Martyrs to the Pilgrim Fathers* (London: Oxford University Press, 1971), 117.

[4]*Smyth*, 1:44; White, 117.

[5]*Smyth*, 2:331.

[6]Ibid., 2:337; White, 121.

[7]*Smyth*, 1:252.

[8]Ibid.

[9]Ibid., 1:567.

[10]The "Hoffmanite" Christology of the Waterlanders will be discussed later in this chapter.

[11]Champlin Burrage, *Early English Dissenters in the Light of Recent Research*, 2 vols. (Cambridge: Cambridge University Press, 1912), 1:238.

[12]Thomas Helwys, *A Short Declaration of the Mistery of Iniquity*, 97; Ernest A. Payne, *Thomas Helwys and the First Baptist Church in England* (London: Baptist Union of England and Ireland, 1962), 3.

[13]White, 125.

[14]Ibid.

[15]Burrage, 2:185.

[16]For the entire English text, see W. J. McGlothlin, ed., *Baptist Confessions of Faith* (Philadelphia: American Baptist Publication Society, 1911), 85-93.

[17]A facsimile of this letter is reproduced in W. T. Whitley, *Thomas Helwys of Gray's Inn and Broxtowe Hall* (London: Kingsgate Press, n.d.), n.p.

[18]Michael R. Watts, *The Dissenters: From the Reformation to the French Revolution* (Oxford: Clarendon Press, 1978), 160, 270; Thomas Kent Gulley, "The General Baptists in Early Stuart and Revolutionary England," Ph.D. diss., University of Wisconsin, 1994, ix-x.

[19]See James Edward McGoldrick, *Baptist Successionism: A Crucial Question in Baptist History* (Metuchen: Scarecrow, 1994).

[20]W. T. Whitley, *A History of British Baptists* (London: Charles Griffin and Company, 1923), 17-18; Lonnie D. Kliever, "General Baptist Origins: The Question of Anabaptist Influence," *Mennonite Quarterly Review* 36 (1962): 291-321; White, ch. 6; Stephen Brachlow, *The Communion of Saints: Radical Puritan and Separatist Ecclesiology, 1570-1625* (Oxford: Oxford University Press, 1988). I agree with this perspective but still think aspects of Smyth and Helwys's ecclesiology were influenced by the Waterlanders.

[21]James R. Coggins, *John Smyth's Congregation: English Separatism, Mennonite Influence, and the Elect Nation* (Scottdale: Herald, 1991); Jason K. Lee, *The Theology of John Smyth: Puritan, Separatist, Baptist, Mennonite* (Macon: Mercer University Press, 2003).

[22]See Gulley, 24-77, who rehearses every conceivable influence on Smyth and Helwys, from the Lollards to the Separatist social milieu.

[23]Ibid., 207.

[24]White, 139.

[25]Kliever, 313-16 (Kliever would agree with the basic thrust of this essay; however, he conjectures that Smyth probably derived his Arminianism from the English Arminian Peter Baro); R. T. Kendall, "An Investigation into the Theological Controversies that Separated the General Baptists from the Particular Baptists," *Baptist Reformation Review* 8 (1979): 7-28; Goki Saito, "An Investigation into the Relationship between the Early English General Baptists and the Dutch Anabaptists," Ph.D. diss., Southern Baptist Theological Seminary, 1974; Lee, *The Theology of John Smyth*.

[26]Stephen Brachlow, "Puritan Theology and General Baptist Origins," *Baptist Quarterly* ns 31 (1985), 179-94.

[27]Stephen Monroe Johnson, "The Soteriology of the English General Baptists to 1630: A Study in Theological Kinship and Dependence," Ph.D. diss., Westminster Theological Seminary, 1988; James R. Coggins, *John Smyth's Congregation*. Stephen Wright (*The Early English Baptists, 1603-1649* [Woodbridge, Suffolk, UK: Boydell, 2006]) seems to agree with this posture, though he discusses it only briefly.

[28]Ibid., 178. Johnson avers that the correct conclusion must be based on more than circumstantial evidence and cites B. R. White as the prime example of its use.

[29]Thomas Helwys, *A Short and Plaine Proofe by the Word and Workes off God that Gods Decree is not the Cause off Anye Mans Sinne or Condemnation and That All Men Are Redeamed by Christ. As also. That No Infants are Condemned* (1611), sig. A4v.

[30]Johnson, 258-59.

[31]John Smyth, "A Short Confession of Faith in XX Articles by John Smyth," in William L. Lumpkin, ed., *Baptist Confessions of Faith* (Valley Forge: Judson, 1959), 100.

[32]"Propositions and Conclusions Concerning True Christian Religion," in Lumpkin, 127.

[33]Ibid.

[34]Ibid.

[35]Tatha Wiley, *Original Sin: Origins, Developments, Contemporary Meanings* (New York: Paulist, 2002), 71; John M. Rist, *Augustine: Ancient Thought Baptized* (Cambridge: Cambridge University Press, 1996), 317; Augustus Hopkins Strong, *Systematic Theology* (Philadelphia: Judson, 1907), 619-37.

[36]Ibid.

[37]See "The Waterland Confession, 1580," and "A Short Confession of Faith, 1610," in Lumpkin, 44-66, 102-13.

[38]Ibid., 103. Cf. the translation of the 1580 confession in McGlothlin: "The first man fell into sins and became subject to divine wrath, and by God was raised up by consolatory promises and admitted to eternal life at the same time with all those who had fallen; so that none of his posterity, in respect of this restitution, is born guilty of sin or blame" (William J. McGlothlin, ed., *Baptist Confessions of Faith* [Philadelphia: American Baptist Publication Society, 1911], 27).

[39]"Propositions and Conclusions," in Lumpkin, 127.

[40]Ibid., 126-27.

[41]"A Short Confession," in Lumpkin, 103. Italics mine.

[42]Saito, "Appendix B: Translation of Latin *Synopsis of the Faith of the True English Christian Church at Amsterdam*," 198.

[43]McGlothlin, 93. Lumpkin does not include the list of six errors in his edition of the confession.

[44]Thomas Helwys, "A Declaration of Faith of English People Remaining at Amsterdam," in Lumpkin, 117.

[45]*A Short and Plaine Proofe by the Word and Workes of God that Gods Decree is not the Cause of Anye Mans Sinne or Condemnation. And that All Men are Redeemed by Christ. As also, that No Infants are Condemned* (1611), sig. A7r.

[46]Jacobus Arminius, *The Works of James Arminius*, 3 vols, trans. James Nichols and William Nichols (Nashville: Randall House, 2007), 2:156.

[47]Helwys, *A Short and Plaine Proofe*, sig. A7r.

[48]Ibid., 118.

[49]Thomas Helwys, *An Advertisement or Admonition, unto the Congregations, which Men call the New Fryelers, in the Lowe Countries, Written in Dutch, and Published in English* (1611), 91-92.

[50]Ibid., 92.

[51]Ibid., 92-93.

[52]Arminius, *Works*, 2:192.

[53]*An Advertisement or Admonition*, 92.

[54]John Calvin, *Institutes of the Christian Religion*, trans. Henry Beveridge, vol. 2 (Grand Rapids: Eerdmans, 1970), 3.11.23 (58).

[55]Cited in Paul Althaus, *The Theology of Martin Luther* (Philadelphia: Fortress, 1966), 228.

[56]Ibid., 242ff. Calvin was more insistent than Luther on the fact that, though a logical distinction inhered between justification and sanctification, the latter was a guaranteed result of the former.

[57]Smyth, *Works,* 1:164, 209-10. Cf. Johnson, 206-207.

[58]"Short Confession of Faith in XX Articles by John Smyth," in Lumpkin, 101.

[59]"A Short Confession of Faith, 1610," in Lumpkin, 108.

[60]Ibid.

[61]Heiko Oberman's statement about the late medieval theologian Gabriel Biel's view of justification is both noteworthy and relevant: "It does not surprise us that we found [in Biel] no trace of a distinction between justification and sanctification." Heiko Augustinus Oberman, *The Harvest of Medieval Theology: Gabriel Biel and Late Medieval Nominalism* (Durham: Labyrinth, 1983), 356.

[62]"Propositions and Conclusions, 1612," in Lumpkin, 131.

[63]Calvin, *Institutes,* 3.11.23.

[64]"A Short Confession, 1610," in Lumpkin, 106.

[65]See, e.g., Heiko Oberman's discussion of Gabriel Biel's anti-forensic doctrine of justification in *The Harvest of Late Medieval Theology*, 353-56.

[66]Saito, "Appendix B: Translation of Latin *Synopsis of the Faith of the True English Christian Church at Amsterdam,*" 198.

[67]Hoffmanite Christology is the view of the Mennonite Melchior Hoffman called "heavenly flesh" Christology. It opposed the classical orthodox doctrine of the humanity of Christ by positing that Christ's body was not of the same substance as Mary's body.

[68]Helwys opposed Smyth's teaching that magistrates were not allowed membership in Christ's church. This list of grievances is printed in McGlothlin, 92-93.

[69]Ibid.

[70]"A Declaration of Faith of English People Remaining at Amsterdam in Holland, 1611," in Lumpkin, 118.

THE FIRST BAPTIST TREATISE ON PREDESTINATION: THOMAS HELWYS'S *SHORT AND PLAINE PROOFE*

Thomas Helwys is often overshadowed by his mentor, John Smyth. Smyth was the leader of the English Separatist congregation whose voyage to the Netherlands Helwys financed and who later adopted believer's baptism and an Arminian soteriological posture.[1] Yet Helwys was the father of the English Baptist movement, having left Smyth, who had capitulated to the views of the Dutch Waterlander Mennonites. Helwys's decision to leave Smyth and take part of their congregation back to England resulted in the establishment of the first Baptist church on English soil and the subsequent Baptist movement.[2] The General Baptist movement arose from Helwys's activities, while the Particular Baptist (Calvinist) movement arose a generation later.[3]

In 1611 Helwys and his congregation issued a confession of faith, *A Declaration of Faith of English People Remaining at Amsterdam.*[4] In this work, Helwys outlined the major reasons for his separation from Smyth. The confession delineated objections to Smyth's denial of the Reformed doctrine of original sin and the imputation of the righteousness of Christ alone in justification, as well as his acceptance of Hoffmanite Christology[5] and Waterlander positions on succession and the role of the magistracy.[6]

While the layman Helwys was not Smyth's equal in theological acumen, his zealous theological commitments motivated him to put his views into print. His literary output gave voice to the fledgling English Baptist movement, resulting, for example, in the first treatise in the English language advocating liberty of conscience and freedom of religion, *A Short Declaration of the Mystery of Iniquity*.[7] Helwys's sentiments gave rise to the Baptist movement, his soteriological views laying the foundation for a vigorous Arminian Baptist movement in the seventeenth century, which would find expression in General Baptist writers such as Thomas Grantham later in the century.

Later in 1611, after writing his *Declaration of Faith of English People Remaining at Amsterdam*, Helwys wrote a brief work entitled *A Short and Plaine Proofe by the Word and Workes of God that Gods decree is not the cause of anye Mans sinne or Condemnation. And That all Men are redeemed by Christ. As also, That no Infants are Condemned*.[8] This treatise does more than any other General Baptist writing to link General Baptist soteriology with the thought of Jacobus Arminius.

Though Helwys did not mention Arminius's name, in his preface he referred positively to the fact that the truth of general redemption was breaking forth in what even the Calvinist Separatists said were the "best Reformed churches"—that is, the Dutch Reformed churches (sig.A4v). Helwys obviously had in mind the Arminian surge in Dutch Reformed circles that was raging in the Netherlands at the very time he and John Smyth had exiled themselves there. That Helwys would tie his doctrine of general redemption to the Dutch Reformed churches, despite his lack of reference to Arminius personally, indicates he was familiar with early Dutch Arminianism and viewed it favorably.[9] When one adds to this the similarity of Helwys's and Arminius's soteriology, as Helwys moves away from Smyth's Waterlander-influenced soteriology in 1610, it seems probable that Arminius's thought influenced Helwys and General Baptist soteriology.

Helwys intended *A Short and Plaine Proofe* to be an exposition and defense of Article 5 in his *Declaration of Faith*, which dealt with election and reprobation (sig. A3r). As reflected in his title, for Helwys the solution to the problem of election and reprobation lies in the biblical construct of general redemption—God's gracious, universal design for the salvation of humanity. Redemption is not "particular" (wrought only for the elect) but rather general or universal. "God hath not in his eternal decree appointed some particular men to be saved and some particular men to be condemned, and so hath redeemed but some. But . . . Christ is given a ransom for all men, yea even for the wicked, that bring swift damnation upon themselves" (sig. A3r).

Helwys's prayer was that the "clear light of truth" of general redemption would shine on more and more people—starting with his Calvinistic Separatist counterparts.[10] He criticized mainstream Protestants for not going far enough in their reform of the church. They have broken "out of the depths of darkness" of the Church of Rome but are "resting on the faith of the church" rather than Scripture alone, Helwys said. Yet such Protestants still fail to reform the church thoroughly according to scriptural principles and thus distort the scriptural teaching on the divine salvific plan. Helwys hoped that new light would break forth from the Word of God and free them from their error, thus magnifying the universal grace of God in Christ (sig. A4v).

Helwys saw the main solution to the problem of election and reprobation in the doctrine of the general provision of salvation for humanity. Yet he saw the central question at the bottom of the debate as the origin or cause of evil. What caused sin? Was it the unconditional decree of God or the free will of man before the fall? This is the main question that must be answered in any discussion of predestination and human freedom (sig. A4r). Helwys faulted the Calvinists of his day, who wrongly "enter into the secret counsels of God" (sig. A4r). Helwys saw this as vain philosophy that "measur[es] God's thoughts by their thoughts and his ways by their ways" (sig. A4r).

DETERMINISM AND THE FREE WILL OF ADAM

In his preface, Helwys emphasized Adam's free will before the fall. Because Adam had free will to choose to disobey God or not, the divine (supralapsarian) decree to foreordain the fall makes no sense.

> God giving *Adam free will and power in himself not to eat of the forbidden fruit and live, or to eat and die,* could not in his eternal decree ordain or appoint him to life or death, for then had his *free will* been overthrown. And if Adam had not eaten and sinned (which was in his own power), then had not death entered. Therefore God did not decree that death should enter, and thus *God's decree* is not the cause of any man's condemnation (sig. A2r).

Helwys said that it is Adam's unfettered choice to sin that causes condemnation (reprobation), not God's decree.

Another root problem in Calvinism, according to Helwys, is its determinism. He criticized the notion that "*the Almighty* hath decreed all things that come to pass, and that of him, and through him all things are"—that "God is the moving cause of all things" (sig. A4r). This concept logically results in the supralapsarian idea that God foreordained the fall. This view, Helwys argued, results in the belief, whether Calvinists own up to it or not, that God is the author of sin: "They will and do conclude most blasphemously that God hath foredecreed that sin should come to pass" (sig. A4r). Helwys believed that this doctrine was a result of "the craft and subtlety of [Satan] who lieth in wait hereby to deceive" (sig. A4r). Helwys dealt with the Calvinist objection that God did not decree sin itself, just the action that is sinful. Helwys rejected this as faulty logic. If God's providence is "in every action," Helwys argues, then it must also have been in "Adam's eating of the forbidden fruit." Thus, if God foreordained every action, it logically follows that He foreordained sin as well (sig. A4r–sig. A5v). Helwys blasted this approach with stinging rhetoric: "Thus do they walk by their own imaginations and intents, deceiving and being deceived, pretending not to lay sin upon God, when (indeed and in truth) they directly make God the author of sin. Our best thoughts of them are that they do it ignorantly. The Lord give them hearts to repent, all whose conversions should be the joy of our souls" (sig. A5v).[11]

After these opening thoughts about the free will of Adam before the fall and the Calvinist view of the foreordination of all things, Helwys set out his plan for the treatise. He began by humbly telling the reader there was no one more unfit than he to delve into these issues. "Yet to show ourselves faithful with that talent that God hath given us, we have, through the grace of God, taken in hand to do our best service unto the Lord herein, hoping for his assistance and acceptance" (sig. A5v). Helwys's first aim was to show how he differed from Calvinists and how they "digress from the truth" (sig. A5v).

Helwys stated that God decreed all good that comes to pass, "through him are all good things. . . . the Lord is the author, actor, and moving cause in and to every good action"(sig. A5v). Yet God is not the author of evil. However, if Calvinism is true with its system of unconditional election and reprobation, predestination to salvation and predestination to damnation, then God is the author of evil, for He creates people for destruction so "they of necessity must be damned" (sig. A5r). The Calvinist system of reprobation, whether it states that God unconditionally reprobates people to damnation without choice in the matter, or God simply "hath particularly redeemed some and left others to perish," makes God the author of sin and evil (sig. A5r).

THE CAUSE OF DIVINE REPROBATION

Having set forth what is *not* the cause of reprobation—God's decretive will—Helwys proceeded to establish, in "the most plain, easy, and short way that, by the direction of his Spirit, our hearts can devise," (sig. A5r) what *is* the cause of divine reprobation. Citing Romans 5:12, 18, Helwys insisted that sin is the cause of condemnation, not God's decretive will (sig. A5r). Everyone agrees with this, Helwys wrote, but Calvinists wish to make human sin the result of God's decree.

Helwys argued that God's creation of Adam in the *imago dei* with free will to choose between good and evil courses of action frees God of the charge of being the author of sin.[12] "It is proved here," Helwys wrote, "that God gave Adam free will and power to eat, or not to eat, and this all men do confess. How then can it be said, with any spiritual understanding, that God decreed he should sin? For God's forecounsel and decree must of necessity come to

87

pass" (sig. A6v). Whatever God decrees must necessarily come to pass. Thus, if God decreed that Adam would eat of the fruit, then that action becomes a matter of deterministic necessity and not a free action (sig. A6r). "Can men make freedom and bondage in one and the same action, all in one man, and all at one time? How shall men be able with any good conscience to make things so contrary hang together?" (sig. A6r).

Furthermore, God's command to Adam "that he should not sin," means that God is commanding Adam *not* to do something and at the same time decreeing that he *will* do it—making it impossible for him not to do it. Helwys argued that the biblical God does not make commands and then decree states of affairs in such a way that makes it impossible for His creatures to obey those commands (sig. A6r-sig. A7v). Such a decree would place God in opposition to His own revealed will: "In the fear of God, let men take heed how they go about (by subtle arguments) to prove God contrary to himself, which they plainly do, when they say it was the eternal will of God that man should sin, and yet God commands that he should not sin" (sig. A6r).

Just as it would be unjust for God to decree Adam's fall unconditionally, so, Helwys argued, it is unjust for God to decree the condemnation of human beings after the fall without extending divine grace to them. Helwys proceeded to refute the doctrine of divine reprobation, the idea that "God hath decreed to forsake and leave those that he hath appointed to condemnation, to themselves," withholding grace from them, and "leaving them to sin." This, he averred, was an unprovable assertion, "an old, conceived imagination and hath no ground of truth" (sig. A7v-r).

It is interesting that Helwys here aimed, not at what has been called "double predestination" but at "single predestination." Double predestination was much more popular among Calvinists of his day than it is now. Those who held this view believed that God unconditionally predestines people to both salvation and damnation. That is, both election and reprobation are unconditional, both arising from the secret counsel of God. Single reprobation argues that, while God's election of people to salvation is unconditional (that is, not conditioned on foreseen faith or foreseen union with Christ), reprobation of people

88

to damnation is conditioned on foreseen sin or unbelief. Single reprobation is the doctrine that Helwys refuted here. Yet, to him, any doctrine of reprobation in which God condemns people when He commanded them to repent and believe and yet did not give them the grace to repent and believe is equally pernicious, whether single or double. It all amounts to the same thing: God says, "Believe on the Lord Jesus Christ and you will be saved," yet He grants the gracious ability to believe only to the elect, leaving the reprobate in their sins. For Helwys, this is the height of injustice, unworthy of God who is the fountainhead of justice and truth.

FALL IN ADAM, REDEMPTION IN CHRIST

Helwys launched into a discussion of the effects of the fall on the human race. He reiterated the Reformed doctrines of original sin, depravity, and human inability in salvation. Like Arminius, he held to an Augustinian, Traducian, and natural headship understanding of the transmission of sin in the race, as seen in his statement that Adam's posterity "were yet all in his loins" (sig. A7r).[13] Helwys stated that death and condemnation "went over him [Adam], and over all by his transgression" (sig. A8v). After Adam's fall, Helwys explained, we see the first mention of the gospel, Genesis 3:15, which is intended for all Adam's posterity. Helwys used a Reformed approach to original sin to argue for general redemption. As all Adam's posterity are caught up in his sin and guilt, so Christ dies for all Adam's posterity (sig. A8v).

Christ, the second Adam, comes to provide redemption for all people. Yet this redemption becomes actualized in individuals through the condition of personal belief in Christ. Here Helwys's Arminian view of conditional election comes to bear. Predestination to salvation is not unconditional. Rather, "the condition was, that Adam should believe, and under this same condition was Christ promised and sent to all the world" (sig. A8r). Yet this condition is made available to all Adam's posterity, and Helwys illustrates this by quoting from the Gospel of John: "*John 12.46. I am come a light into the world that whosoever believeth in me should not abide in darkness. And John 3.16. God so loved the world that he hath given his only begotten Son that whosoever believeth in him should not perish but have everlasting life"* (sig. A8r).

If God had left people in a state of condemnation for Adam's sin without giving them the opportunity to recover from such a state, He would be unmerciful, Helwys argued (sig. A9v). Yet He does not leave humanity, or any part thereof, without a remedy for original sin. As all of Adam's posterity are guilty in Adam, so Christ provides all of Adam's posterity a remedy—not just the elect, but all of Adam's posterity.

INFANT SALVATION

In this context, Helwys deemed it necessary to discuss infant salvation. Tying the doctrine of infant salvation to the unity of the race in Adam, Helwys explained that infants are saved through the redemption Christ provides for all Adam's posterity (sig. B1v). The difference between infants and adults is that infants have no way to resist the grace of God in Christ that has been proffered to all in general redemption. Adults must meet the condition of belief in order to appropriate the general redemption of all Adam's posterity. Yet, since infants[14] cannot meet the condition of belief, and since they cannot resist Christ's general redemption through unbelief, they are saved through Christ's general redemption. Thus, Helwys posited infant salvation through general redemption (a different kind of "conditionality" for infants than for adults, since they cannot meet—or fail to meet—the conditions set for adults). This is opposed to the constructs in many Anabaptist and later Arminian theories of infant salvation, which are really more infant "safety" views that reject or mitigate original sin, than infant salvation views.

Helwys was interacting directly with Anabaptist theories of original sin (actually, the lack thereof) and infant safety the Waterlanders had confessed and John Smyth had appropriated from them. He distanced himself from Smyth and Waterlander leaders like Hans de Ries in his views on original sin and infant salvation.[15] Again, here Helwys bore the influence of Arminius, the only theologian of that time who sought to combine the notions of general redemption and infant salvation with a thoroughgoing Augustinian approach to original sin and the transmission of Adam's sin to the human race. The foregoing distinctions are not meant to imply Helwys believed that infants were guilty of actual sins. His primary concern here was to provide a rationale for the salvation of infants, and he did so in the context of general redemption rather than mere infant safety or a denial of the doctrine of original sin.[16]

PROBLEMS WITH DIVINE REPROBATION

After this excursus on original sin, general redemption, and infant salvation, Helwys again took up the subject of reprobation. He reiterated his earlier point, that reprobation makes God the author of sin. He then argued that the doctrine of reprobation, which rests on the Calvinistic system of particular redemption, mitigates the biblical witness to the love of God. It "restraineth the love of God to the world in giving his Son for a Savior" (sig. B2v). Helwys's argument from the universal love of God in Christ is penetrating and powerful, as seen in the following passage:

> . . . whereas our Savior Christ saith, John 3.16, *God so loved the world, that he hath given his only begotten son that whosoever believeth in him should not perish but have eternal life.* This opinion of particular redemption saith that God did not so love the world, but he loved some few particular persons, as he gave his son for them, and they only shall believe and shall be saved. And the greatest part of mankind, God loved them not, but hath decreed they shall be damned, and he hath not given his Son for them but hath left them to perish. Thus denying the greatest part of the world to have any means of salvation, and that there is no Savior for them (sig. B2v).

This excerpt brings Helwys's general-redemption approach into sharp relief with the particular-redemption theology of regnant seventeenth-century Calvinism. It also illustrates Helwys's method, which veers from the scholastic method and uses a more plain-style expositional approach to Scripture to establish Arminian arguments.

Another reason Helwys rejected the Calvinistic scheme of particular redemption and reprobation is that, like the decree to cause the fall, the decree to reprobate certain people puts God at cross-purposes with Himself. In Scripture God commands people to repent and even calls them to faith universally with the gospel. Yet in the Calvinistic view, Helwys charged, God is commanding them and calling them to do what they cannot possibly do because He has not graciously given them the capacity to do it.

> . . . This lamentable opinion of particular *redemption* and *reprobation* saith they [the reprobate] can have no part nor portion in Christ. So is their judgment enlarged for not receiving Christ, with whom they have nothing to do. And thus do they make Christ to offer himself to them that he would not have receive him, and which he hath decreed shall not receive him, nor believe him, and make the words of the Lord feigned words, and words of dissimulation (sig. B2v).

Helwys went on to cite Luke 13:34, which he interpreted as giving human beings the freedom to resist and reject divine drawing grace. Here again, he pressed, a particular-redemption scheme seems to make Christ conflicted with Himself, using words He does not really mean, holding out promises on which He cannot, or does not intend to, deliver. Helwys quoted Jesus's words of "unfeigned earnestness" to Jerusalem, "how often would I have gathered thy children together as the hen gathereth her brood under her wings, and ye would not." It is "impiety," he insisted, to "account these words feigned," and if Calvinists say they are not doing this, then they have to admit that "God would have had all Israel and all their posterity in uprightness of heart, to have feared him, and kept his commandments, that it might have gone well with them forever, and so did not decree any of them, nor of their posterity, to be condemned." If Jesus's words were not "feigned," then He would have "gathered the children of Jerusalem together which would not be gathered and so would have had them believe in him that would not. And yet they that hold this fearful opinion hold that God would not have some men, yea the most men, to believe, but hath decreed their condemnation" (sig. B2r).

Helwys quoted Acts 17:30, "*That now God admonisheth all men everywhere to repent*," continuing his engaging line of argument: "Yet they of this opinion . . say, he would not have all, but some to repent. And if they would speak plainly, and not halt betwixt opinions, they must say that God would have some to be unbelievers and wicked and disobedient, and that is the highest blasphemy" (sig. B2r).

Another difficulty Helwys had with particular redemption was that it diminishes Christ's gracious work of redemption and His suffering for sins. This view, which makes Christ a "particular private redeemer for some private men" dishonors Christ "in that his great sufferings are not accounted sufficient to take away Adam's sin, and so hath he not yet utterly broken, but only bruised, the serpent's head, making Adam's sin to abound above the grace of God by Christ, overthrowing that word of God, Rom. 5:20, which saith, *Where sin abounded grace abounded much more*, speaking of Adam's sin"(sig. B3v). Again Helwys invoked his theory that Christ's redemption makes available a remedy for original sin for the entire human race, so that all who meet the condition of faith personally appropriate Christ's redemptive work.

SPIRITUAL EFFECTS OF THE DOCTRINE OF UNCONDITIONAL ELECTION

Helwys rooted his discussion of the doctrine of unconditional election to practical, spiritual concerns, warning that Calvinism has numerous negative spiritual effects. First, he argued that the doctrine of unconditional election "works presumption in men" (sig. B3v). People who believe they are elect and have no possibility of being condemned will become presumptuous about their salvation. This relates to their security in salvation as well:

If men can but once get a persuasion in themselves that God hath elected them, then they are secure. They need not work out their salvation with fear and trembling. For God having decreed them to be saved, they must be saved. They need not fear: If they increase and grow in knowledge and grace, it is well but if they do not, it is all one, for it is decreed they must be saved, and this causeth all slothful, careless, and negligent profession. . . . But for all their presumption, it shall be said unto them, *I know you not. Depart from me all you workers of iniquity. Luke 13.26, 27* (sig. B3v).

Second, Helwys argued, particular redemption causes those who fear they might be among the reprobate to despair and not to attempt to respond to God at all. This, in turn, leads to their own condemnation. It "makes some despair utterly, as thinking there is no grace for them, and that God hath decreed their destruction. And it makes others desperately careless, holding that if God hath decreed they shall be saved, then they shall be saved, and if God hath decreed they shall be damned, they shall be damned, and so in a desperate carelessness run headlong to destruction" (sig. B3v).

Third, Helwys asked, why preach? If God has already decided that certain people are necessarily saved and others are necessarily damned, the biblical command to preach the gospel is incoherent. How can the gospel be preached to everyone, Helwys asked, if preachers do not know whether or not Christ died for the ones to whom they are preaching? "Here is all faith in preaching the Gospel to the World destroyed. For what faith can there be to preach the Gospel when we know not whether Christ belong to them or not?" (sig. B3r).

Fourth, Helwys argued, praying for the conversion of unregenerate people makes no sense if Christ did not die to provide them with salvation. If a Christian prays for an unbeliever to be converted, he might be praying against the decretive will of God. Helwys asks, how can "a man of faith pray for any man, when he cannot know, whether God hath decreed him to condemnation, and so he pray against God's decree" (sig. B3r).

Fifth, Helwys brought the discussion back to the question of assurance of salvation. Before, Helwys had said that the doctrine of unconditional election might cause people to be presumptuous about their security in salvation. In this point, he argued that the doctrine has the effect of causing some truly regenerate people to doubt whether they are among the elect. This gets to the heart of the problem of assurance (or lack thereof) in sixteenth- and seventeenth-century English Calvinism (Puritanism): How can one prove (even to himself) that he is elect? Helwys said, "For thou must first believe that Christ is given a Savior for thee before thou canst know that he is a Savior for thee, which cannot be, that a man should believe what he knows not" (sig. B4v). Helwys went on to say, "Let the mystery of iniquity the man of sin himself devise (whose device this particular redemption is) how any man shall know by the word of God that Christ is given a Savior for him, but by knowing that he is given a Savior for all men, except he can show his name especially set down in the Word" (sig. B4v).

GENERAL REDEMPTION

Helwys followed his discussion of the practical, spiritual effects of the doctrine of particular redemption with a more direct discussion of general redemption or general atonement *per se*. He proposed to "prove by plain evidence of Scripture that Christ by his death and sufferings hath redeemed all men." He began with a consideration of the *protoevangelion* in Genesis 3:15. Here again, Helwys marshaled his Traducian and natural headship view of Adam's relationship to his posterity to argue for general redemption. Key to Helwys's construct was his belief that all Adam's posterity were "in him" or "in his loins," though they had not yet been born. Reformed theologians have often referred to this Augustinian concept as the doctrine of Adamic unity. In Genesis 3:15, Helwys argued, the promise to send Christ to redeem Adam and Eve was, by extension, made to the entire race, because the entire race were in Adam and Eve at the time the promise was made. The "promise of Christ is made of Adam and Hevah, in which were all mankind, and in whom were all mankind

95

in whom all had sinned, and for the taking away of the condemnation due for that sin, Christ was there promised and given" (sig. B4v-r). This interpretive device sets certain Calvinistic categories on their head while at the same time appealing to Augustinian-Reformed categories (e.g., regarding Adamic unity).

Helwys's other arguments for Christ's universal atonement for humanity appealed to proof texts that were common to the Dutch Arminians and the Amsterdam Waterlander Mennonites. He cited, for example, 1 John 2:2, "*And he is a reconciliation for our sins* (speaking of all the faithful to whom he wrote) *and not for ours only, but also for the sins of the whole world.*" Helwys argued that this passage clearly teaches that Christ's atonement is not merely for believers, but also for unbelievers. "How is it possible that the Holy Ghost should speak more plainly, to show that Jesus Christ is a reconciliation for the faithful which are not of the world, and for the unfaithful which are the world" (sig. B4r).

In this connection, Helwys cited 2 Corinthians 5:15, which states that Christ is dead for all; 2 Corinthians 5:19, which affirms that Christ reconciled the world to himself; and 1 Timothy 2:5-6, which asserts that Christ Jesus gave himself a ransom for all (sig. B4r). Helwys was appealing to proof texts that were part of both Arminian and Mennonite doctrinal teaching, with which he was familiar. He continues this with his citation of 2 Peter 3:9; 1 Timothy 2:4; and Colossians 2:20: "*The Lord of that promise is not slack as some men count slackness but is patient towards us and would have no man perish but would all come to repentance*" (B4). "*God will that all men shall be saved and come to the acknowledging of the truth*" (sig. B5v). "*And through peace made by that blood of that his cross to reconcile to himself through himself all things both which are in earth and which are in heaven*" (sig. B5v).

Having cited these proof texts, the plain sense of which Hewlys believed should be clear to anyone who is "tractably minded," Helwys moved back to a reiteration of his main theological framework for understanding both original sin and general redemption: Adamic unity. He stated that "when man had of his own free will (being tempted) yielded unto the temptation of the serpent, neglecting the commandment of his God and Creator, and brought condemnation upon himself and all mankind, God, of his infinite mercy, would not leave

Adam and in him all mankind to perish under that condemnation, but hath sent a Savior to redeem Adam and all mankind from that sin" (sig. B5v).

Furthermore, Helwys argued, both the mercy and justice of God demands that He send His Son to die equally for all people. Yet Helwys tied even this to the concept of Adamic unity. In the atonement, God was "equally merciful and equally just unto all, being no respecter of persons, not pardoning Adam and giving him a Savior and condemning the greatest part of his posterity for that his sin: but hath given his son a Savior for all, if through unbelief they deprive not themselves" (sig. B5v-r).

Finally, Helwys discussed the practical spiritual benefits of believing the doctrine of general redemption. "And what a comfortable doctrine is this unto all, when every poor soul may know, that there is grace and salvation for him by Christ, and that Christ hath shed his blood for him, that believing in him he may be saved, and that God would not the death of him, but that he should repent and live. Thus is all despair taken away, . . . and all careless presumption cut off . . . " (sig. B5r).

In his concluding paragraph on proofs for general atonement, Helwys recapped some of the arguments he had already made. He discussed, for example, the agreement of the doctrine with "the whole Word of God," the fact that the doctrine sets forth the mercy of God and advances the justice of God. Yet then he added to his understanding of the universality of Christ's atonement being an example of God's justice. Before he had said that general atonement illustrates God's justice in that God is not partial to one segment of humanity over another (e.g., Adam over his posterity or the elect over the reprobate). Here Helwys says that general atonement also illustrates the justice of God in that it leaves human beings "without excuse" in God's condemnation of those who have rejected Christ and remain alienated from God in sin. General redemption "advances the justice of God, in condemning unbelievers seeing he hath left them without excuse, in that he hath given them a Savior, in whom because they believe not, they are justly condemned" (sig. B5r).

It is clear that Helwys believed doctrine has not merely a cognitive function but also an affective one. This is seen in his constant appeal to the fact that the doctrine of general redemption brings with it emotional benefits: " We doubt not that comfort will follow abundantly" (sig. B5r-sig. B6v).

In his conclusion, Helwys summarized his treatment of the doctrine of particular versus general redemption. However, he spent the most time on the unique keystone of his interpretation: that the unity of the race in Adam, which demands the Reformed doctrine of original sin, also demands the doctrine of general redemption, based on the *protoevangelion* in Genesis 3:15. Yet, while this general redemption is accomplished for all, it is not indiscriminately applied to all, but must be subjectively appropriated to be salvifically efficacious.

> And we have shown that, as Christ the promised seed was given and sent to Adam to be his Savior, for the same end he was given and sent to all the world as also under the same condition, which was that he should believe in him. For if Adam had not believed, he must have been condemned, and if all the world had not believed, all the world must have been condemned, and as Adam, believing in the promised seed, was (through the grace and mercy of God in Christ) to be saved, even so all the world, believing in the promised seed, was (through the grace and mercy of God in Christ) to be saved (sig. B6v-r).

FREE WILL

In an epilogue, Helwys clarified what his beliefs were concerning human free will after the fall. He argued that the belief in free will as Calvinists commonly define it is often attached to the doctrine of general redemption. Yet he wished to distance himself from that doctrine. If by free will is meant the Pelagian or semi-Pelagian belief (which, for example, John Smyth and the Waterlander Mennonites held) that man after the fall has the natural free will to choose the good without the interposition of divine grace, then Helwys does not believe in it. He says,

It is a custom amongst men to conclude that free will must needs follow this understanding of universal redemption: and if their meaning were free will in Christ, and that we have free power and ability through Christ to work out our salvation, and that through Christ we are made able to every good work, such a free will we hold. But that man hath any free will or power in himself to work his own salvation or to choose life, we utterly deny. . . . Thus Christ offering himself, man hath power and doth reject Christ, put the Word of God from him, resist the Holy Ghost, and freely of his own will work his own condemnation. But he hath no power at all to work his own salvation, and so much only to clear ourselves from that gross and fearful error of free will, from the which the Lord in great mercy hath freed us (sig. B7v).

CONCLUSION

Many who are unfamiliar with Baptist origins will be surprised to learn that Helwys, the first Baptist, was Arminian. As seen in the last paragraph, his Arminianism, like that of Arminius, was of a different sort from the more semi-Pelagian tendencies of the Waterlander Mennonites, which he rejected, the English Arminianism gaining popularity in his day, or the later Wesleyan-Holiness Arminianism of those who would follow John Wesley.[17] It was a more grace-oriented Arminianism that emphasized that salvation was by grace alone, through faith alone, by the imputed righteousness of Christ alone, though divine grace is resistible. Helwys's plain-style approach in this first Baptist treatise on predestination laid the groundwork for more extensive works by General Baptist thinkers such as Thomas Grantham (e.g., *Christianismus Primitivus*).[18] Probably because the Free Will Baptists are the only modern denomination historically connected to the seventeenth-century General Baptists, the Arminianism of Helwys and his successors has not been studied in the wider Baptist movement. Yet it remains a vital resource for understanding Arminian Baptist approaches to soteriology.

[1]On Smyth and Helwys, see B. R. White, *The English Separatist Tradition: From the Marian Martyrs to the Pilgrim Fathers* (London: Oxford University Press, 1971).

[2]See Chapter Three.

[3]The "General" in General Baptists signifies general or universal atonement—that Christ died for all humanity, whereas the "Particular" in Particular Baptist stands for particular or limited atonement—that Christ died only for the elect. For more on both the General Baptists and Particular Baptists, see H. Leon McBeth, *The Baptist Heritage: Four Centuries of Baptist Witness* (Nashville: Broadman, 1987), 21-123; B. R. White, *The English Baptists of the Seventeenth Century* (London: Baptist Historical Society, 1996). On the English General Baptists in the context of their relationship with their American descendants, the Free Will Baptists, see William F. Davidson, *The Free Will Baptists in History* (Nashville: Randall House, 2000); Michael R. Pelt, *A History of Original Free Will Baptists* (Mount Olive: Mount Olive College Press, 1996); and J. Matthew Pinson, *A Free Will Baptist Handbook: Heritage, Beliefs, and Ministries* (Nashville: Randall House, 1998).

[4]For the entire English text, of Helwys's *Declaration*, see W. J. McGlothlin, ed., *Baptist Confessions of Faith* (Philadelphia: American Baptist Publication Society, 1911), 85-93.

[5]Hoffmanite Christology taught that Christ's flesh was celestial or heavenly rather than derived from the Virgin Mary.

[6]See Champlin Burrage, *Early English Dissenters in the Light of Recent Research,* 2 vols. (Cambridge: Cambridge University Press, 1912), 2:185.

[7]Thomas Helwys, *A Short Declaration of the Mystery of Iniquity*, ed. Richard Groves. Classics of Religious Liberty I (Macon: Mercer University Press, 1998).

[8]Hereafter, in this chapter, the spelling in quotations from Helwys is modernized.

[9]Many authors did not document their sources back then; thus, it is sometimes difficult to discern who their influences are.

[10]This phrase is reminiscent of Separatist leader John Robinson's phrase, "The Lord has yet more truth and light to break forth out of His Holy Word." Cited in Timothy George, *John Robinson and the English Separatist Tradition* (Macon: Mercer University Press, 1982), vii.

[11]Sometimes in his writings, Helwys—beleaguered, persecuted, imprisoned, and in the context of theological polemics much more heated than those in our own day—made extreme statements about the spiritual state of his opponents, whom he believed had rejected the truth.

[12]Helwys assumed the classic Reformed tying of Genesis 1:26-27 with Ephesians 4:24 in his understanding of the divine image in humanity.

[13]See Chapter Three.

[14]And, as later General Baptists specified, children and mentally incapable adults who have not reached an age of moral and spiritual responsibility.

[15]See Chapter Three.

[16]Helwys's statements on infant salvation here must be compared to his statements in his *Declaration of Faith* to get the full impact of these distinctions.

[17]See Chapters Three and Six.

[18]See Chapter Four.

THOMAS GRANTHAM
AND THE DIVERSITY OF
ARMINIAN SOTERIOLOGY

Thomas Grantham, the foremost English General Baptist of the latter half of the seventeenth century, is the quintessential representative of Arminian Baptist theology, combining classical Arminian soteriology with a distinctly Baptist view of church and state.[1] To say, however, that Grantham's or his General Baptist contemporaries' soteriology was Arminian requires much qualification. This is not because it differed exceedingly from Arminius's own soteriology. Rather, it is because of the shape Arminian theology took in the early part of the seventeenth century and in the centuries that followed. A study of Grantham's soteriology serves to enable one to understand the nuances of that unique Arminian Baptist stream of theology. Yet it also helps one grasp the diversity of Arminianism (or, as some have quipped, "Arminianisms"[2]) as a theological phenomenon.

To study Grantham's views in the context of the whole of Arminian theology prior to him would be a daunting task.[3] But to examine them in the context of a representative English Arminian in the half-century that preceded Grantham would serve at least two purposes. It would uncover Grantham's unique middle ground between orthodox Calvinism and what has come to be known as Arminianism since the time of Arminius. However, it would also serve as a starting point for the discussion of doctrinal Arminianism in the seventeenth and succeeding centuries. Thus this study will comprise an exposition of Grantham's theology of sin and redemption with reference to John Goodwin (d. 1665), the Arminian Puritan.[4]

THOMAS GRANTHAM

Thomas Grantham was born in 1634 in Halton, near Spilsby, in eastern Lincolnshire, the son of a farmer and tailor.[5] Grantham made his living, like his father, as a tailor and mainly a farmer. Grantham recalled that the "Lord wrought faith and repentance" in his heart when he was around fourteen or fifteen years of age, and at age nineteen (1653), he joined a small General Baptist church in Boston, Lincolnshire, and was baptized by immersion. Three years after his baptism, Grantham was chosen as pastor, which involved him in preaching in his own town as well as neighboring villages. This activity brought persecution on Grantham and others.

In 1660, after the restoration of the monarchy, Grantham and a fellow believer, Joseph Wright, presented a plea for toleration to King Charles II. This plea included a statement of General Baptist loyalty to the crown as well as a confession of faith, which later become known as the *Standard Confession, 1660.* (Grantham subsequently reprinted it with annotations in his *Christianismus Primitivus.*) The crown was not receptive, and many General Baptist leaders soon found themselves imprisoned. Grantham himself was in and out of jail during the 1660s, which occasioned his tract *The Prisoner Against the Prelate* (1662). In 1666, he was elected a messenger "by the consent of many congregations, and ordained . . . by those who were in the same office before [him]," in essence an itinerant minister who aided the churches in the planting of churches, giving counsel to local churches and associations, and assisting in the ordination of ministers. Grantham then began to establish himself as an author, debater, and pamphleteer. He debated Roman Catholics, Anglicans, Quakers, Presbyterians, and Particular Baptists, gaining a reputation as an able and articulate spokesman for the General Baptists. His most monumental work was *Christianismus Primitivus, or, the Ancient Christian Religion*, published in 1678, of which the eminent General Baptist historian Adam Taylor said: "From the universal approbation it received, [it] may be considered almost a public document."[6] In this massive work, Grantham aimed to restore primitive Christianity, which he said had been abused and neglected for centuries. Like Grantham's other works, *Christianismus Primitivus* is the product of a well-read theologian who cited numerous contemporary authors but relied primarily on the Bible and the church fathers.

Grantham's work as an author and messenger made him the foremost leader of the General Baptists in the latter half of the seventeenth century. He also gained the respect of many outside the General Baptist community. Grantham died on January 17, 1692. He was to be buried in the yard of St. Stephen's Cathedral in Norwich. Upon rumors that the body would be dug up, John Connould, the vicar of St. Stephen's, with whom Grantham had previously debated and become friends, had Grantham's body interred "before the West Doors, in the Middle Aisle" of the building. Connould conducted the burial service. A plaque in the General Baptist chapel in Norwich contains the following inscription:

> When at closing the Book he [Connould] added
> This day is a very great man fallen in our Israel:
> For after their epistolary dispute in sixty letters, ended
> That very learned Vicar retained,
> The highest esteem and friendship for him while living,
> And was at his own desire buried by him, May MDCCVIII.

Grantham's theology can accurately be described as Arminian because it was strikingly similar to the soteriology of Jacobus Arminius. But Grantham was not fond of the label "Arminian," just as he did not like the title "Anabaptist." This was not because he was unsympathetic with either of these doctrinal positions, but because of the negative connotations attached to these names.

"Anabaptist" conjured up images of raving revolutionaries at Munster, and "Arminian" invoked notions of semi-Pelagianism (if not outright Pelagianism),[7] works-righteousness, synergism, Romanism, rationalism, and even Socinianism. Grantham lamented that he was accused of preaching "Arminianism, the life and Soul of Popery." Yet in another place, in a polemic against the "dangerous and impious Doctrines of those of Calvin's Way," he asserted the "purity of the Doctrine of those called Arminians, concerning the sinful Acts of Men."[8]

Grantham had read many contemporary Calvinist and Arminian theologians, including John Goodwin, but his General Baptist soteriology was unique among the thinkers of his day. He differed from the Calvinists in his doctrines of election, the extent of atonement, the resistibility of grace, and the perseverance of the saints. On these subjects he agreed with his fellow Arminians. Yet he differed substantially with his Arminian counterparts on the doctrines of sin and depravity, human inability, the nature of atonement and justification by faith, and what was involved in falling from grace. Grantham stridently avoided a semi-Pelagianism that would take the focus off the sovereign grace of God and place it on humanity's own merit. Hence he differed from traditional Reformed theology in his view of predestination and the resistibility of grace, but not in his understanding of how redemption is accomplished by God in Christ and applied to the believer.

An examination of Grantham's similarities with Calvinism and his differences with the Arminianism of his day defies the contrived classifications usually assigned to Protestant soteriological positions and gives one insight into the complexities of soteriological thought in the post-Reformation period. Consequently, it moves beyond the simplistic "Calvinism-Arminianism" debate so often discussed in studies of historical theology.

JOHN GOODWIN

The distinctiveness of Grantham's soteriology becomes most evident when contrasted with that of the better known English Arminian, John Goodwin.[9] While Grantham and Goodwin were both known as Arminians, they were far apart on many issues. Grantham was more radical than Goodwin on matters of ecclesiology, yet Goodwin moved much further from Calvinist orthodoxy than Grantham did. Goodwin was the chief advocate of what has been referred to as the "New Arminianism" or "Radical Arminianism" which took root during the Cromwellian era. Though some scholars have assumed that Goodwin's soteriology exerted great influence over other Arminian sectaries, such as the General Baptists, a comparison of the thought of Grantham and Goodwin demonstrates the inaccuracy of this assumption.[10]

Goodwin was educated at Queens' College, Cambridge, and had by 1633 become vicar of St. Stephen's, Coleman Street, London. By this time, Goodwin had become an Independent, under the influence of John Cotton, and from his pulpit at St. Stephen's, Goodwin proclaimed his gospel of nonconformity combined with Arminianism. Precisely when Goodwin embraced anti-Calvinism is a matter of debate, but his magisterial *Imputatio Fidei* (1642) betrayed an understanding of atonement and justification that had moved a great distance from Reformed orthodoxy and even beyond Arminius himself and was much like that of Hugo Grotius. If Goodwin was not a full-blown Arminian when he wrote *Imputatio Fidei*, he was certainly thought to be one by the more strident Calvinists of the period. Indeed, Thomas Edwards, in his *Gangraena* (1646), described Goodwin as "a monstrous sectary, a compound of Socinianism, Arminianism, antinomianism, independency, popery, yea and of scepticism."[11] At any rate, Goodwin outlined a fully-developed anti-Calvinism in his 1651 work, *Redemption Redeemed*.[12]

Goodwin is best known as a controversialist, in matters not only theological and ecclesial but also political. As the historian Edmund Calamy said, Goodwin "was a man by himself, was against every man, and had every man against him."[13] Goodwin's ecclesiological stance was radical enough to result in his ejection from his living in May 1645 for refusing to administer infant baptism indiscriminately (though he continued to serve a gathered congregation at Coleman Street). His political views were perhaps even more radical. These opinions were reflected in such works as *Anti-Cavalierisme* (1642) and *Ossorianum* (1643), which attacked the divine right of kings. He was a stringent supporter of Cromwell, and he applauded Pride's Purge in a 1648 work, *Right and Might Well Met*. Because of his political affiliations, Goodwin was arrested in June of 1660, but was soon exonerated. He continued his activity as a vibrant preacher and prolific writer until his death in 1665.

Goodwin's legacy to later Arminian theology was mediated through John Wesley. Wesley, who made positive numerous references to Goodwin in his works, republished Goodwin's *Imputatio Fidei* in 1765. Goodwin probably had more influence on Wesley's doctrine of justification in the last thirty years of Wesley's life than any other single thinker, as is evidenced by his preface to Goodwin's treatise.[14]

GRANTHAM ON ORIGINAL SIN, DEPRAVITY, AND HUMAN INABILITY

Grantham's view of original sin and depravity had been articulated by the Magisterial Reformers as well as by Arminius. Arminius had said (contrary to popular belief) that every human being "existed in Adam, and [was] by [Adam's] will involved in sin and guilt" and that "the whole of this [original] sin . . . is not peculiar to our first parents, but is common to the entire race and to all their posterity, who, at the time when this sin was committed, were in their loins, and who have since descended from them by the natural mode of propagation."[15] These are essentially Grantham's views on original sin. Grantham believed that all humanity sinned in Adam, and that Adam's sin was attributed to the entire human race. He articulated

> that the Sin of Mankind is either *Original* or *Actual*. The first is come upon all, even the very Infant State of Mankind lie under it; of whom that saying is true, *Rom. 5. They have not sinned after the similitude of Adam's Transgression.* Yet Death reigning over them, proves the Transgression of Adam to be upon them. This is the Root Sin, called *the Sin of the World, John 1.29,* whereof none are free. . . . We also may say, Our Father hath sinned, and we have borne his Iniquity.[16]

Thus, *original* sin consists in Adam's transgression being imputed to all humanity, the end result being that no human being is free of Adam's "root" sin and guilt. In another place, replying to those who said his doctrine of infant salvation was a denial of original sin, Grantham declared, "I do not deny Original Sin, for I know it is come upon all *Adam's* Posterity, and Death passeth upon them, for that all have sinned in him."[17]

Not only is humanity guilty of original sin itself, but original sin, for Grantham, is the root that makes humanity wholly depraved and dead in sin and hence unable to desire or perform the things of God without divine aid. In his section on depravity in *Christianismus Primitivus,* Grantham says:

> Nor is it convenient to extenuate or lessen this [original] Sin, either in its nature, or the punishment it brings with it; It being indeed the *filum certissimum,* or leading Thred to all other Iniquities, Mankind being hereby corrupt . . . and wholly deprived of the Glory of God, without the intervening Mercy of a Saviour. And hence we find *David,* when complaining of his sinful State, looks back to his corrupt Original, *Psal. 51.5. Behold I was shapen in Iniquity, and in Sin did my Mother conceive me.* Knowing (as *Job* saith) none can bring a clean thing out of an unclean thing.[18]

Original sin is the root of or thread to all other sins and brings about corruption and depravity in the human soul, indeed deprivation of the glory of God, and finally, except for the intervention of a Savior's mercy, eternal death. The result of original sin for Grantham is a depravity that is total and complete.

Even the human will is depraved, wretched, and entirely corrupt, blind in understanding, and unable to subordinate itself to the will of God.[19] "*The Will of Man,*" says Grantham, is "*corrupted, and as such, made the Rule of his Actions.*"[20] Grantham ardently disagreed with the doctrine that human reason is not fallen. Though God desires that the human will should be subject to reason and to the law of God, "Men are actuated by the impulse of their desires, without regard to the Will of God, or Rational Principles, as regulated by the Will of

God."[21] While Grantham believed the human will is free in the sense that it is not "chained" of "necessity," Grantham's account of free will is not optimistic when it comes to the effects of depravity. Human depravity is so great that people cannot depend on their own "Liberty or Power" for salvation but must depend on "the strength of God."[22] Man cannot "be converted by the power of his own freewill."[23] Sinners can be converted only through divine prevenient grace, which, "at one time or other," is provided to all people, but God gives them the freedom to resist that grace.[24]

Grantham's doctrines of original sin and the resultant depravity of humanity are basically Reformed and in essential agreement with Arminius. However, they differ radically from the English Arminianism of his day as well as from later Arminianism, which betrays a conspicuous departure from the "Reformed Arminian" theology of Arminius.

GOODWIN ON ORIGINAL SIN, DEPRAVITY, AND HUMAN INABILITY

Goodwin did not drift as far from the Reformed shore as some Arminians before and after him. Indeed his theology was quite conservative compared to that of some Arminians of the seventeenth century. Yet he nonetheless self-consciously departed from Reformed thinking in his understanding of the imputation of Adam's sin. In his *Imputatio Fidei,* Goodwin stated unequivocally that the "sinne of *Adam is* no where in Scripture said to be imputed to his posterity."[25] He continues, "The Scriptures wheresoever they speake of *Adams* sin, and the relation of it to his posterity, wholly abstaine from the terme of imputation, neither doe they use any other word or phrase in this Argument of like signification."[26] Though Goodwin did not deny that Adam's posterity were in Adam when he committed his sin, he made clear that *"Adams* sinne comes to relate or to have reference to his posteritie, in matter of pollution and defilement."[27]

That which is borne of the flesh (corrupted and weakened by sinne) is (by the course of nature, whereunto God himselfe hath righteously consented) *flesh,* a creature or thing of the same sinful and weake nature and condition with it. . . . The Apostle, *Rom. 5.19.* expresly affirmeth, that *by the disobedience of one* (meaning *Adam) many were made sinners:* not by the imputation of the Act of his sinne to them . . . but by corrupting and defiling his owne person, by reason whereof, all that are born of him in a way of naturall dissent and propagation, must needs be borne sinners.[28]

Goodwin's theory of original sin is unique in its claim that, though humanity sinned in Adam, it had not, as Grantham stated, "borne his iniquity." The reason for this interpretation seems to be Goodwin's concern to create a disjunction between the method of one's becoming sinful and the method of one's being redeemed: "Though justification and salvation came unto the world by Christ the second Adam, as condemnation and death came by the first Adam; yet are there many different considerations and circumstances, between the coming and bringing of salvation by the one and of condemnation by the other."[29] Goodwin spends a great deal of time on details, but the end result of his doctrine of sin is something less than the Reformed doctrine of original sin. Though the differences between Grantham's and Goodwin's doctrines of original sin and depravity may appear subtle, the contrasts between the two regarding the nature of redemption—atonement and justification—are stark.

GRANTHAM ON ATONEMENT AND JUSTIFICATION

It goes without saying that Grantham and Goodwin, as Arminians, held fervently to a general atonement. This theme resounds throughout both men's works. Grantham, for example, argues:

When we are bid to behold the Lamb of God, which taketh away the Sins of the World, John I. 29. Are we to except any Person in the World, or the greatest part of the World? God forbid. Are they all become guilty *per* force (except *Adam*) and have none to justify them? Where is then the *Lamb*? Behold here is Fire, the Wood, and

109

the Knife, but where is the Sacrifice, may many say, if indeed the Lamb of God died not for them? But the Holy Ghost resolves the Query to the full, I John 2. 2. *He is the Propitiation for our Sins, and not for ours only, but also for the Sins of the whole World.*[30]

The crucial differences between Grantham and other English Arminians of his day arose, not with regard to the extent of the atonement, but rather with respect to the nature of the atonement and, consequently, the character of justification. Grantham aligned himself with the Reformers and with Arminius.[31]

As a Reformed theologian, Arminius had taught that God must punish sin with eternal death unless one meets the requirement of total righteousness. God is portrayed as a judge who must sentence individuals to eternal death if they do not meet his righteous requirements. In typical Reformed fashion, Arminius employed the analogy of "a judge making an estimate in his own mind of the deed and of the author of it, and according to that estimate forming a judgment and pronouncing sentence."[32] The sentence pronounced on the sinner who cannot meet the requirements of God's justice is eternal death. Yet, since no one has this righteousness, it must originate from someone else. It can come only from Christ, who undergoes the penalty for sin on the cross, paying "the price of redemption for sins by suffering the punishment due to them."[33] For Arminius, this emphasis on justice does not militate against God's mercy, as some later Arminians held. God never had to offer Christ for the redemption of humanity in the first place. If God had not made a way of satisfaction for His justice (through mercy), *then,* Arminius says, humanity would have truly been judged according to God's "severe and rigid estimation."[34] This view has been called the penal satisfaction theory of atonement, and these were Grantham's sentiments exactly.

Grantham's doctrine of atonement is rooted in his perspective on the justice and righteousness of God. Grantham believed that God's righteousness is not merely something to be posited of Him but is in His essence as God. Justice is "essential to him." Without it, He would cease to be God."[35] While justice and righteousness in human beings is "mutable," not being a part of their being or essence, in God, "to be righteous, is the same as to be God, and therefore he is called Righteousness itself, *the Lord our Righteousness*. Like as it is said, *God dwelleth in the Light*, so it is as truly said, That *God is Light, and in him is no Darkness at all*, I John I. 5."[36]

God's essential justice evidences itself in the righteous "Judgment which he executeth" against people for their sin.[37] According to Grantham, an accurate understanding of God's justice and righteousness enables one to see the serious nature of sin, the intensity of divine wrath against it, and the necessity that it be punished. When one comprehends the chasm between God's justice and righteousness and humanity's sinfulness, and the latter's "dreadful Nature and Effects," only then can one understand the need for atonement and for the gospel.[38] "To see Sin to be exceeding sinful," Grantham avers, "is an excellent Introduction to Christianity, and so necessary, that the internal part thereof is not rightly founded without it."[39]

Grantham understands the need for atonement in the context of the "condemning Power and Curse of the Law" over sinners.[40] "The whole World stands Guilty" before the law, which makes it "subject to the judgment of God."[41] Grantham distinguishes between two sorts of righteousness: human beings' own futile attempts to obey the law and the "Righteousness of God." In this vein, he cites Philippians 3:9 and Romans 3:21: "*And be found in him, not having on my own Righteousness which is of the Law, but that which is through the Faith of Christ, the Righteousness which is of God by Faith. Again, The Righteousness of God without the Law, is manifested, being witnessed by the Law and the Prophets.*"[42] Since people were unable to fulfill the law, Christ fulfilled it for them. He "cancelled the Law, which stood as an hand-writing against us, and was contrary to us, nailing it to the Cross of Christ. And hath manifested, or shewed forth a way to be made Righteous, without the Law; yea, by which we may be justified from all things, from which we could not be justified by the Law."[43] According to Grantham, the only way to keep the handwriting of the law from being held against believers was for Christ to fulfill the law in their place: "Nor can I see to what end Christ did so exactly fulfil the Law, if he did it not for us, or in our stead: and so is the end of the Law for Righteousness to every one that believeth, Rom. 10. For though it is true, he was born under the Law, and so stood bound to keep the Law, yet for our sakes he was so born; and so consequently all that he did in that capacity, was on our account also, as well as his Sufferings."[44]

In *St. Paul's Catechism,* Grantham, in a discussion of justification, explains the nature of atonement to clarify why the righteousness of Christ must be imputed to individuals for them to be justified. His reasoning is almost identical to that of Arminius: "God having made a Righteous Law, it must be fulfilled; and none was able to do this but Christ, and he did fulfil it in our behalf. *Heb. 10.5, 6, 7, 8, 9, 10. Psal. 4.5, 6, 7.* and thus the Righteousness of the Law is fulfilled in the Children of God, because Christ's righteousness is made theirs through believing. *Rom. 10.3, 4. Phil 3.9.*"[45] Grantham taught that, since no one could satisfy God the judge's requirement of absolute righteousness, the only way for individuals to be freed from the penalty of sin and justified before God was for God to provide a righteousness by which people could be saved and to suffer the penalty for their sins. "The justice of God cried against us for Sin committed; and Sin must be purged by the Blood of Christ; He bare our sins, that is, the punishment of our Sins, in his own Body on the Tree, I Pet. 2.24."[46]

Grantham summarized his theology of atonement in the title of Section V in book two, chapter three of *Christianismus Primitivus,* which reads, "According to the Will of God, and his Eternal Wisdom, Christ did, in the place and stead of Mankind, fulfil that Law, by which the whole World stood guilty before God."[47] In this section, Grantham explained "how deeply Mankind stood indebted to the Righteous God of Heaven and Earth, and how unable he was to pay that score; and how consequently he must inevitably undergo the eternal displeasure of God, with the malediction of his Righteous Law."[48] Humanity is subject to the harsh judgment and wrath of God, says Grantham, on account of "fall[ing] short" of the Law of God. Yet God in His wisdom has "designed to magnifie his Mercy in Christ, as the only Physician to Cure the Malady of Mankind," providing a

Plaister commensurable with the Sore, that none may cry out and say, I am undone, I am wounded with the unavoidable wound of Mankind: And there is no Balm for me, the Physician hath made the Plaister so narrow, that Thousands, and ten Thousands, cannot possibly have Healing by it; nay, he hath determined to see us perish without Remedy. Alas! there is none to save us, neither could we come whole and sound into the World; we are born to be destroyed, and destroyed we must be. To quell which hideous (and indeed most just) complaint . . . we are bid to behold the Lamb of God.[49]

Christ, the Lamb of God, is the only individual who can "pay the score" or the debt of sin that men and women have accrued to God.

Because, for Grantham, the essence of the atonement is Christ's fulfilling the law and taking on himself "the Punishment due for our Sin,"[50] he goes into great depth eschewing a moral influence view of atonement, which was popular among the Socinians of his day. "How it cometh to pass, that any should take the Righteousness of Christ's Performances, or actual Obedience, to be designed by God only as an excellent Pattern, or Example to Men, is not easie to conceive."[51] One can see between the lines of Grantham's discussion an interaction with the merit-theology of the Council of Trent. Christ alone can be called our righteousness, Grantham argues, not the saints. Yet if the righteousness of Christ consists merely in His being our example or pattern, then the saints' pattern or example could suffice. "Now if Christ should be called our Righteousness only because he is our Pattern," Grantham argued, "he alone could not be called our Pattern; and consequently, he alone would not be called our Righteousness. But seeing Christ, and Christ alone, may truly be said to be our Righteousness, Jer. 23. 6. We must therefore look upon his Righteousness to be of far greater Concernment to us, than the Righteousness of the most holy Saint that ever yet lived."[52] Grantham believed that it is "easie to demonstrate the Transcendent Advantages that accrue to us from his Righteousness, and from his only: For where are we bid to look to the Saints for

113

Righteousness? Or where are they said to be made of God unto us Righteousness? But unto Christ we are thus directed."[53]

Grantham held that there are two aspects of atonement, passive and active obedience. Passive obedience refers to Christ's submission to the wrath of God for the sins of humanity—the satisfaction of the penalty for sin—while active obedience refers to Christ's satisfaction of the justice of God in meeting the standards of God's righteous law. Christ obeys God the Father passively through His death on the cross to satisfy the penalty for the violation of God's law. Christ obeys God the Father actively by fulfilling the righteous law in His sinless life. Grantham noted that "it is true, he was born under the Law, and so stood bound to keep the Law, yet for our sakes he was so born; and consequently all that he did in that capacity [active obedience], was on our account also, as well as his Sufferings [passive obedience]: For the Transgressions committed against the Law, was he crucified in our place and stead."[54]

Grantham's penal satisfaction theology of atonement resulted in a penal satisfaction doctrine of justification like that of Reformed thought common in seventeenth-century England. This view of justification held that believing sinners are justified by the merit of Christ alone imputed to them through faith alone. This was also Arminius's doctrine of justification, namely that the righteousness of Christ is "made ours by gracious imputation."[55]

Grantham explained in *St. Paul's Catechism* that there are two kinds of righteousness, the one "imputative," the other "practical." The first, he said, "is called the *Righteousness of God*, Mat. 6.33. or *God's Righteousness*, Rom. 10.3." This is "a Righteousness to us *without the* Law. . . . It is the Righteousness of Christ, who is the Lord our Righteousness, *Isa. 45.24, 25. Christ made of God unto us Righteousness*, 1 Cor.1.30."[56] This imputative righteousness is to be sharply distinguished from practical righteousness. Grantham described practical righteousness as "a comely, yea, and a necessary Ornament." Yet he went on to say that practical righteousness "is not so immediately signified" as imputative righteousness, because the latter is "said to be *granted to the* Saints," whereas practical righteousness "is acquired by Industry."[57] Practical righteousness, for Grantham, is associated with sanctification, and hence is progressive in nature,

114

while imputative righteousness is the righteousness that justifies believers. Since people cannot by their own works of righteousness justify themselves, they can be justified only by the righteousness of God in Christ:

> That God imputes Righteousness to Men without Works, is so plain, that it can never be denied. What is thus imputed, is not acted by us, but expressly reckoned as a matter of free Gift, or Grace; and this can be the Righteousness of none but Christ . . . because no other way can the Righteousness of God be made ours. . . . There is none righteous, no not one. Except therefore the Righteousness of Christ be laid hold on, there is no Righteousness to be imputed to Sinners.[58]

Grantham's theory of active and passive obedience as essential aspects of the atonement is brought directly to bear on his doctrine of justification: "Now whether the Passive Righteousness of Christ only, or his Active Righteousness also, be that which is imputed to Sinners, is doubtful to some; but for my part I take it to be both. . . . The whole Righteousness of Christ, Active and Passive, is reckoned as ours through believing."[59] Grantham referred to the active and passive obedience of Christ imputed to believers as "that fine Linnen, white and clean, which arrayeth the Church of God, *Rev.* 19. 7. And the best Robe which God puts upon returning Sinners, *Luke* 15."[60]

Grantham strove to distance himself from an emphasis on good works as a contributor to salvation, approaches that the Reformed were quick to decry, not only in Roman Catholic authors, but also in Arminian, Anabaptist, Quaker, and Socinian writers. Believers' justification rests wholly in their in-Christ status, without regard to their own works or merit: "We must therefore in no wise place our Justification in our Repentance," he wrote, "For that were to place our Justification from the guilt and condemning Power of Sin, in our Duty, and not in Christ Jesus."[61]

A key element in Grantham's doctrine of justification is identification with Christ. Grantham argued that Christ identified with the believer in the atonement, and that through faith the believer identifies with Christ.[62] Grantham preached that the individual who exercises saving faith is brought into union with Christ and is hence identified with Christ. In this identification, the active obedience of Christ becomes the active obedience of the believer, and the death of Christ, the payment of the penalty for sin, becomes the death of the believer. In turn, the believer's sin becomes Christ's. As Grantham explains, "Christ was made Sin for us only by imputation, for he had no Sin; and as he was made Sin, so are we made the Righteousness of God in him, which must needs be by the free Imputation of his Righteousness to us."[63]

Thus, for Grantham, justification is completely *by* the imputed righteousness of Jesus Christ, apprehended *through* faith; Christ's righteousness is the *ground* of justification, and faith is the *condition*. Against the Roman Catholics on one hand and many Arminians on the other, Grantham's hallmark was *sola fide:* not by our works, but by God's gracious imputation of the righteousness of Christ which is ours through faith.[64]

GOODWIN ON ATONEMENT AND JUSTIFICATION

Because most Arminian theology has taught a less robust view of the nature of atonement and justification than Grantham's penal satisfaction, it is instructive to contrast Grantham's views with those of the more influential Arminian John Goodwin. As intimated earlier, Goodwin's views on atonement and justification may be said to be more influential on the subsequent Arminian movement because Wesley re-published *Imputatio Fidei* and was heavily influenced by Goodwin's thought. Grantham's more Reformed Arminian approach, by contrast, survived only in the smaller General-Free Will Baptist tradition.

Goodwin's doctrines of atonement and justification differ extensively from Grantham's. Goodwin bears the influence of Hugo Grotius's governmental theory of atonement, which held that God could freely pardon sinners without any satisfaction for the violation of divine law, because such a pardon was within God's discretion as governor or sovereign.[65] Thus the sacrifice of Christ is accepted by God as governor or ruler rather than as judge. The death of

Christ, in this view, is a symbol of the punishment sin may induce. God uses this symbol as a deterrent. The penalty for sin is thereby set aside rather than paid. Therefore, upon faith, the believer is pardoned as a governor would pardon a guilty criminal, and all past sins are forgotten.

Goodwin articulated such a view of atonement and justification in *Imputatio Fidei*. The sole purpose of this book of over four hundred pages was to disprove the doctrine that Christ's righteousness is imputed to believers for their eternal acceptance with God. Goodwin's disavowal of the penal satisfaction theory of atonement was unabashed. He argued, "The sentence or curse of the *Law*, was not properly executed upon *Christ* in his death, but this death of *Christ* was a ground or consideration unto *God*, whereupon to dispence with his *Law*, and to let fall or suspend the execution of the penalty or curse therein threatened."[66] Whereas Grantham's whole explanation for *cur Deus homo* is to meet the demands of the "Righteous Law of God," Goodwin's reason for Christ's coming was so God could dispense with His law. Not until God dispensed with His law, said Goodwin, could He pardon men and women and forgive their sins: "But God in spareing and forbearing the transgressors (who according to the tenor of the *Law* should have bin punished) manifestly dispenceth with the *Law*, and doth not execute it."[67] It was not absolutely necessary, according to Goodwin, for Christ to die on the cross to pardon sinners, but it was the method that God in His government chose. Goodwin explains:

> Neither did *God* require the death and sufferings of Christ as a valuable consideration whereon to dispence with his *Law* towards those that beleeve, more (if so much) in a way of satisfaction to his justice, than to his wisdome. For (doubtlesse) *God* might with as much justice, as wisdome (if not much more) have passed by the transgression of his *Law* without consideration or satisfaction. For him that hath the lawfull authority and power, either to impose a *Law*, or not, in case he shall impose it, it rather concerns in point of wisdome and discretion, not to see his *Law* despised and trampled upon without satisfaction, then in point of justice.[68]

117

Christ's death was for Goodwin, therefore, an exhibition of public justice, not a penal satisfaction, as Grantham held.

Goodwin rooted his doctrine of justification in his perspective on atonement. Inasmuch as God can, in His government, set aside the penalty for sin since it does not of necessity have to be suffered, God can freely forgive the believer, and the imputation of Christ's righteousness is not necessary. Nor is it desirable, for to impute Christ's righteousness to the believer would be to admit that God did not set aside the demands of the law after all. Thus Goodwin concluded that justification consists primarily in the forgiveness or remission of sins (the nonimputation of sins).[69] Goodwin maintained that "the Scriptures constantly speake of this act of God justifying a sinner, not as of such an act whereby he will either make him or pronounce him legally just, or declare him not to have offended the Law, and hereupon justifie him; but of such an act, whereby he freely forgives him all that he hath done against the Law, and acquits him from all blame and punishment due by the Law."[70]

As a consequence of his doctrine of atonement, Goodwin asserted that it would be erroneous to posit that Christ's righteousness is imputed to the believer, for this would be admitting that God's free acquittal or pardon of the sinner is not enough. Thus Goodwin spends the entire first part of his book arguing against the imputation of Christ's righteousness to the believer. It is not His righteousness that is credited or imputed to the believer, but faith is counted as righteousness.[71]

Incidentally, Arminius had argued that the Pauline phrase "faith counted for righteousness" is fully compatible with the notion of the imputation of the righteousness of Christ to believers. Arminius's enemies had charged him with teaching that "the righteousness of Christ is not imputed to us for righteousness, but to believe (or the act of believing) justifies us."[72] Arminius replied that he never said the act of faith justifies a person. He held that Christ's righteousness is imputed to the believer and that our faith is imputed for righteousness. He believed both views were held by St. Paul: "I say that I acknowledge, 'The righteousness of Christ is imputed to us,' because I think the same thing is contained in the following words of the Apostle, 'God hath made Christ to

118

be sin for us, that we might be made the righteousness of God in him.' . . . It is said in the third verse [of Romans 4], 'Abraham believed God, and it was imputed unto him for righteousness.' . . . Our brethren therefore do not reprehend ME, but the APOSTLE."[73]

Goodwin's emphasis, in the last analysis, was on God's freedom to dispense with the law and freely pardon or forgive the sinner. The doctrines of atonement and justification are the most apparent disparity between Grantham's and Goodwin's types of Arminianism. The most practical difference is that, for Grantham, salvation consisted totally in Christ's righteousness, whereas for Goodwin, it hinged on the individual's faith.[74]

GRANTHAM ON PERSEVERANCE AND APOSTASY

In Reformation and Post-Reformation theology, one's view of perseverance, or enduring in the faith, was conditioned on other doctrines. Reformed theology had traditionally taught that, because grace is irresistible, the elect or predestined individual will of necessity persevere in faith, whereas Arminian theology posited that God had granted humanity the freedom to resist divine salvific grace.[75] It is understandable, then, why an Arminian theory of the resistibility of grace would result in its continual resistibility after conversion. Grantham's doctrine of the perseverance of the saints was an outgrowth of his doctrines of the resistibility of grace and of justification.

Because the grace of God is resistible, taught Grantham, it must of necessity continue to be so throughout one's life.[76] Yet one cannot comprehend Grantham's understanding of perseverance outside the context of his doctrine of justification. His teaching that the believer is justified solely by the righteousness of Christ, apprehended by faith, necessitated a view of perseverance consistent with the *sola fide* principle: One could not fall from grace because of failure to be righteous or do righteous works, because the believer stood justified before God based solely on the righteousness of Christ rather than his own merits. As long as saving faith is intact, the believer remains justified on account of Christ's righteousness.

Grantham's emphasis in perseverance was enduring *in faith* and hence in Christ. As long as people maintain faith, they will remain in Christ; one falls from grace only when he or she "destroys a state of faith."[77] Grantham cannot be viewed as teaching a semi-Pelagianism in which the believer maintains salvation by works of righteousness that he or she performs. Rather, only when the believer again becomes an unbeliever will he or she fall from the salvific grace of God, for the believer is, as the *Standard Confession, 1660* repeats, "kept by the power of God through faith unto salvation" (1 Peter 1.5). Falling from grace is for Grantham a much more serious matter than merely committing sin or drifting from God. It amounts to a reversal of the *ordo salutis*: after an individual renounces faith in Christ, he or she is no longer a partaker in Christ and hence loses the benefits of salvation. Thus, with reference to the fourth, sixth, and tenth chapters of Hebrews, Grantham described falling from grace as that state in which "Men have destroyed a state of Faith (in respect of themselves) trodden under foot the Son of God; counted the blood of the Covenant wherewith they were Sanctified an unholy thing, and thus [done] despite to the Spirit of Grace."[78]

Grantham also viewed apostasy or falling from grace as an "irrecoverable Estate" from which the apostate can never return.[79] Those who have once been in Christ but who have resisted and rejected the grace of God and fallen from grace are, Grantham says, "Trees *twice dead, plucked up by the Roots*: and consequently uncapable of bearing fruit in Gods Vineyard for ever." Thus, Grantham rejected the doctrine some have called "repeated regeneration," which holds that, if believers sin enough they will lose their salvation and must repent to regain it. On the contrary, Grantham states that those who have committed such apostasy "cannot, (as *Chrysostom* notes upon the place) be twice made Christians; and there being but one Sacrifice for Sin, there remains no more. . . ."[80]

GOODWIN AND PERSEVERANCE AND APOSTASY

Goodwin's view of the perseverance of the saints differed substantially from Grantham's. Though there was fundamental agreement on the possibility of a believer's apostasy, significant disagreement existed on how a believer may fall from grace and on the remediability of apostasy. Whereas Grantham's emphasis is on continuance in faith, Goodwin's stress is on continuance in good works. Thus impenitency is the cause of a believer's fall from grace rather than shipwreck of faith. In an extensive treatment of David as an example of a believer who had fallen from grace, Goodwin said, "Our Adversaries themselves . . . generally acknowledge him to have bin a man truly godly and regenerate, before the guilt of the two enormous sins mentioned clave unto Him." He further contended: "The Question is, Whether He continued such, truly Godly, under the guilt of the said sins, viz., from the time of the perpetration of them, until the time of His Repentance: They affirm, I deny."[81] David, said Goodwin, "during his impenitency aforesaid, was cut off from all right of entering the new *Jerusalem*."[82] Goodwin was not clear just how many or what kind of sins cause one to fall from grace, but he made it plain that particularly reprehensible sins will bring about apostasy. In his comments on Ezekiel 18.24, he declared: "The Text saith, *In His Trespass* (in the singular number) *that He hath trespassed,* shall he dye; implying, that any one sin, of that kinde of sins, which the Scripture calls, *abominations,* whilest unrepented of, translateth him from life unto death, casteth Him in to the state and condition of an Unbeleever."[83]

It is clear from Goodwin's treatment of David that he believed apostasy was a remediable state. Yet in his comments on Hebrews 6 he was even more explicit, saying that the biblical author's statement that it is impossible for the one who has fallen away to be renewed again to repentance "was not asserted by him with an eye to the state or condition of ordinary believers . . . as if he intended to conclude them under the heavy doome of such an *impossibility,* but with an eye only to the most deplorable condition of [other believers]."[84] For Goodwin, most cases of falling away are remediable.

The differences between Grantham and Goodwin on the doctrine of perseverance arise from other elements in their doctrinal systems that touch the nature of justification, its relation to sanctification, and the resultant relationship of faith and works in the Christian life. Whereas Goodwin's Arminian approach to the doctrine is a complete reversal of the Calvinistic system,

121

Grantham's Arminianism retains key Reformed soteriological elements, most notably the *sola fide* formula.

CONCLUSION

The essence of the disparity between Grantham and Goodwin lay in their respective understandings of the gravity of sin and the nature of divine justice. Grantham viewed sin as such an egregious violation of divine holiness that God, out of justice, must punish it. Goodwin, on the contrary, believed that the law of God (divine justice) "may be relaxed without contradiction to the divine nature."[85] Goodwin would have heartily agreed with Grotius's statement that "the law is not something internal with God or the will of God itself, but only an effect of that will. It is perfectly certain that the effects of the divine will are mutable,"[86] or that divine law is promulgated by God as "a positive law which at some time he may wish to relax."[87] This is why, as Goodwin stated, God could "dispense with his Law" in pardoning sinners.

Grantham would hear nothing of this. For him, the law of God is a necessary outcome of the divine nature, not simply an effect of the divine will. For Grantham, God's holiness demands intolerance of sin. God's holy nature necessarily repels sin. Consequently, divine wrath is not a capricious anger at sin. It is rather the necessary outcome of God's nature. Because of this, divine justice must be satisfied. God's requirement of absolute righteousness cannot be met by humanity, so people must undergo, as Grantham put it, "the malediction of his Righteous Law." This, Grantham held, is why Christ's death and righteousness must be imputed to believers. Christ's sinless life and sacrificial death is the only thing that will satisfy the justice or holy nature of God.

These dissimilarities on the seriousness of sin and the nature of divine justice in turn caused Grantham and Goodwin to come down on different sides of the soteriological debate. For Goodwin, God dispenses with holy law and pardons sinners; for Grantham, God cannot do away with His holy law. So sinners must be imputed the righteousness of Christ through faith to be saved. Accordingly, Grantham held that this righteousness remains the possession of the believer as long as he or she remains in Christ through faith, whereas Goodwin emphasized the necessity of penitence for persevering in salvation, as though the believer must continue to be pardoned over and over again.

The traditional categories of Calvinism and Arminianism on which historians and theologians usually rely are somewhat imprecise and misleading. Calvinists and Arminians alike have been predisposed to understand Arminianism as even more semi-Pelagian than Goodwin's version. Yet Grantham defied such classification, striving instead for a *via media* which, he firmly believed, was the way of the Bible and the primitive churches.

[1]The English General Baptists are the forefathers of those now known as Free Will Baptists. The early Free Will Baptists in the American South were influenced by Grantham's *Christianismus Primitivus,* and their confession of faith was the *Standard Confession, 1660,* which Grantham delivered to King Charles II in 1660 and which he reprinted with annotations in *Christianismus Primitivus.*

[2]See J. I. Packer, "Arminianisms," in *The Collected Shorter Writings of J. I. Packer,* vol. 4, (Carlisle, UK: Paternoster, 1999). In his insightful essay, Packer is right to posit several "Arminianisms," and to see the differences between Remonstrant and Wesleyan Arminianism. However, he posits all Arminianism as having rejected the doctrine of a penal satisfaction view of atonement and justification by the imputed righteousness of Christ alone.

[3]The purpose of this essay is not to discuss the five points of Calvinism or the five articles of the Remonstrance, but rather to point out the divergencies that can and do occur within Arminianism. It will be assumed, for the purposes of this essay, that all Arminians disagree with at least the last four of the five points of Calvinism: unconditional election, particular atonement, irresistible grace, and the unconditional perseverance of the saints.

[4]The best treatment of Grantham's theology is Clint C. Bass's monograph, *Thomas Grantham (1633-1692) and General Baptist Theology* (Oxford: Regent's Park College, 2013). The general nature of his book does not permit his delving into Grantham's thought on atonement. However, he correctly understands that Grantham viewed justification as the imputation of the active and passive obedience of Christ to the believer. While I think Bass misinterprets Grantham as having a more optimistic anthropology than he actually does regarding human reason, depravity, and free will, Bass is quick to note significant differences between Grantham and the other Arminians of his day. I believe that, despite Grantham's anti-predestinarianism, his anthropology is quite pessimistic, like Arminius's, and closer to the Reformed thought of his day than to that of most other Arminians. Despite these nuances, Bass's volume is excellent.

[5]The biographical information in the next three paragraphs is based on Samuel Edward Hester, "Advancing Christianity to Its Primitive Excellency: The Quest of Thomas Grantham, Early English General Baptist (1634-1692)," Th.D. diss., New Orleans Baptist Theological

Seminary, 1977, 9-32. For an in-depth critical biography of Grantham, see John Inscore Essick's excellent monograph, *Thomas Grantham: God's Messenger from Lincolnshire* (Macon: Mercer University Press, 2013).

[6]Adam Taylor, *History of the English General Baptists*, vol. 1 (London: T. Bore, 1815), 362.

[7]For a discussion of the semi-Pelagian tendencies John Smyth took from the Dutch Waterlander Mennonites, and which Thomas Helwys rejected, see Chapter Three. Cf. Alvin J. Beachy, *The Concept of Grace in the Radical Reformation* (Nieuwkoop: B. De Graaf, 1977).

[8]Thomas Grantham, *A Dialogue Between the Baptist and the Presbyterian* (London, 1691), 27; *The Infants Advocate* (London, 1688), 2.

[9]The best treatment of Goodwin is John Coffey, *John Goodwin and the Puritan Revolution: Religion and Intellectual Change in Seventeenth-Century England* (Woodbridge, Suffolk, UK: Boydell and Brewer, 2006).

[10]Cf. Ellen More, "John Goodwin and the Origins of the New Arminianism," *The Journal of British Studies* 22 (1982), 52.

[11]*Dictionary of National Biography*, vol. 22, eds. Leslie Stephen and Sidney Lee (New York: Macmillan & Co., 1890) 22.145.

[12]A new edition of this work was recently published: John Goodwin, *Redemption Redeemed: A Puritan Defense of Unlimited Atonement*, ed. John Wagner (Eugene: Wipf and Stock, 2001).

[13]*Dictionary of National Biography*, 22.146.

[14]Goodwin's influence on Wesley, though profound, seems to be later in his life. His earlier influences seem to be more from Anglican Arminianism, including authors such as Jeremy Taylor and William Cave, as well as Hugo Grotius. For more on Wesley's doctrine of atonement and justification, see Chapter Six.

[15]Jacobus Arminius, *The Works of James Arminius,* 3 vols., trans. James Nichols and William Nichols (Nashville: Randall House, 2007), 2:12, 156.

[16]Thomas Grantham, *Christianismus Primitivus, or The Ancient Christian Religion* (London, 1678), Book 2, part 1, 76-77. Grantham here echoes the sentiments of his General Baptist forebear, Thomas Helwys, who said in *A Declaration of Faith of English People Remaining at Amsterdam* (1611): "Through [Adam's] disobedience, all men sinned (Romans 5:12-19). His sin being imputed unto all; and so death went over all men" (Article 2). This document is reprinted in J. Matthew Pinson, *A Free Will Baptist Handbook: Heritage, Beliefs, and Ministries* (Nashville: Randall House, 1998), 123-31.

[17]Thomas Grantham, *The Controversie about Infants Church Membership and Baptism, Epitomized in Two Treatises* (London, 1680), 14.

[18]Grantham, *Christianismus Primitivus*, Book 2, part 1, 78. Grantham, like the other General Baptists, did not believe that infants, if they died in infancy, would be eternally condemned solely on account of original sin. Instead, infants are saved by Christ's atoning work, which takes away the "condemning power" of original sin but not the depravity that results from it (Grantham, *St. Paul's Catechism: Or, A Brief Explication of the Six Principles of the Christian Religion, as recorded Heb. 6.1,2* [London, 1687], 21). He said in *The Infants Advocate* that there is no doubt infants are "born again in God," but how they are, he said, "is a secret" (29). Thus Grantham

has the same tension in his thought as Helwys, attempting to maintain both original sin and its effects in total depravity, together with the salvation (not the mere safety) of infants.

[19]Ibid., Book 2, part 1, 76-77.

[20]Ibid., Book 2, part 1, 76.

[21]Ibid.

[22]Grantham, St. Paul's Catechism, 21, 22. Grantham's language here is similar to Arminius's. The latter taught that the human will was free from necessity but not from the bondage of sin, apart from divine grace. See, e.g., Arminius, 3:179-80. "Friendly Conference with Francis Junius."

[23]Grantham, The Infants Advocate. The Second Part (London, 1690), iii.

[24]See his citation of the Standard Confession, 1660, in Christianismus Primitivus, Book 2 part 2, 63: "All men at one time or other, are put into such a capacity, as that through the grace of God they may be eternally saved."

[25]John Goodwin, Imputatio Fidei. Or A Treatise of Justification (London, 1642), Part II, 13. It is interesting to note that John Wesley later reprinted and wrote a preface to this work and was greatly influenced by Goodwin's theology.

[26]Ibid.

[27]Ibid., 15.

[28]Ibid., 15-16.

[29]Ibid., 16.

[30]Grantham, Christianismus Primitivus, Book 2, part 1, 63.

[31]For more on Arminius's theology of atonement and justification, see Chapters One and Two.

[32]Arminius, 2:256.

[33]Ibid., 1:419.

[34]Ibid.

[35]Grantham, Christianismus Primitivus, Book 2, part 1, 46.

[36]Ibid., Book 2, part 1, 46-47.

[37]Ibid., Book 2, part 1, 46.

[38]Ibid., Book 2, part 1, 80.

[39]Ibid.

[40]Ibid., Book 2, part 1, 62. Grantham states that Christ's death was "the Punishment due for our Sin, with the condemning Power and Curse of the Law" (Ibid.).

[41]Ibid.

[42]Ibid., Book 2, part 1, 67. "So then, we see there is a Law, by which the whole World stands Guilty; and upon that account subject to the judgment of God" (Ibid., Book 2, 62).

[43]Ibid.

[44]Ibid. In typical Reformed fashion, Grantham comments that Christ's fulfillment of the Law does not take away the responsibility of his people to submit to it and conform to it (Ibid.).

[45]Grantham, St. Paul's Catechism, 28.

[46]Ibid.

[47]Grantham, *Christianismus Primitivus,* Book 2, part 1, 62.

[48]Ibid.

[49]Ibid., Book 2, part 1, 63.

[50]Ibid., Book 2, part 1, 62.

[51]Ibid., Book 2, part 1, 66.

[52]Ibid.

[53]Ibid. "Thus then the whole World being found guilty before God, could not, by any Righteousness which they have done, lift themselves out of that state of Sin and Misery; wherefore God, in the greatness of his love to Mankind, hath laid help upon One that is mighty to save; who brings near his Righteousness, to those that were far from Righteousness, that in him they might have Righteousness through Faith; though in themselves there is too much demerit, to bear the Appellation of Righteousness" (Ibid., Book 2, 67).

[54]Ibid., Book 2, part 1, 68.

[55]Arminius, 2:256-57, 406.

[56]Grantham, *St. Paul's Catechism*, 28.

[57]Grantham, *Christianismus Primitivus,* Book 2, part 1, 68.

[58]Ibid.

[59]Ibid., Book 2, part 1, 67.

[60]Ibid., Book 2, part 1, 67-68.

[61]Grantham, *St. Paul's Catechism*, 22.

[62]In Anselmian fashion, Grantham emphasized that God had to identify with humanity to atone for sin. Even angels could not atone for humanity's sin. Atonement required someone who was both divine and human, a being with a "Divine Nature" who could "sympathize with the Human Nature in his Sufferings for us" (*Christianismus Primitivus*, Book 2, part 1, 62).

[63]Ibid., Book 2, part 1, 68.

[64]Although scholars have historically held this understanding of atonement and justification to be the domain of strict, orthodox Calvinism, Grantham and the General Baptists held to such a view. Even Richard Baxter, who has been described as a "mild Calvinist," rejected the penal satisfaction theory of atonement and the doctrine of justification by the imputed righteousness of Christ through faith. Revisionists such as R. T. Kendall and Alan C. Clifford argue that Calvin and Luther, contrary to received opinion, did not subscribe to the penal satisfaction theory of atonement and its attending doctrine of justification. Ironically, this was also the interpretation of John Goodwin. R. T. Kendall, *Calvin and English Calvinism to 1649* (Oxford: Clarendon, 1979); Alan C. Clifford, *Atonement and Justification: English Evangelical Theology 1640-1790: An Evaluation* (Oxford: Clarendon, 1990).

[65]Grotius also influenced Richard Baxter and John Tillotson with his governmental view of atonement.

[66]Goodwin, *Imputatio Fidei*, part 2, 33.

[67]Ibid.

[68]Ibid., 34-35.

[69]Ibid., 177.

[70]Ibid., part 1, 3.

[71]Ibid., 14.

[72]Arminius, *Works*, 2:42.

[73]Ibid., 2:43-45.

[74]This distinction has dramatic consequences for the doctrines of sanctification and the perseverance of the saints.

[75]All Arminians agreed on the doctrine of the resistibility of grace.

[76]Grantham, *A Dialogue Between the Baptist and the Presbyterian*, 19-20.

[77]Grantham, *Christianismus Primitivus*, Book 2, part 2, 155.

[78]Ibid.

[79]Ibid., Book 2, part 2, 154.

[80]Ibid., Book 2, part 2, 155.

[81]Goodwin, *Redemption Redeemed* (London, 1651), 345. It is worthy of note that in a letter to Walter Sellon, John Wesley wrote, "I am glad you have undertaken 'Redemption Redeemed.' But you must in no wise forget Dr. Owen's answer to it: otherwise you will leave a loop-hole for all the Calvinists to creep out. The Doctor's evasions you must needs cut in pieces."

[82]Ibid., 347.

[83]Ibid., 348.

[84]Ibid., 288.

[85]Henry C. Sheldon, *History of Christian Doctrine* (New York: Harper and Brothers, 1897), 2:142. This statement is made with reference to Grotius's theory of atonement.

[86]Hugo Grotius, *A Defence of the Catholic Faith Concerning the Satisfaction of Christ, against Faustus Socinus*, trans. Frank Hugh Foster (Andover: Warren F. Draper, 1889), 75. Interestingly, Clint Bass, in making a case for Grantham's identification with Dutch Arminianism, says that Grotius was one of Grantham's "favorite authors" (Bass, 163), thus unintentionally giving readers the impression that Grantham was influenced by Grotius's soteriological views. Yet Grotius was one of the scores of widely quoted authors of the day whom Grantham cited, and Grantham never cited him on soteriological matters. Grantham cited Grotius only six times, and only on baptism (which many Calvinistic Baptists have done), basic Christian doctrines on which any Christian would agree with Grotius, and the injustice of Calvin's procuring of Servetus's execution (Grantham actually cited the Reformed Oecolampadius in support of his position). Using Bass's logic, Grantham's favorite authors are Calvin and Augustine, whom Grantham favorably cites far more than he does Grotius.

[87]Grotius, 75.

6

ATONEMENT, JUSTIFICATION, AND APOSTASY IN THE THEOLOGY OF JOHN WESLEY

Reformed Arminians are indebted to John Wesley for his dedication to Christ and an extension of a Kingdom mentality in the church and society. They are also heirs to a wonderful tradition of scriptural exposition that eschews predestinarian Calvinism, which was strong in Wesley's day and is reasserting itself in our own day. Charles Wesley, John's brother, beautifully represents a broadly Arminian theological tradition in his hymns. If it is true that people learn their theology from hymns, we would do well to sing Charles Wesley's hymns.[1]

Yet, despite these affinities that we have with John Wesley, Reformed Arminians differ strongly with Wesley and the Wesleyan tradition on some important points regarding salvation and the Christian life. This is because they hearken back to a *pre-Wesleyan Arminianism*. Their Arminianism goes back to the theology of Thomas Helwys (1550-1616), the first Baptist who was a General or Arminian Baptist, influenced by the Dutch Reformed theologian Jacobus Arminius (1560-1609).[2] This pre-Wesleyan stream of Arminianism retains much in Reformed theology and spirituality that the later Wesleyan movement would discard. As I have said elsewhere, while Arminius "veered from Calvinism on the question of how one *comes to be* in a state of grace (predestination, free will, and grace) he retained Reformed categories on the *meaning* of sin and redemption."[3] The same can be said of his, and Helwys's, views on sanctification and Christian spirituality, although Helwys emphasized the baptism of disciples and the importance of Christian conversion more than Arminius.

In their view of sanctification and Christian spirituality, for example, Free Will Baptists have typically sympathized more with the practical, warm-hearted Puritan piety of a John Bunyan than the crisis-oriented, higher-life spirituality of Wesleyanism. The Wesleyan movement has emphasized a second work of grace and Christian perfection, which non-Wesleyan Arminians have avoided. Yet these views are in harmony with other Wesleyan beliefs about salvation. In the traditional Wesleyan view, Christ did not pay the penalty for sins but only pardoned sinners as a governor pardons a guilty criminal. Or He paid the penalty only for past sins and not for sin in general. If this were true, and if Christ's righteousness were not "imputed to all believers for their eternal acceptance with God,"[4] it would make sense that believers have little or no assurance of salvation until they have reached a state of entire sanctification or perfection, and that they must be "re-justified" every time they sin. Free Will Baptists differ with doctrines such as these.[5]

A thoroughgoing understanding of Wesley's soteriology will help to engender a clearer understanding of biblical and historic Free Will Baptist and Reformed Arminian understandings of salvation. This chapter will do that by examining Wesley's views on atonement, justification, and apostasy, with special attention to the historical context of his thought.

Wesley's understanding of atonement and justification and the implications of these doctrines for his view of continuance in the Christian life are indicative of the eclectic nature of his theology. Modern scholars have variously attempted to place Wesley firmly within certain streams of the Christian theological tradition. This has resulted in such designations as "the Calvinist Wesley," "the

Anglican Wesley," and "the Catholic Wesley." Such classifications, however, fail to grasp the complexity of Wesley's theology and the diversity of intellectual influences brought to bear on his intellectual development.

By examining Wesley's doctrines of atonement and justification and the ramifications of these concepts for his view of perseverance in the Christian life, one recognizes that he cannot be forced into a particular mold. On the contrary, Wesley's theology will be seen as a symbiotic blending of diverse elements in his own background that aided in shaping his theological perspectives. Such a study must begin with a discussion of the perspectives on Wesley's theology in modern scholarship[6] and proceed to consider the various people and schools of thought that influenced Wesley's theology. After this background has been laid, an analysis of Wesley's views on the nature of atonement, justification, and continuance in the Christian life will be undertaken.

INTERPRETATIONS OF WESLEY'S INTELLECTUAL INFLUENCES

Modern Wesley scholarship has produced disparate opinions on Wesley's place in the Christian tradition. Four main schools of thought have developed in Wesley studies: one highlights the Catholic elements in Wesley's theology; the second stresses his Calvinist or "Reformation" tone, while the third emphasizes Wesley as Anglican. A fourth school consists of those few scholars who have emphasized the eclecticism of Wesley's theology.

The "Calvinist Wesley"

Certain scholars have stressed Wesley's indebtedness to Reformation theology and the Reformed tradition as mediated through the Anglican Church. These scholars have characterized Wesley as "the Calvinist Wesley," emphasizing Wesley's statement that he was within "a hairsbreadth of Calvinism." George Croft Cell was the first twentieth-century scholar to advance this interpretation of Wesley. Cell argued that, despite Wesley's divergence from Calvin on the doctrine of predestination, he was in agreement with Calvin on original sin and on justification.[7] Since Wesley emphasized the priority of

131

divine grace over against a Pelagian anthropocentrism, Cell lumps Wesley into the Reformation camp. Thus he highlights Wesley's similarities rather than his differences with Luther, Calvin, and the other Magisterial Reformers.[8] Many subsequent Wesley scholars, such as William R. Cannon, Martin Schmidt, and Colin W. Williams, have followed Cell in stressing Wesley's dependence on Reformation theology and downplaying his differences with Luther, Calvin, and the English Puritans on atonement and justification.[9]

The "Catholic Wesley"

Ironically, the person who opened Wesley studies to new considerations of Wesley's place in the Christian tradition was the Catholic scholar Maximin Piette. His influential revisionist work *John Wesley in the Evolution of Protestantism* broke with the older view of Wesley as essentially anti-Catholic. Piette emphasized Wesley's benefit from the Roman Catholic tradition by both his high esteem for patristic theology and his use of the Catholic tradition as mediated through the Anglican Church.[10] Piette's basic understanding of "the Catholic Wesley" has been shared by such scholars as Jean Orcibal.[11] These scholars tend to deemphasize the importance of Wesley's Aldersgate experience—a theme highlighted by the "Calvinist Wesley" advocates. They also offer a lower estimate of the influence of the Reformers on Wesley's doctrines of grace, justification, and the nature of atonement.[12]

The "Anglican Wesley"

Some scholars have asserted that Wesley's theological orientation owes itself primarily to his Anglican[13] heritage. Scholars such as C. F. Allison, Richard P. Heitzenrater, John English, Herbert McGonigle, and David Eaton have pointed to the influence of seventeenth-century Anglican Arminianism as assimilated through Wesley's parents. These authors have also emphasized his reading of Jeremy Taylor and other representatives of the Anglican "Holy Living School."[14] H. R. McAdoo characterizes Wesley's theology as Anglican in "spirit" or method rather than in content.[15]

132

The Eclectic Wesley

David Hempton is representative of an approach to Wesley's intellectual influences that emphasizes the eclectic nature of Wesley's thought. He remarks that Wesley was influenced by

> a bewildering array of Christian traditions: the church fathers, monastic piety, and ancient liturgies; continental mystics such as Jeanne-Marie Guyon . . . Byzantine traditions of spirituality approached through Macarius and Gregory of Nyssa; the English and Scottish Puritan divines; the Moravians and other channels of European Pietism; his mother and through her to Pascal; classics of devotional spirituality including Thomas à Kempis, Jeremy Taylor, and William Law; and the canon of Anglican writers from Hooker to the seventeenth- and eighteenth-century High Churchmen. Writers on each of these traditions are prone to compete for the preeminent influence over Wesley, but the truth of the matter is that Wesley's eclecticism is itself preeminent.[16]

Albert Outler, though sometimes classified within the "Wesley as Calvinist" school, has come closer than most scholars to recognizing the eclectic nature of Wesley's theology. Thus, he has emphasized Wesley as a "folk theologian" whose pastoral and homiletical aims, together with his diverse influences, uniquely shaped his theological views. Despite this characterization, however, Outler tends to place great emphasis on the Reformation tributaries (particularly within the Church of England) that flowed into the Wesleyan stream.[17]

The first three approaches to Wesley's theology are unsatisfactory because they overemphasize one current of the diversity of influences on Wesley's thought. These perspectives employ a synchronic method of understanding Wesley's theology that has Wesley choosing between polarities in his theological experience. Only Hempton's and Outler's diachronic or symbiotic approach, which understands Wesley as absorbing and synthesizing several influences from a spectrum of theological expressions in his own intellectual development, is adequate to explain the uniqueness of Wesley's theology. This approach is borne out in an examination of Wesley's doctrines of justification, the nature of atonement, and continuance in the Christian life, as will be demonstrated in the course of this chapter.

WESLEY'S INTELLECTUAL INFLUENCES

Wesley did not selectively choose between Reformation and Anglican Arminian theological expressions of these doctrines. Rather, he, seemingly unconsciously, absorbed central motifs from both traditions and amalgamated them into a unique theology that differed substantially from both systems. An understanding of Wesley's doctrines of justification, atonement, and continuance in the Christian life can be gained only by comprehending the variant intellectual influences on Wesley's thought in the context of his intellectual development.

Anglican Arminianism

Of the two most significant broad influences on Wesley's theology, the Reformation and Anglican Arminianism, the latter is more basic. The most formative of influences was that of Wesley's parents, who were steeped in Anglican Arminianism. Both Samuel and Susanna Wesley had converted to Anglicanism from Nonconformity and had reacted vehemently against their own dissenting backgrounds. Their resistance to the rigid predestinarianism of their upbringings precipitated a vigorous acceptance of seventeenth-century Anglican Arminianism.[18] Samuel Wesley credited William Cave's *Primitive Christianity*, in which Cave sought to demonstrate Anglican Arminianism's consistency with patristic theology, with his own decision to convert to Anglicanism.[19] Wesley's parents immersed him in Anglican Arminianism, as is evidenced in numerous letters and discussions between Wesley and his parents. His mother had encouraged him to read Jeremy Taylor (just as his father had recommended Hugo Grotius as the best biblical commentator he knew of).[20] Wesley's Anglican Arminian rearing was confirmed as he came into contact with the works of the most distinguished Arminian writers. Wesley began reading Taylor in 1725, and he spoke of the latter's inestimable influence on him. Indeed, Taylor can be said to have been the vehicle through which Wesley was introduced to the Anglican Arminianism of the seventeenth century.[21] In addition to Taylor, Wesley was greatly influenced by William Law's *Christian Perfection* and *A Serious Call to a Devout and Holy Life* as well as the works of Thomas a Kempis.[22] Wesley's circle at Oxford was saturated in both Dutch and English Arminian sources.[23] For example, Wesley's close friend at Oxford, Benjamin Ingham, recorded eleven separate readings of Hugo Grotius in his diary in the year 1733.[24]

Prior to his connection with the Moravians, Wesley's primary influences were from Anglican Arminianism. As C. F. Allison has persuasively argued, seventeenth-century Anglican Arminianism was thoroughly imbued with moralism, diverging from the *sola fide* emphasis of the Reformation. This perspective stressed the ethical example of Christ's atonement. It neglected the atonement's juridical aspects and tended toward semi-Pelagianism in its doctrine of justification and the relation of faith and works, and the resultant doctrines of sanctification and the Christian life.[25]

Reformation Theology

The Anglican Arminians of the seventeenth century were exceedingly influential on Wesley's theology. However, Reformation theology as mediated through the Moravians, the Reformation Anglicanism of thinkers such as Thomas Cranmer, and Wesley's reading of the continental Reformers themselves, was also influential. There has been scholarly disagreement on the nature and extent of the influence of Reformation thought on Wesley. G. C. Cell, Colin Williams, and others have painted Wesley as an heir of the continental reformers. Yet Outler has stated that it is inaccurate to speak of Wesley as directly influenced by Luther and Calvin, and that Wesley would have been surprised by Cell and Williams's assessment of him.[26] Part of this debate arises from the problem of identifying Wesley's influences, since he rarely documented his sources. Although it is difficult to assess the extent of Wesley's indebtedness to the continental Reformers, his absorption of certain aspects of Reformation theology through the Moravians, the doctrinal standards of the Church of England, and Thomas Cranmer is indubitable.[27] Outler states that Wesley's investigation of the Homilies of the Church of England during his controversy with the Moravians constituted the mature phase of Wesley's theology.[28]

John Goodwin and Richard Baxter

In addition to the Anglican Arminianism of the seventeenth century and Reformation thought, Wesley was enormously influenced by two non-Anglican theologians—the Independents John Goodwin and Richard Baxter. Affirmative quotations of Goodwin and Baxter abound in Wesley's writings. In 1745 he reprinted an extract of Baxter's *Aphorisms of Justification*, which had originally been published in 1649. Wesley's *Predestination Calmly Considered* bears striking resemblance to numbers XIX-XLV of Baxter's *Aphorisms*, and Wesley's doctrine of justification reveals Baxter's influence.[29] Despite the numerous positive references to Goodwin in Wesley's works and Wesley's 1765 republication of Goodwin's *Imputatio Fidei, or A Treatise of Justification* (1642), scholars have largely ignored Goodwin's influence on Wesley. However, Goodwin had perhaps more influence on Wesley's doctrine of justification in the last thirty years of his life than any other single thinker, as is evidenced by his preface to Goodwin's treatise.

This short summary of Wesley's intellectual influences argues that Wesley's early theological development was shaped primarily by the Anglican Arminianism of the seventeenth century. It was offset, however, by the Reformation theology he imbibed from the Moravians, his reading of the continental Reformers, and more directly from Thomas Cranmer and the doctrinal standards of the Church of England. This amalgamation was in turn augmented by the influence of two seventeenth-century Nonconformists, Richard Baxter and John Goodwin.

INTERPRETATIONS OF WESLEY'S THEOLOGY

The scholarship on Wesley's view of atonement, justification, and continuance in the Christian life has been diverse. Of these three doctrines, Wesley's understanding of justification has been studied the most, but it has not been analyzed in the context of his doctrines of the nature of atonement and perseverance in the Christian life. The difficulty with many of the studies of Wesley's doctrine of justification, however, is the lack of understanding of the nuances of seventeenth- and eighteenth-century theology that often accompanies them.

While much has been written on Wesley's view of the extent of atonement, precious little has been done on his understanding of the nature of atonement. The three principal scholars who have deliberated it are Williams, Renshaw, and Deschner. In his brief treatment on the nature of atonement, Williams fails to see the strong juridical overtones in Wesley's doctrine of atonement. He mistakenly asserts that "Wesley does not put the penal substitutionary element of his teaching inside a legal framework in which God is made subject to an eternal unchangeable order of justice."[30] Renshaw, while understanding Wesley's emphasis on God as judge, is simplistic in characterizing Wesley's view of atonement as a mix between Reformational and Grotian categories.[31] Deschner is more sophisticated in his view of Wesley's doctrine of atonement, seeing it essentially as a modified penal satisfaction theory. He fails, however, to ground Wesley's doctrine of the nature of atonement in its historical or theological contexts.[32]

Scholars have deliberated Wesley's doctrine of justification considerably. While some scholars have noted Catholic overtones in Wesley (Piette, Orbical, Lee), most (Cannon, Cell, Schmidt, Skevington Wood, Williams) have seen Wesley's doctrine of justification as basically similar to that of the continental Reformers. The latter group of scholars, however, has failed to unveil the complex distinctions between the Catholic and Reformation influences with regard to the imputation of Christ's righteousness. Furthermore, they have missed the significance of Baxter's and Goodwin's influence on Wesley. A few scholars (Clifford, Lindstrom, Outler) correctly interpret Wesley's doctrine of justification but fail to tie it in any significant way to his doctrine of the nature of atonement. Only Deschner succeeds in this regard, but his study of these doctrines, limited to Wesley's Christology, is brief and fails to understand how these doctrines shaped Wesley's view of continuance in the Christian life.[33]

WESLEY'S VIEW OF THE NATURE OF ATONEMENT

In his doctrine of the nature of atonement, Wesley betrays the clear influence of the Reformers and Reformation Anglicanism in his retention of a basic, though modified, penal satisfaction theory of atonement. The Reformers' view of atonement had been rejected by the seventeenth-century Anglican Arminians such as Jeremy Taylor as well as by Richard Baxter and John Goodwin. Despite Wesley's acknowledged debt to these thinkers, he diverged from them in his doctrine of atonement. Though he failed to reveal the sources for his penal satisfaction doctrine of atonement, it is safe to assume that Cranmer, the Homilies of the Church of England, and the Reformers themselves influenced Wesley to maintain central elements of the Reformation doctrine of the nature of atonement.[34]

Wesley maintained the Reformation understanding of God as judge and humanity as the violator of divine justice. The sins of humanity have accrued the penalty of the wrath of God, which is eternal death.[35] The only way for individuals to escape the wrath of God is for Christ to bear the penalty for sin, which He does on the cross. In explaining this concept, Wesley retained the Reformation language of passive obedience. In his passive obedience, Christ voluntarily submitted to the wrath of God and took humanity's punishment for sin, thus averting the wrath of God. Christ's death is a "propitiation—to appease an offended God. But if, as some teach, God was never offended, there was no need of this propitiation."[36] Thus, the divine penalty for sin, meted out by God, is satisfied by Christ's passive obedience on the cross.

Wesley here aligned himself with the satisfaction tradition that originated with Anselm of Canterbury and found its fullest expression in Luther, Calvin, and Cranmer. Despite his basic reliance on the seventeenth-century Anglican Arminians, Baxter, and Goodwin, his doctrine of atonement was radically distinct from theirs. These thinkers relied on Hugo Grotius's governmental theory of atonement, which held that God could freely pardon or forgive sinners without any satisfaction for the violation of divine justice. In the governmental view, the death of Christ is accepted by God as governor or ruler rather than as judge. Christ's death is a symbol of the punishment of sin rather than punishment itself. The penalty for sin, rather than being fulfilled or satisfied, is set aside, and the believing sinner is pardoned as a governor would pardon a guilty criminal. Goodwin's statement of this theory in his *Imputatio Fidei* (1642) is especially relevant in view of the fact that Wesley republished this work in 1765: "The sentence or curse of the Law, was not properly executed upon Christ in his death, but this death of Christ was a ground or consideration unto God, whereupon to dispense with his Law, and to let fall or suspend the execution of the penalty or curse therein threatened."[37] Goodwin's statement contrasts sharply with Wesley's comment on Romans 3:26, where he speaks of God "showing justice on his own Son" so that God "might evidence himself to be strictly and inviolably righteous in the administration of his government, even while he is the merciful justifier of the sinner that believeth in Jesus. The attribute of justice must be preserved inviolate; and inviolate it is preserved, *if there was a real infliction of punishment on our Saviour.*"[38] Thus Wesley was at great pains to affirm a retributive or penal satisfaction view of atonement over against a governmental view. In this view, Wesley was in complete agreement with article 31 of the Thirty-nine Articles, which says Christ made "perfect redemption, propitiation, and satisfaction" for sin and "there is none other satisfaction for sin, but that alone." Unlike the governmentalists in his Anglican Arminian background, Wesley believed, with the Reformers, that the penalty for sin must be paid and that it has been satisfied by Christ in His passive obedience on the cross.

However, before one thinks the case is tied up for Wesley's absolute reliance on Reformation categories, it must be emphasized that, while Wesley stressed the penal satisfaction nature of Christ's atonement, he modified it.

Yet his modification of this theory was unique in that it avoided the govern-
mentalist overtones of much of early English Arminianism. In much Reformation theology, the atonement of Christ included not only passive obedience
but also active obedience.[39] Active obedience consists of Christ's perfect righteousness and His complete obedience to and fulfillment of divine law. Most
Reformed theologians held that both aspects of Christ's obedience go together
in satisfying the just demands of the divine law. Divine justice requires absolute righteousness on the part of human beings for their acceptance before
God, and human beings cannot themselves provide such absolute righteousness. Hence, Christ's absolute righteousness must be imputed or credited to
them for their justification. Here Wesley diverged from the mainstream penal
satisfaction theory of atonement, insisting that the efficacy of Christ's atonement subsists primarily in His passive obedience, or His bearing the divine
penalty for sin, rather than in His positive fulfillment of the law. In his preface
to John Goodwin's *Imputatio Fidei,* which he retitled "A Treatise on Justification," Wesley stated that Christ's death is "certainly the chief part, if not the
whole" of the atonement.[40] "Although I believe Christ fulfilled God's law, yet
I do not affirm he did this to purchase redemption for us. This was done by his
dying in our stead."[41] Christ's active obedience, for Wesley, was coincidental,
not formally essential, to the atonement. Thus, though Wesley affirmed the
reality of Christ's active obedience, he denied its salvific efficacy.

Wesley further modified the penal satisfaction view of atonement with his
distinction between past and future sins. Whereas Reformation Anglicanism
insisted that Christ's oblation for the sins of humanity was for all sins, original
and actual (Thirty-Nine Articles, 31), Wesley asserted that Christ atoned only
for the believer's past sins. Christ's atonement was not for the *condition* of sin,
nor was it to remove the curse of original sin, but it was a propitiation for
"the remission of past sins."[42] Neither sin in general nor the sinner, but only
past sins are forgiven, for God cannot forgive sins before they happen. This
concept is borne out in "A Dialogue between an Antinomian and His Friend,"
in which the Antinomian says Christ "did then heal, take away, put an end to,
and utterly destroy, all our sins." Then his friend replies, "Did he then heal the

wound before it was made, and put an end to our sins before they had a beginning? This is so glaring, palpable an absurdity, that I cannot conceive how you can swallow it."[43] Wesley's conception that Christ atoned only for past sins rather than for sin generally exerted great influence on his view of justification and continuance in the Christian life.

It has been argued here that Wesley's doctrine of the nature of atonement was firmly rooted in the penal satisfaction categories of Reformation theology and was theologically distinct from the governmental theory of Grotius, which was employed by the Anglican Arminians as well as Baxter and Goodwin. Yet Wesley modified this penal satisfactionism in his disavowal of Christ's active obedience in the atonement as well as his notion that Christ atoned only for past sins. This theory of atonement relies on the logic of penal satisfaction but on the spirit of governmentalism. It is an unambiguous example of the creative amalgamation that made Wesley's theology unique.[44]

WESLEY'S VIEW OF JUSTIFICATION

Wesley's doctrine of justification betrays his reliance on his Anglican Arminian heritage and his appreciation for John Goodwin and Richard Baxter as well as a total divergence from Reformation categories. "The plain scriptural notion of justification," asserted Wesley, "is pardon, the forgiveness of sins. It is the act of God the father, whereby, for the sake of the propitiation made by the blood of his Son, he 'showeth forth his righteousness (or mercy) by the remission of sins that are past.'"[45] The above statement reveals Wesley's notion that justification is "the atonement of Christ actually applied to the soul of the sinner now believing on him."[46] Wesley's theory of atonement is brought directly to bear on his view of justification. As was seen above, the principal aspect of atonement is Christ's passive obedience. The believing sinner is justified because of or *for the sake of* the "propitiation made by the blood" of Christ, that is, the punishment of Christ for the sake of sinful humanity. This propitiation is applied to the sinner, the result of which is remission of sins, that is, pardon or forgiveness.

Wesley believed that Christ's passive obedience only and not His active obedience is applied to the sinner in justification. Therefore, Christ has borne the believer's punishment and deflected the wrath of God from him or her, but has not provided a positive righteousness for the believing sinner. Wesley veered from the Reformation doctrine of justification which insisted on a forensic justification—a divinely provided righteousness that is imputed to believers for their acceptance with God. The English General Baptist Thomas Grantham was exemplary of this forensic view of justification: "That God imputes Righeousness to Men without Works, is so plain, that it can never be denied. What is thus imputed, is not acted by us, but expressly reckoned as a matter of free Gift, or Grace; and this can be the Righteousness of none but Christ . . . because no other way can the Righteousness of God be made ours . . . there is none righteous, no not one. Except therefore the Righteousness of Christ be laid hold on, there is no Righteousness to be imputed to Sinners."[47]

Wesley differed strongly from such a view. Far from believing that the righteousness of Christ is imputed to believers so that they are (forensically) accounted righteous in God's sight, Wesley asserted that justification

> does by no means imply that God judges concerning us contrary to the real nature of things, that he esteems us better than we really are, or believes us righteous when we are unrighteous. Surely no. The judgment of the all-wise God is always according to truth. Neither can it ever consist with his unerring wisdom to think that I am innocent, to judge that I am righteous or holy, *because another is so. He can no more, in this manner, confound me with Christ than with David or Abraham.*[48]

Wesley had no use for forensic justification or the imputed righteousness of Christ. Such language, warned Wesley, is so often used as "a cover for unrighteousness."[49] He found it difficult to conceive of a gospel that would allow a believer to commit sin with impunity because he has been imputed with the righteousness of Christ:

A man has been reproved, suppose for drunkenness: "O," said he, "I pretend to no righteousness of *my own; Christ is my righteousness.*" Another has been told, that "the extortioner, the unjust, shall not inherit the kingdom of God:" He replies, with all assurance, "I am unjust in myself, but I have a spotless righteousness in Christ." And thus, though a man be as far from the practice as from the tempers of a Christian; though he neither has the mind which was in Christ, nor in any respect walks as he walked; yet he has armour of proof against all conviction, in what he calls "the righteousness of Christ."[50]

Wesley's view of forensic justification has been debated because of his use of the word "imputed" in speaking of righteousness in the believer. However, to clear up any lingering misconceptions, Wesley stated in his 1773 writing entitled, "Remarks on Mr. Hill's Farrago Double-Distilled," that "that phrase, *the imputed righteousness of Christ,* I never did use," and he advised everyone "to lay aside that ambiguous, unscriptural phrase."[51]

Wesley's notion that Christ's death atoned only for sins committed prior to conversion applies to his idea of justification. If atonement is only for past sins, then justification is only for past sins. Thus Wesley could equate justification merely with pardon or forgiveness—remission of past sins—without any recourse to a doctrine of imputation. This formulation of the doctrine of justification deviated from Reformation theology and aligned with Goodwin, Baxter, and the seventeenth-century Anglican Arminians, with their reliance on Grotius's governmentalism. Wesley, however, arrived at the same position in a different way. He did not assert, like the governmentalists, that Christ's righteousness is not imputed to the believer because the penalty for sin has been set aside and God has freely forgiven the sinner. Rather, Wesley averred that the penalty for sin has been satisfied in Christ's death and that this satisfaction is appropriated to the believer, but that this justifies the believer from only past sins. Thus, the governmentalists worked from the perspective of God's free pardon of the sinner based on the sweeping aside of the law, whereas

Wesley held that the believer's past sins are remitted because of Christ's oblation. But with regard to the imputation of the righteousness of Jesus Christ, the end result is identical: righteousness in the believer is purely practical; it is inherent and not forensic.

WESLEY'S VIEW OF PERSEVERANCE

Wesley's doctrine of justification is enormously crucial for his doctrine of perseverance in the Christian life. Wesley agreed with his Arminian forebears that it is possible for a believer to fall from grace, to apostatize from the Christian life. For Wesley, this possibility manifests itself in two ways: the first is through irremediable apostasy; the second is through willful sin.

Irremediable Apostasy

In his notes, Wesley found examples of irremediable apostasy in such scriptural passages as 1 Timothy 1:19-20 and Hebrews 6:4-6. In 1 Timothy 1, Paul states that some have "made shipwreck of their faith." Wesley viewed this condition as irremediable, "for ships once wrecked cannot be afterwards saved."[52] His exegesis of Hebrews 6:4-6 fell in line with the standard Arminian exposition: "The apostle here describes the case of those who have cast away both the power and the form of godliness. . . . Of these wilful total apostates he declares, *it is impossible to renew them again to repentance* (though they were renewed once)."[53] This "total" or "final" apostasy, Wesley contended, is a result of the defection from faith—the renunciation of the atonement of Christ—and hence cannot be remedied.[54]

However, while Wesley affirms repeatedly in a number of writings that shipwreck of faith constitutes final, irremediable apostasy, in a few instances he struggled with the concept. For example, in his sermon, "A Call to Backsliders," he indicated that even those guilty of the kind of apostasy described in 1 Timothy 1:19-20 and Hebrews 6:4-6 can still be restored:

> If it be asked, "Do any real apostates find mercy from God? Do any
> that have 'made shipwreck of faith and a good conscience,' recover

what they have lost? Do you know, have you seen, any instance of persons who found redemption in the blood of Jesus, and afterwards fell away, and yet were restored,—'renewed again unto repentance?'" yea, verily and not one or an hundred only, but, I am persuaded several thousands. . . . Indeed, it is so far from being an uncommon thing for a believer to fall and be restored, that it is rather uncommon to find any believers who are not conscious of having been backsliders from God, in a higher or lower degree, and perhaps more than once, before they were established in faith.[55]

Apostasy through Willful Sin

The second avenue of apostasy, Wesley taught, is willful sin. Whereas the first type of apostasy, total apostasy, logically follows from Wesley's doctrine of the resistibility of divine salvific grace, the second ensues from his view of justification. Because only past sins are atoned for and forgiven in justification, future sins must likewise be forgiven. One must remember Wesley's assertion that it is absurd to say God can forgive sins that have not yet occurred. Just as God pardoned the believer for past sins, so the believer's future sins must be pardoned.[56] Failure to receive pardon for post-conversion sins results in apostasy.

Wesley believed that sin in itself brings about apostasy, thereby breaking one's relationship with God. Wesley uses David as an example of the pattern of apostasy through willful sin:

To explain this by a particular instance: David was born of God, and saw God by faith. He loved God in sincerity. He could truly say, "Whom have I in heaven but thee? and there is none upon earth," neither person nor thing, "that I desire in comparison of thee." But still there remained in his heart that corruption of nature, which is the seed of all evil.

"He was walking upon the roof of his house," (2 Sam. 11:2) probably praising the God whom his soul loved, when he looked

145

down, and saw Bathsheba. He felt a temptation; a thought which tended to evil. The Spirit of God did not fail to convince him of this. He doubtless heard and knew the warning voice; but he yielded in some measure to the thought, and the temptation began to prevail over him. Hereby his spirit was sullied; he saw God still; but it was more dimly than before. He loved God still; but not in the same degree; not with the same strength and ardour of affection. Yet God checked him again, though his spirit was grieved; and his voice, though fainter and fainter, still whispered, "Sin lieth at the door; look unto me, and be thou saved." But he would not hear: He looked again, not unto God, but unto the forbidden object, till nature was superior to grace, and kindled lust in his soul.

The eye of his mind was now closed again, and God vanished out of his sight. Faith, the divine, supernatural intercourse with God, and the love of God, ceased together: He then rushed on as a horse into the battle, and knowingly committed the outward sin. [57]

Unlike total apostasy, this second type of apostasy is remediable. Wesley termed this kind of apostasy "backsliding." In his *Journals,* he offered several examples of people he believed had apostatized and been restored to salvation. [58] In his sermon "A Call to Backsliders," Wesley described believers who think they can never fall from grace but nonetheless "have utterly lost the life of God, and sin hath regained dominion over them." [59] "It is remarkable," declared Wesley, "that many who had fallen either from justifying or sanctifying grace . . . have been restored . . . and that very frequently in an instant, to all that they had lost. . . . In one moment they received anew both remission of sins, and a lot among them that were sanctified." [60]

This works-oriented view of continuance in the Christian life emanates naturally from Wesley's doctrine of justification. If only past sins are remitted, then believers are "left on their own" with regard to future sins:

Wilt thou say, "But I have again committed sin, since I had redemption through his blood?". . . It is meet that thou shouldst abhor
thyself. . . . But, dost thou now believe? . . . At whatsoever time
thou truly believest in the name of the Son of God, all thy sins
antecedent to that hour vanish away. . . . And think not to say, "I
was justified once; my sins were once forgiven me:" . . . "He that
committeth sin is of the devil." Therefore, thou art of thy father the
devil. It cannot be denied: For the works of thy father thou doest.
. . . Beware thou suffer thy soul to take no rest, till his pardoning
love be again revealed; till he "heal thy backslidings," and fill thee
again with the "faith that worketh by love."[61]

Thus, Wesley emphasized the necessity of personal holiness and continual penitence for continuance, asserting that individuals fall from grace by committing
sins and must repent to be restored, thus reappropriating the benefits of the
atonement.

It is important to note the striking similarity between Wesley and John
Goodwin. In his 1651 work, *Redemption Redeemed,* Goodwin offered the same
two-fold analysis of apostasy that Wesley later proposed.[62] Wesley revealed
his appreciation for *Redemption Redeemed* in a July 1768 letter to Walter Sellon,
who was embarking on a reprinting of the work: "I am glad you have undertaken the 'Redemption Redeemed.' But you must nowise forget Dr. Owen's
answer to it: Otherwise you will leave a loophole for all the Calvinists to creep
out. The Doctor's evasions you must needs cut in pieces, either interweaving
your answers with the body of the work, under each head, or adding them in
marginal notes."[63]

Wesley's understanding of the nature of atonement, justification, and
continuance in the Christian life are somewhat unique in Christian theology. His modified penal satisfaction theory of atonement, which entails that
Christ atoned only for the believer's past sins, is a distinctive contribution to
Western Christian thought. His view results in a notion of justification and
the Christian life that has the inherent holiness of the individual believer at

its core. These doctrines in turn lay the foundation for an understanding of sanctification—Christian perfection—that is also unique. Wesley's theological originality makes him difficult to assess. Those who attempt, however, to pigeonhole him by forcing him into a preconceived theological mold, whether Anglican, Arminian, Calvinist, or Catholic, fail to comprehend the complexity of his symbiotic absorption and amalgamation of the sources of his own intellectual history.

[1] As this chapter will note, there is often tension in early Wesleyan thought between a more grace-oriented Arminianism and a semi-Pelagian approach, but John Wesley in the end comes out on the more works-oriented side of things rather than the grace-oriented side that Arminius and Helwys represent. Yet the hymns of Charles Wesley emphasize the grace-oriented side and are usually very amenable to Reformed Arminianism.

[2] See Chapters One and Three.

[3] J. Matthew Pinson, "Introduction," in J. Matthew Pinson, ed., *Four Views on Eternal Security* (Grand Rapids: Zondervan, 2002), 14-15.

[4] This phrase is from the *1812 Abstract*, which says, "We believe that no man has any warrant before God through his own works, power, or ability which he has in and of himself, only as he by Grace is made able to come to God, through Jesus Christ; believing the righteousness of Jesus Christ to be imputed to all believers for their eternal acceptance before God." The *1812 Abstract* is the earliest Southern Free Will Baptist confession of faith. It was an abstract of the 1660 *Standard Confession* of the English General Baptists, which the early Southern Free Will Baptists brought with them from England. It is reprinted in J. Matthew Pinson, *A Free Will Baptist Handbook: Heritage, Beliefs, and Ministries* (Nashville: Randall House, 1998), 142-47.

[5] For contemporary treatments from this perspective, see the following: F. Leroy Forlines, *Classical Arminianism: A Theology of Salvation* (Nashville: Randall House, 2011); Robert E. Picirilli, *Grace, Faith, Free Will: Contrasting Views of Salvation: Calvinism and Arminianism* (Nashville: Randall House, 2002); Stephen M. Ashby, "Reformed Arminianism," in J. Matthew Pinson, ed., *Four Views on Eternal Security* (Grand Rapids: Zondervan, 2002).

[6] This initial historiographical discussion will lay out the general understandings of where Wesley fits in the Christian tradition. Historiographical analysis with specific regard to Wesley's doctrines of justification and the nature of atonement will be reserved for the section of the essay that explicates these doctrines.

[7] George Croft Cell, *The Rediscovery of John Wesley* (New York: University Press of America, 1983. First edition, 1935), 19.

[8] Ibid., 243-45.

[9] William R. Cannon, *The Theology of John Wesley, with Special Reference to the Doctrine of Justification* (New York: Abingdon, 1946); Martin Schmidt, *John Wesley: A Theological Biography*, 3

vols. (Nashville: Abingdon, 1972-73. First German edition, 1967); Colin W. Williams, *John Wesley's Theology Today* (New York: Abingdon, 1960).

[10]Maximin Piette, *John Wesley in the Evolution of Protestantism* (London: Sheed and Ward, 1937). Though this work was first published in 1925, it still figures greatly into the discussion, and is referred to by most scholars of Wesley's theology.

[11]Jean Orcibal, "The Theological Originality of John Wesley and Continental Spirituality," Translated by J. A. Sharp. In *A History of the Methodist Church in Great Britain,* vol. 1, eds. Rupert Davies and Gordon Rupp (London: Epworth, 1965), 102-10.

[12]See also U. Lee, *John Wesley and Modern Religion* (New York, 1936).

[13]The term "Anglican" here, while anachronistic, is employed for purposes of convenience. It is used here to denote the non-Puritan wing of the Church of England in the seventeenth century.

[14]C. F. Allison, *The Rise of Moralism: The Proclamation of the Gospel from Hooker to Baxter* (New York: Seabury, 1966); Richard P. Heitzenrater, "John Wesley and the Oxford Methodists, 1725-1735," Ph.D. diss., Duke University, 1972; John C. English, *The Heart Renewed: John Wesley's Doctrine of Christian Initiation* (Macon: Wesleyan College, 1967); Herbert Boyd McGonigle, *Sufficient Saving Grace: John Wesley's Evangelical Arminianism* (Milton Keynes, UK: Paternoster, 2001); and David E. Eaton, "Arminianism in the Theology of John Wesley," Ph.D. diss., Drew University, 1988.

[15]Henry R. McAdoo, *The Spirit of Anglicanism: A Survey of Anglican Theological Method in the Seventeenth Century* (New York: Charles Scribner's Sons, 1965), 1.

[16]David Hempton, *Methodism: Empire of the Spirit* (New Haven: Yale University Press, 2005), 714.

[17]Albert C. Outler, "The Place of Wesley in the Christian Tradition," in *The Place of Wesley in the Christian Tradition,* ed., Kenneth E. Rowe (Metuchen: Scarecrow, 1976), 11-38.

[18]Adam Clarke, *Memoirs of the Wesley Family Collected Principally from Original Documents,* 2nd ed. (New York: Lane and Tippett, 1848), 89.

[19]Schmidt, vol. 1, part 1, 44.

[20]Richard P. Heitzenrater, *The Elusive Mr. Wesley* (Nashville: Abingdon, 1984), vol. 2, 23.

[21]*The Works of John Wesley,* XI, 366 (hereafter cited as *Works*; all quotations from Wesley's works are from the Thomas Jackson edition reprinted by Zondervan Publishers); John Deschner, *Wesley's Christology: An Interpretation* (Dallas: Southern Methodist University Press, 1960, 1985), 197.

[22]Albert C. Outler, ed., *John Wesley* (New York: Oxford University Press, 1964), 7.

[23]Eaton, 255-70.

[24]See Richard P. Heitzenrater, ed., *Diary of an Oxford Methodist: Benjamin Ingham, 1733-34* (Durham: Duke University Press, 1985).

[25]See Allison, 65-70.

[26]Outler, ed., *John Wesley,* 119-20.

[27]Ibid., 121-33.

[28]Ibid., 16.

[29]Ibid., 148-49.

[30]Colin W. Williams, *John Wesley's Theology Today* (New York: Abingdon, 1960), 84.

[31]John Rutherford Renshaw, "The Atonement in the Theology of John and Charles Wesley," Ph.D. diss., Boston University, 1965, 126.

[32]Deschner, 152-57.

[33]Few scholars have sought to extend their studies to encompass an understanding of Wesley's view of continuance in the Christian life. The closest most writers come to this is to study Wesley's doctrine of entire sanctification, which is logically and theologically distinct from his understanding of continuance in the Christian life. Some scholars make reference to Wesley's view of "backsliding," but fail to understand how crucial his view of atonement and justification is to his larger understanding of Christian perseverance.

[34]I am indebted to John Deschner's *Wesley's Christology: An Interpretation* for his insights on Wesley's doctrine of atonement, which have been helpful to me.

[35]*Works*, IX, 481-82; "Of Hell," *Works*, VI, intro, 4; II, 2.

[36]*Notes*, Romans 3:25.

[37]John Goodwin, *Imputatio Fidei. Or A Treatise of Justification* (London, 1642), Part II, 13.

[38]*Notes*, Romans 3:26. Italics added.

[39]Some Reformed thinkers, even among the framers of Reformed confessional documents such as the Westminster Confession, Canons of Dort, Heidelberg Catechism, Belgic Confession, and Thirty-Nine Articles of the Church of England, did not insist that one affirm the active obedience of Christ to hold a satisfaction view of atonement. Wesley's view, while different from most Protestant satisfaction theories, still meets the rigorous demands of a more general penal substitutionary understanding of atonement.

[40]*Works*, X, 331.

[41]*Works*, X, 386.

[42]*Notes*, Romans 3:25. Wesley defines "past sins" here as "all the sins antecedent to their believing."

[43]*Works*, X, 267.

[44]It might be stated as a sidelight (though it is beyond the scope of this paper) that Wesleyan theologians after the first generation jettisoned Wesley's eclectic view of atonement for the more logically consistent Grotian theory.

[45]"Justification by Faith," V, II, 5.

[46]"Salvation by Faith," V, II, 7.

[47]Thomas Grantham, *Christianismus Primitivus, or The Ancient Christian Religion* (London, 1678), Book 2, chapter 3, 67.

[48]"Justification by Faith," V, II, 4.

[49]"The Lord Our Righteousness," V, II, 19.

[50]Ibid.

[51]*Works*, X, 430.

[52]*Notes*, I Timothy 1:20.

[53]*Notes*, Hebrews 6:6.

[54]"Serious Thoughts on the Perseverance of the Saints," X, 284-298.

[55]"A Call to Backsliders," *Works*, VI, 525.

[56]*Notes,* I John 1:9.

[57]"The Great Privilege of Those Who Are Born of God," *Works,* V, 230.

[58]*Works,* II, 33, 278, 337, 361; III, 21.

[59]*Works,* VI, 526.

[60]Ibid.

[61]"The First Fruits of the Spirit," *Works,* V, 95-96.

[62]John Goodwin, *Redemption Redeemed* (London, 1651), 345-48. See Chapter Five for more on Goodwin's doctrine of perseverance.

[63]*Works,* VIII, 44.

7

CONFESSIONAL, BAPTIST, AND ARMINIAN: THE GENERAL-FREE WILL BAPTIST TRADITION AND THE NICENE FAITH

CONFESSIONAL, BAPTIST, AND ARMINIAN

"Confessional, Baptist, and Arminian." That sounds like an oxymoron, probably because of common caricatures of Baptist and Arminian theology. After all, Baptists are supposed to be anti-confessional because of soul competency and the absolute right of private judgment, their mantra "No creed but the Bible," and supposedly this has fostered in them an anti-traditional posture. Arminians are supposed to be pietistic holiness folk who define the essence of Christianity as experience, not orthodox doctrine. Further, the Arminian and Baptist movements are supposed to be modern, evangelical movements that were birthed out of the Enlightenment and imbued with the genius of Romanticism, thus averse to the strong confessionalism of Protestant orthodoxy. The term *confessional* is inconsistent with all these stereotypes. Perhaps that is why some Baptist and some Arminian scholars have jettisoned confessional orthodoxy. This chapter will argue that it is consistent for one to be orthodox, confessional, Baptist, and Arminian. It will do so by appealing to the General-Free Will Baptist tradition: the seventeenth-century English General Baptists, with emphasis on their major theologian, Thomas Grantham, and their progeny in America, the Free Will Baptists.[1]

Ecclesial

The General-Free Will Baptist tradition is an Evangelical, Arminian, and Baptist communion the origins of which predate the Enlightenment, Romanticism, Pietism, and the transatlantic awakenings of the eighteenth and nineteenth centuries. This historic tradition represents a different way of being Baptist and Arminian than many modern stereotypes allow. Its spirituality was less individualistic and more ecclesial than that of many modern Protestants.[2] The General Baptist cry for religious liberty was not a prototypical version of Romantic liberal-individualism. Curtis Freeman correctly argues that Baptist founder Thomas Helwys's primary concern was "the sovereignty and freedom of God, who alone is Lord of the conscience . . . a romantic reading of Helwys fails to account for the main question of *The Mystery of Iniquity*: What must the church teach and practice to be the true and faithful church?"[3] These early Baptists were persecuted for their views on religious liberty and the priesthood of all believers. They interpreted those ideas not primarily in terms of modern concepts of soul competency and personal autonomy but in more ecclesial terms. They did not cast their view of the priesthood of all believers merely in the language of individual rights.[4] Rather, they viewed it in terms of believers covenanting together, serving as priests to each other. They would have agreed with the following statements from "Re-Envisioning Baptist Identity: A Manifesto for Baptist Communities in North America":

> We affirm following Jesus as a call to shared discipleship rather
> than invoking a theory of soul competency. . . . Such discipleship
> requires a shared life of mutual accountability in the church. Disciples may not remain aloof from the church and its life. . . . Only

154

as we stand together under the Lordship of Christ can we discern by the Spirit that from which we are liberated and that to which we are obligated. . . . In this life together, God has chosen us to serve as priests, not for our ownselves, but to one another.[5]

Confessional

In fact, the General-Free Will Baptist tradition has historically taken these principles so seriously that it has engaged in a rather rigorous sort of confessionalism.[6] Affirming this "shared life of mutual accountability," these believers have required their churches and ministers to subscribe to corporate confessions of faith.[7] This confessionalism has been a free church confessionalism, not "creedalism," which Timothy George rightly says Baptists "never advocated." Because they believe God alone is "Lord of the conscience," they do not believe that the state has "any legitimate authority to regulate or coerce" the internal lives of believers and churches. They are also non-creedalists in the sense that they "deny that any humanly constructed doctrinal statement can be equal to, much less elevated above, Holy Scripture."[8] Thus, unlike some Protestant communions, the General-Free Will Baptist tradition has always held that its confessions are revisable. Yet this hearty confessionalism requires churches to unite in conferences or associations in a corporate confession of the faith once delivered to the saints, as they understand it to be taught in Holy Scripture. The presbyteries of these conferences require their ministers to assent to that confession or be disciplined by the conference.[9]

Warm-Hearted Orthodoxy

In addition to the autonomous individualism and lack of confessionalism that often accompanies it, Arminian evangelicals are usually cast in terms of the Holiness movement and even Charles Finney. Calvinists too often equate Arminianism with the perfectionism, semi-Pelagianism, and ultra-pietism of Finney, the Holiness movement, and the Second Great Awakening. Michael Horton, for example, has questioned whether Arminians are real evangelicals.[10] However, many Arminians are also guilty of painting all Arminians with the same broad brush.

There is a cottage industry of defining the nature and essence of evangelicalism.[11] The debate is cast between the "Presbyterian" interpretation of scholars like George Marsden and the "Holiness" interpretation of those like Donald Dayton. Twentieth-century fundamentalism and neo-evangelicalism are thought of as an amalgamation of two historical streams: Protestant orthodoxy and Holiness pietism. Postconservative thinker Roger Olson states:

> On the one hand, evangelicalism has inherited from Protestant orthodoxy and Puritan Reformed theology a strongly confessional emphasis that seeks to preserve orthodoxy. Conservative evangelicals tend to work out of that side of the heritage. On the other hand, evangelicalism has inherited from Pietism and Revivalism a strong emphasis on the experience of the transforming power of God. Postconservatives tend to work out of that side of the heritage. Some might even argue that there are two evangelicalisms and that these two movements have been somewhat artificially pasted together by their common opposition to liberal defection from authentic Christianity.[12]

But is this not a false dichotomy? The General-Free Will Baptist tradition has managed to combine a warm-hearted Puritan spirituality, appropriating the best of mild pietism and revivalism, with a tradition of strong theological orthodoxy and confessional subscription. The same could be said of many Baptists who are neither strongly Calvinist nor fully Arminian (the vast majority), and who do not fit either caricature.[13] Thomas Oden is right in his analysis of Olson's false dichotomy:

> A lingering pietism surfaces in [Olson's] annoyance with "theological correctness." His polarities may also have the unintended consequence of tending to keep the evangelical theological dialogue

trapped in the Protestant scholastic versus pietistic quarrel between doctrine and experience. Evangelical teaching worthy of the gospel will frame both salvific experience and sacred doctrine as derivative from revelation, from God's own merciful presence in history. Revelation is not first thought then experienced but first occurs in history, and only then thought and experienced.[14]

Mark Noll correctly maintains that the extremes of Pietism shaped much North American revivalism. A needed corrective to dead orthodoxy, Pietism and revivalism, in their extremes, encouraged religious individualism and subjectivism and de-emphasized the "objective realities of revelation," as well as the church and its tradition.[15]

The General-Free Will Baptist movement, like evangelicalism at large, has struggled with the excesses of Pietism and revivalism. Yet the historic spirituality of the General-Free Will Baptist tradition is a mildly Arminian form of Puritan spirituality, different from the higher-life, perfectionist spirituality of the modern Holiness movement.[16] In its warm-hearted Puritan spirituality, it made room for the best of pietism and the awakenings while remaining distinct from the excesses of pietism and revivalism as seen in Charles Finney and the Holiness movement.

Reformed Arminianism

The theology of the General-Free Will Baptist movement, even in the twentieth century, diverges from a Finneyesque model of Arminianism toward the more Reformed categories of Arminius. Some call this approach "Reformed Arminianism."[17] Unlike Wesleyan-Arminian theology as it developed in the Holiness movement, Reformed Arminianism posits a traditional Reformed notion of original sin and radical depravity that only the grace of God via the convicting and drawing power of the Holy Spirit can counteract. It puts forward a thoroughgoing Reformed, penal satisfaction view of atonement, with the belief that Christ's full righteousness is imputed to the believer in justification. Thus, it demurs from the perfectionism, entire-sanctification, and crisis-

157

experience orientation of much Arminianism, believing that one perseveres in salvation through faith alone. While believers can apostatize from salvation and be irremediably lost, this apostasy comes about through defection from faith rather than through sin.[18]

Tradition

Historically, the General-Free Will Baptist tradition has seen itself in continuity with the saints and martyrs of the Christian past—and the further back that goes, the better it is! With the individualism, consumerism, and consequent "amusing of ourselves to death" so ascendant in American evangelicalism, this mentality is most in need of revival.[19] So, with "paleo-orthodox" thinkers such as Thomas C. Oden, this chapter hopes to mine the General-Free Will Baptist tradition for resources for renewal from the church's past.[20] That Reformational tradition prized the ancient, apostolic Christian faith. It emphasized recovering what had been lost from the New Testament and ante-Nicene churches. It also stressed the orthodox, consensual wisdom of the ecumenical creeds, councils, and fathers of the early church. Thus, *sola scriptura* is a vital, essential theme in the General Baptist tradition—rooted deeply as it is in the Reformation—but not *nuda scriptura*.[21]

Consequently, the individual's "communion with God," to use a phrase Thomas Grantham used so often, is balanced by a respect for the *communio sanctorum* (communion of the saints) past and present, and in this *communio* there is a *consensus fidelium* (consensus of the faithful) that guides the church in its orthodox confession and commitment. As Grantham and the General Baptist confessions (especially the *Orthodox Creed*) modeled, the church should "read the Bible with the dead."[22] Thus, the historic General-Free Will Baptist tradition eschews the individualism and anti-traditionalism of modernity.[23]

This chapter commends Thomas Grantham and the orthodox General Baptists as a model for how to be confessional, Baptist, and Arminian today. They worked out an orthodox, Reformational, confessional theology together with a warm-hearted Puritan piety. Yet they did this while maintaining Arminian and Baptist doctrines of salvation and the church, confessing the faith once delivered to the saints, holding ministers accountable for preaching and teaching that confession, and valuing the consensual exegesis of the church's past. This model has abiding relevance for today.

THE ENGLISH GENERAL BAPTISTS AND THE NICENE FAITH

The first Baptists, John Smyth and Thomas Helwys, were General Baptists. Smyth and Helwys were Radical Puritans who separated from the Church of England and fled to Amsterdam. There they came to believe that the church was a gathered community of baptized believers called out of the world and covenanted together as a counter-cultural kingdom community of God in the world.[24] Helwys left Smyth and went back to England with his small band of followers because Smyth had wholeheartedly embraced Mennonite doctrine. Helwys's ecclesiology, like Smyth's, was influenced by the Dutch Waterlander Mennonites, but Helwys rejected their Anabaptist views of the illegitimacy of the Christian magistracy as well as baptismal succession. Anabaptist anthropology and soteriology was more semi-Pelagian than Helwys could tolerate.[25] Rather, like Arminius, Helwys affirmed Reformed concepts of original sin and depravity as well as justification by the imputation of Christ's righteousness through faith alone.[26] Furthermore, Helwys regarded as heterodox the Hoffmanite "heavenly-flesh" Christology that Smyth had imbibed from the Waterlander Mennonites. A few General Baptists in the early seventeenth century would toy with these Mennonite doctrines. However, the mainstream of General Baptists who convened the first-known General Assembly in 1654 and put forth the *Standard Confession, 1660* were like Helwys in their faith and practice.[27] Thomas Grantham, of Lincolnshire, was the most influential theologian among the General Baptists, representing the mainstream General Baptist movement to the religious community of seventeenth-century England.

Churchliness

Grantham and the early General Baptists' approach to the church and its orthodoxy, tradition, and confession of faith was very different from the indi-

159

vidualistic, anti-confessional, and anti-traditional views of many modern Baptists. These early Baptists emphasized the church as a covenanted body of believers under the lordship of Jesus Christ. Thus they differed from the modern emphasis on the sole believer who answers to God alone and believes as he or she pleases rather than submitting to the corporate confession of the church. Philip Thompson is correct when he asserts that Grantham and the early General Baptists viewed God's freedom over the human conscience as the basis for their doctrine of freedom of conscience.[28]

Grantham argued that each individual retains a "judgment of science [knowledge]" in "what he chuseth or refuseth." This judgment gives individuals the right to differ from church authority without fear of coercion by church or state.[29] Yet this was very different from modern Baptist concepts of people such as Francis Wayland, who championed "the *absolute right* of private judgment in all matters of religion."[30] Rather, the church has the right and obligation to require individuals in communion with it to maintain harmony with the corporate confession of the church. Thus, Grantham states, the church retains "a Judgment *Authoritative*; the latter I know cannot be excercised by me, nor any other Member of the Church, because this Power lieth in the Church as imbodied together." This corporate judgment supersedes even that of church councils, whose conclusions must bow to the judgment of the church "taken collectively." Individuals can dissent from the church's leaders, helping keep the church on track and holding its leaders accountable. Yet the emphasis of Grantham and the early General Baptists was on the "judgment authoritative" of the gathered church, not the church's leaders nor individuals.[31]

In *The Baptist against the Papist*, Grantham remarked that the primacy of Scripture in establishing doctrine does not detract from the Christian church's judgment regarding true doctrine: "You here wrong us, to say, That we will not trust the Judgment of the Church; for the Church, truly and universally taken, we do credit, as Her that is appointed of the Father to be the Pillar and Ground of the Truth; of which Church, we take the Prophets and Apostles to be the principal Members, and so in all Points of Faith, to be credited in the first place."[32] This meant that individuals must believe certain doctrines to be admitted as members of the church. Grantham held that Christians in "Communion" in "Church-Assemblies" are to hold and observe one "form of Doctrine or word of Faith." Because God has delivered only this "one Form of Doctrine to the Churches," it is "the duty of all Christians to hold and diligently observe the same, and not to be *carried about with divers and strange Doctrines, Heb. 13. 9.*"[33]

Confessional Orthodoxy

These non-individualistic, churchly sentiments led Grantham and the General Baptists to hold strong views on the centrality of orthodox doctrine. They believed in the importance of "the truly Ancient and Apostolical Faith, that was once delivered unto the Saints, by our Lord Jesus Christ."[34] This led Joseph Hooke, a Lincolnshire General Baptist whom Grantham mentored and ordained, to say, "Tho we have extensive Charity, and a tender regard to the Good of all Mankind, yet [we must] join in Communion with such Christians only, who we believe are found in the Faith: seeing we are of Opinion, That *our Fellowship is founded in our Faith.*"[35]

These Christians expressed their faith in creeds and confessions. While like many Dissenters they would not recite the creeds in public worship, they were zealous in their assent to the doctrinal content of the ancient ecumenical creeds.[36] Thus, as a preface to his reprinting and discussion of the *Standard Confession* in his *magnum opus, Christianismus Primitivus,* Grantham reprinted the English and Latin texts of the Nicene Creed (reprinting it again a decade later in his *St. Paul's Catechism*). He commended it and the Apostles' Creed as "of most venerable estimation, both for Antiquity, and the solidity of the matter, and for their excellent brevity," and wished to "declare to the world that we assent to the Contents thereof." He stated that the contents of these two creeds are "digested and comprehended" in the *Standard Confession,* hoping that, by his public assent to these creeds, "all men may know that we are no devisers, savourers of Novelties or new Doctrines." He hoped that the Nicene Creed "might be a good means to bring to a greater degree of unity, many of the divided parties professing Christianity."[37]

161

The other orthodox General Baptists shared Grantham's approach to the creeds. This is seen no more clearly than in the *Orthodox Creed* of 1679, which was put forth by Thomas Monck and a number of other General Baptists from the Midlands. The *Orthodox Creed*, designed to demonstrate the orthodoxy of the General Baptists to the larger Protestant community in England, contained an article entitled "Of the Three Creeds." In language adapted from the Thirty-Nine Articles of the Church of England, the article confessed that the Nicene, Athanasian, and Apostles' creeds "ought throughly to be received, and believed. For we believe they may be proved by most undoubted Authority of holy Scripture, and are necessary to be understood of all Christians; and to be instructed in the knowledg of them, by the Ministers of Christ, according to the Analogie of Faith, recorded in sacred Scriptures (upon which these Creeds are grounded)."[38]

The General Baptists did not make much of a distinction between creeds and confessions of faith.[39] They defended written confessions of faith as vital for maintaining the orthodox belief of the church and holding people accountable for confessing that belief. Joseph Hooke, for example, self-consciously saw himself as following in Grantham's footsteps in his *Creed-Making and Creed-Imposing Considered*, which was designed to defend the confessional posture of the orthodox General Baptists from their heterodox detractors. He stated that it is "lawful to compose *Creeds*, or *Confessions of Faith*, in other than Scripture Words, while we retain the true Sense of those Oracles of God."[40] However, he argued against imposing creeds and confessions on four categories of people: infidels, heretics, apostates, and weak believers. Infidels, heretics, and apostates have liberty of conscience and should not have creeds or confessions imposed on them. Coercing heretics, Hooke said, is the way of Rome, not of the baptized churches.[41]

Hooke's statements on not imposing creeds and confessions on weak believers is a classic example of the distinction made in the General-Free Will Baptist tradition between ordained church leaders and laypeople. He did not wish to impose confessions of faith on laypeople, but he clarified what he was saying, stating that "professed Ignorance" and "willful Opposition" are "two far different Things." If a weak believer is ignorant of some of the terms used in describing the Trinity, Hooke said, "*we ought not to impose upon his Understanding*, but may, and ought to receive him to Communion as such a one that is *weak in the Faith*." However, "if a Man profess to understand this Mystery better than We, and *will oppose and contradict our Confessions of Faith*, and maintain a *contrary* Faith," this is "not to be allowed, this must not be tolerated; we cannot suffer this, if we must *contend earnestly for the Faith once delivered to the Saints* . . . neither can such things be permitted, and the faith be preserved."[42] Thus, for the General Baptists, there was an orthodox doctrinal center but also a circumference.

The General Baptists believed that it was the job of pastors to protect the flock of God from heresy. This involved what Grantham called "Gospel separation" from "such as pervert the Gospel by wicked Doctrine, or walk disorderly."[43] Their main concern was the well-being of the people of God. Weak believers should be nurtured and cared for, but ordained officers of the church must be held to a higher standard in protecting the corporate confession of the church's faith. Thus Grantham says, "The Apostle was not more industrious to gain the *Galatians* who were fallen into Heretical Opinions, than sharp and severe against those that seduced them. *Gal.* 5. 12. *I would they were cut off which trouble you!*"[44] As Hooke said, "But if he be a *Weak Believer*, yet he is a Believer; tho he cannot understand *Our Confessions of Faith*, he owns and professes the Truth in general which is *explained in them*; he is one of Christ's Lambs that must be fed, a Babe in Christ that must be cherished; we must receive him, *Rom.* 14. 1. And *labour to perfect that which is lacking in his Faith*, 1 Thess. 3. 10."[45] Ministers, however, are not weak believers. Hooke recalled an ordination sermon by Grantham in which he urged, "Brethren (said he) as you are obliged to teach and maintain the Truth, beware that you be not led away with new and strange Doctrines."[46]

In these statements by Grantham and Hooke can be seen, to use Thomas Oden's phrase, the "sister disciplines" of irenics and polemics. Oden maintains that, while false teaching must be met with "bold and persuasive argument," the argument "must be grounded firmly in a charitable irenic spirit that understands where the center lies."[47] The General Baptists, like most Dissenters who had been in and out of prison for their beliefs, were very clear about where they stood on doctrine and with whom they would fellowship in "church communion." Yet Grantham had very strong relationships with Christians in other communions. This is witnessed, for example, by his warm friendship with the Church of England priest John Connould (whom Grantham often debated), whose friendship with Grantham was so close that he had Grantham's body interred in his parish church.[48] One sees this same spirit in the *Orthodox Creed*'s intent to "unite and confirm all true Protestants."[49] Unlike their Free Will Baptist descendants, for whom open communion was an article of faith, most General Baptists in the seventeenth century were closed communionists. Still, they desired to manifest unity with other Christians on the gospel and the consensual orthodoxy of the Christian faith.[50]

Tradition

The English General Baptists defied the anti-traditionalism that would later infect many modern Baptists. Quoting of the church fathers was common among the General Baptists, especially Grantham.[51] He is very much like earlier reformers in all wings of the Reformation in his use of the church fathers. However, he is atypical of those of his own time, because, as D. H. Williams argues, Protestant reliance on the patristic tradition declined in the seventeenth century.[52] After his reprinting of the Nicene Creed in *Christianismus Primitivus*, he reprinted the *Standard Confession*. After each article of the confession, Grantham provided quotations from various church fathers "to shew that though the composition of these Articles be new, yet the Doctrine contained therein, is truly ancient, being witnessed both by the Holy Scriptures, and later writers of Christianity."[53] With the exception of Augustine, from whom a fourth of Grantham's patristic citations came, he showed a preference for the ante-Nicene fathers, from which came a third of his citations of the fathers. If frequency of citation is any indication, Augustine was his favorite, followed by Tertullian, Eusebius, Jerome, and Chrysostom.

Grantham was much like Calvin in his use of the church fathers.[54] He was identical to Calvin in maintaining *sola scriptura* side-by-side with a high esteem for the church fathers and ecumenical councils. While enthusiastically commending and modeling the study of the church fathers, Calvin said, "We have always held them to belong to the number of those to whom such obedience is not due, and whose authority we will not so exalt, as in any way to debase the dignity of the Word of our Lord, to which alone is due complete obedience in the Church of Jesus Christ."[55] Further, like Calvin, who said that "these holy men . . . often disagreed among themselves, and sometimes even contradicted themselves," Grantham, in *The Baptist against the Papist*, stated that "the Fathers and Councils of the Church . . . could not agree to themselves; for they are opposite each to other to this day, insomuch as you are utterly unable to reconcile them."[56]

Grantham's *sola scriptura* is unmistakable. He held it both against the Roman Catholics, who he said believed the Holy Spirit speaks infallibly "in the Church"—that is, in church tradition, and the Quakers, who he said believed the Holy Spirit speaks infallibly "in the Quakers"—that is, through private revelations to them. This, he said, made the Roman Catholics and Quakers "near neighbors," because both exalted other sources of authority over the infallible Word. This, he believed, led the Roman Church to erect a sort of foundationalism of infallible church tradition,[57] and it led the Quakers to a sort of relativism of private revelation which relativized Scripture, causing them to doubt its inspiration and infallibility.[58]

Grantham managed to place great value on the wisdom of the Christian tradition, relying heavily on the church fathers, creeds, and councils of the first five centuries of the Christian church, while maintaining a strong posture of *sola scriptura*.[59] Though his aim was to "restore Christianity to its primitive excellency," he was not a restorationist in the modern sense of the word. Grantham would have agreed wholeheartedly with the sentiments of J. I. Packer:

> The evangelical emphasis on the uniqueness of Holy Scripture as
> the verbalized revelation of God and on its supreme authority over

> God's people is sometimes misunderstood as a commitment to the
> so-called restorationist method in theology. This method sets tra-
> dition in antithesis to Scripture, and places the church's heritage
> of thought and devotion under a blanket of permanent suspicion,
> thus reducing its significance to zero. . . . But the authentic evan-
> gelical way has always been to see tradition as the precipitate of the
> church's living with the Bible and being taught by the Holy Spirit
> through the Bible—the fruit, that is, of the ministry that the Holy
> Spirit has been fulfilling in the church since Pentecost, according to
> Jesus' own promise.[60]

The General Baptists were much like the reformers, believing, as George says, in *sola scriptura*, not *nuda scriptura*. Thus they were like Luther and the other reformers, who argued for the "coinherence of Scripture and tradition, Holy Writ and Holy Church, while never wavering in [their] commitment to the priority of the former."[61]

The Trinitarian Controversy

Suspicions of Hoffmanite Christology began to surround the General Baptist minister Matthew Caffyn and his followers around 1670.[62] An anonymous publication entitled *A Search for Schism* criticized the General Assembly for not dealing with Hoffmanites in their midst.[63] Grantham responded in *A Sigh for Peace* (1671), indicating his surprise at these allegations. He said that most General Baptist churches had never heard of Hoffmanite doctrine until the anonymous authors informed them of it. He argued that not a single General Baptist church held that doctrine and proceeded to defend unequivocally the orthodox Christology of the General Baptists, which he himself had learned. To dispense with the fully divine and human natures of Christ, he averred, would be to destroy any possibility of redemption and salvation.[64] Thomas Monck followed in 1673 with a scathing denunciation of the Caffynite "heavenly-flesh" Christology entitled *A Cure for the Cankering Error of the New Eutychians*.[65] In 1678, Grantham carefully refuted anti-Trinitarianism of all sorts in *Christianis-*

166

mus Primitivus.[66] A year later Thomas Monck and a number of General Baptists in the Midlands published the *Orthodox Creed*, putting the self-conscious Nicene orthodoxy found in *Christianismus Primitivus* in confessional form.

It is hard to determine the degree of Caffyn's influence among General Baptists in the seventeenth century, though most historians of the movement have considered it very limited, both geographically and numerically.[67] Caffyn and his followers were equivocal in their views, publicly subscribing to orthodox confessions of faith while privately encouraging people to question those views. The orthodox General Baptist Christopher Cooper spoke of them as deceptive—"privily" discussing their views while publicly subscribing to orthodox confessions of faith.[68] Most of their writings that did come out and affirm heterodox views were anonymous, and the absence of extant writings on the subject by Caffyn complicates matters.[69] The Caffyn group said one thing in public and something else in private, shrouding their anti-Trinitarian views under the cloak of wanting to use scriptural language. This, together with the full-blown anti-Trinitarianism of many eighteenth-century General Baptists, has caused some scholars to exaggerate the extent of anti-Trinitarianism among the General Baptists of the seventeenth century.[70]

Perhaps this perception is why Curtis Freeman has called Thomas Grantham only a moderate Trinitarian, citing Daniel Allen's 1699 book *The Moderate Trinitarian*.[71] But, as Clint Bass cogently argues, Grantham was not moderate but robust in his Trinitarianism.[72] Daniel Allen was not moderate either but actually heterodox in his views of the Trinity.[73] Bass's view, and the view of this essay, is that Grantham and the mainstream General Baptists—the vast majority—in the seventeenth century were robustly orthodox. This is the traditional view laid out in Adam Taylor's classic *History of the English General Baptists* and all the other standard histories.[74] The confusion originates from Grantham's statement that "the Trinity" is "a phrase no way offensive to Christianity . . . [yet] it is not necessary to impose words on any man which God himself has not used. Yet truly this term, the Trinity, hath very near affinity with the language of the Holy Ghost."[75] However, in this statement Grantham is making it very plain to his detractors that, while it is not *necessary* to *impose* words not found

167

in Scripture on people, still he believes that the word *Trinity* is *not offensive* to Christianity *in any way* (his detractors believe it is) and that it has "*very near affinity*" with the Spirit's language in Scripture.[76] Grantham seems to be like Luther in this regard. As George remarks, Luther "personally disliked terms such as *homoousios* and *Trinity*," yet he still thought they were useful, *contra* reformers such as Martin Bucer, "who wanted to resort to strictly biblical language."[77] Grantham's statement, especially when taken together with his whole-hearted Trinitarian views throughout his works, substantiates his strong Trinitarian orthodoxy. Furthermore, the firebrands of the orthodox General Baptists in the early eighteenth century, such as Grantham's disciple Joseph Hooke, saw themselves as carrying on the thoroughgoing Trinitarian orthodoxy of their mentor, who, said Hooke, "lived and died" with those orthodox beliefs.[78]

In the 1680s and 1690s, Caffyn and his disciples became more heretical in their views, espousing not only Hoffmanite but also subordinationist views. Joseph Wright brought charges against Caffyn before the General Assembly in the mid-1680s, but Caffyn denied being heterodox.[79] Grantham again strongly articulated Nicene orthodoxy in 1687 with the publication of his *St. Paul's Catechism*.[80] The controversy raged on until, in 1691, the General Assembly, in an attempt to quell it once and for all, revised the *Standard Confession* to reflect changes made by Grantham that made the Christological article even more explicitly Trinitarian.[81] Caffyn publicly subscribed even to this unambiguously Trinitarian confession![82] Yet the controversy intensified[83] until the General Assembly of 1696, after which a large group of orthodox General Baptists withdrew from the General Assembly to form a new, orthodox assembly, the General Association. That body called on the General Assembly to "purge themselves from ye said heresye for which we made our separation from them."[84]

The irony in all of this is that the General Assembly always condemned as heterodox the views ascribed to Caffyn. In the interests of unity, they did not want to engage in the sort of heresy hunting of which they accused their brothers and sisters in the General Association. The General Association never accused the General Assembly itself of heresy, but rather of not dealing with the heresy in their midst.[85] History shows that the General Association was justified in its concerns regarding the anti-Trinitarian heresy of the Caffynites.[86] The ranks of the General Association increased, and it crystallized its orthodox confessionalism.[87] Despite failed attempts, the two groups did not reunite until 1734. Though they came back together on the basis of the Trinitarian 1691 *Standard Confession*, problems of anti-Trinitarianism plagued the body until the beginning of the New Connexion of General Baptists in 1770.

THE CONFESSIONAL HERITAGE
OF THE FREE WILL BAPTISTS

Laker, Palmer, and the North Carolina General Baptists

By the time of the reunion of the General Association and the General Assembly in 1734, English General Baptists had been in the colonies of the American South for more than five decades, and in the North longer than that. The only major group of American descendants of these General Baptists eventually came to be dubbed "Free Willers," and the name stuck.[88] American Free Will Baptists trace themselves to the work of Paul Palmer, a North Carolina General Baptist minister and church planter who had converted to the General Baptist movement from the Quakers.[89] Palmer married the daughter of Benjamin Laker, a General Baptist layman who was a friend of Thomas Grantham and had signed the 1663 edition of the *Standard Confession*.[90] Laker, though not an ordained minister, had discipled a small band of General Baptist worshipers who continued after his death. In 1702, this group wrote a letter to the General Association, the orthodox group that had separated from the General Assembly. In that letter, the struggling band of General Baptist believers asked the General Association to provide them with a minister or books.[91] At its meeting with White's Alley Church, London, June 3-5, 1702, the General Association adopted the following resolution:

> Whereas our Brethren of the Baptist perswation and of the Gener
> all Faith who haue their aboad in Caralina haue desired us to Supply

them with a Ministry or with books, we being not able at present
to doe the former haue collected ye Sum of Seuen pounds twelve
Shillings whch wth wt can be farther obtain'd we haue put into
the hands of our Bror S Keeling to Supply ym wth ye latter. & yt
ye sd Bror Keeling doe wright a letter to them in the name of this
Assembly.[92]

This is significant for Free Will Baptist historians, in view of the sparse re-
cords from this early period, because it ties the North Carolina General Baptists of the early eighteenth century to the orthodox General Association. This
is strengthened by the fact that the North Carolina General Baptists came from
the Midlands, a strongly orthodox area.[93]

The General Baptists of North Carolina utilized the *Standard Confession* as
their corporate confession of faith.[94] This is natural, given Laker's public subscription to the 1663 edition of the confession. Laker's copy of Grantham's
Christianismus Primitivus was one of his prized possessions, which he bequeathed
to a daughter in his will.[95] Free Will Baptist historians would love to have a
listing of the books the General Association sent their brothers and sisters in
North Carolina. Given the orthodox polemical fervor of the General Association in 1702 and the spate of recent books that had been produced by General
Association ministers, *Christianismus Primitivus* was no doubt joined by more
recent volumes such as Joseph Taylor's *Brief Enquiry* (1698), Joseph Hooke's
The Socinian Slain with the Sword of the Spirit (1700) and *A Necessary Apology for
the Baptized Believers* (1701), and Christopher Cooper's *The Vail Turn'd Aside*
(1701).

Owing to the leadership of Paul Palmer and his colleague Joseph Parker,
the General Baptists moved from a small band of struggling believers in the
early eighteenth century to a strong group of newly planted churches by mid-
century.[96] However, in the 1750s, the strongly Calvinistic Philadelphia Baptist
Association set its sights on the North Carolina General Baptists, aiming to
proselytize the Arminian congregations and convert them to Calvinism. Sev-

eral General Baptist churches became Calvinistic, leaving the remaining group struggling but even more entrenched in their confession of faith.[97]

The 1812 Abstract

Under leaders such as William Parker, the General Baptists (soon called Free Will Baptists) continued to grow, and by 1812, they adopted a new confession of faith and book of discipline entitled *An Abstract of the Former Articles of Faith Confessed by the Original Baptist Church Holding the Doctrine of General Provision with a Proper Code of Discipline.*[98] This document, which came to be known as the *Discipline*, tells a great deal about the nineteenth-century Free Will Baptists' confessionalism. First, it was a condensed version of the *Standard Confession*, "the former Confession of Faith, put forth by the former Elders and Deacons," which they had been confessing since the seventeenth century. Second, it is notable that it was a revision: "the General Conference . . . judg[ed] it expedient to examine and re-print the former Confession of Faith. . . . " This indicated their belief that confessions of faith are revisable. Third, the document was binding on the conference's ministers, stating that they were required to abide by the "ordinances and decrees" of the conference, that they must be "found orthodox" and "believe the Faith and Order of this Church to be altogether consonant with the Holy Scriptures" to receive ordination.[99] As the Free Will Baptists migrated from the Carolinas and other types of Baptists became Free Will Baptists, this same pattern held true. For example, many Separate Baptists in the nineteenth century became Free Will Baptists. Although as Separate Baptists they did not believe in having written confessions of faith, after they became Free Will Baptists, they drew up and published confessions of faith and required their ministers to assent to them.[100]

Confessionalism and the Disciples Controversy

This confessionalism was challenged in a protracted controversy in the 1830s and 1840s between the Disciples of Christ (the followers of Thomas and Alexander Campbell) and the Free Will Baptists. The Free Will Baptists of North Carolina are an outstanding example of the loss of members to the Disciples of Christ, a phenomenon that occurred across the Protestant spectrum in the mid-nineteenth century. The Disciples set about actively proselytizing Free Will Baptists, and a number of churches were lost. One of the major issues in this controversy was the Disciples' slogan, "No creed but the Bible." Free Will Baptists who came under the influence of the Disciples were required to renounce their traditional commitment to written confessions of faith—to "discard as utterly useless all human creeds, traditions, or commandments of uninspired men."[101] Some Free Will Baptist ministers and laymen began to teach against the use of written confessions of faith. For example, Reuben Barrow, a layman who himself had served on the 1836 revision committee for the *Discipline*, stated in 1842 that all rules of discipline "written by uninspired men, are altogether useless and unprofitable; and that they are one great cause of the divisions and contentions which pervade the Christian world at the present day."[102] Over and over again, churches were asked to vote to choose whether to "take the written discipline or the word of God, upon which [some] voted to take the word of God."[103] But those Free Will Baptists who remained committed to their received faith and practice saw this as a false dichotomy and continued to confess the *Discipline*. This controversy strengthened the confessional posture of the continuing Free Will Baptist movement.[104]

Continuing Confessionalism

The Free Will Baptists of the South continued the orthodox confessional tradition of their forebears, despite the isolation and lack of theological education that characterized most of them during the nineteenth century. A perusal of Free Will Baptist minutes and other documents throughout the nineteenth and twentieth centuries shows a solidifying of orthodox confessionalism. This intensified as the Free Will Baptists witnessed the Free Baptists of the North (with whom they were never in union) succumb to a more liberal version of Protestantism and unite with the Northern Baptist Convention in 1911. E. L. St. Claire, the foremost leader of the General Conference in the first two decades of the twentieth century, is a representative example of the continuation of the Grantham dynamic of polemics and irenics. St. Claire engaged

172

in numerous debates over orthodox doctrine as well as distinctive Free Will Baptist doctrines. Yet despite important differences, St. Claire wished to co-operate with orthodox Christians of other communions for the proclamation of the gospel and benevolent enterprises.[105] The tradition of confessional sub-scription by ministers has continued, with strong conferences and associations maintaining the responsibility of the ordination and discipline of ministers, despite the intrusion in some areas of alien forms of church government such as the radical autonomy and independency of the Independent Baptist and non-denominational megachurch movements.[106]

CONCLUSION

The task at hand for contemporary Arminian Baptists is to re-connect with their past: their own scripturally permeated tradition, the tradition of the Ref-ormation, and the Reformation's rooting of itself in and appropriation of the consensual orthodoxy of the creeds, councils, and fathers of the early church. The greatest temptation of modern-day Arminian Baptists, as it is of all evan-gelicals, is to make Christianity acceptable to its "cultured despisers." In our case, these are not so much anti-Trinitarians or elite liberals and modernists. Our greatest threat is not to reject our orthodoxy in favor of heterodoxy, but to water it down in our craving after the spirit of this present evil age, which is passing away with its desires. Instead, we need to tap into the powers of the age to come, which are enduring, which transcend our passing moment with its consumerism and narcissism and amusement. Engaging in the *ressourcement* of our tradition will aid us in this task.

[1]For lack of space and other considerations, this chapter will not consider the Randall movement of Free Baptists in the North, which merged with the Northern Baptist Convention in 1911. In 1935, a small remnant of that movement united with the larger Free Will Bap-tist General Conference of the South to form the National Association of Free Will Baptists. Probably about fifteen percent of present-day Free Will Baptists originated with the Randall movement.

[2]A poignant symbol of this ecclesial, communal orientation is the ritual of the washing of the saints' feet, which was widespread among English General Baptists and was prescribed in

the American Free Will Baptist confession of faith, the *1812 Abstract*, as one of nine gospel or-dinances that must be practiced by churches in fellowship with the conference. See A. C. Un-derwood, *A History of the English Baptists* (London: Kingsgate, 1947), 123; J. Matthew Pinson, *A Free Will Baptist Handbook: Heritage, Beliefs, and Ministries* (Nashville: Randall House, 1998), 147; J. Matthew Pinson, *The Washing of the Saints' Feet* (Nashville: Randall House, 2006).

³Curtis W. Freeman, "A New Perspective on Baptist Identity," *Perspectives in Religious Stud-ies* 26 (1999): 59-65. Both Freeman and Philip E. Thompson trace a shift in Baptist life to Ro-mantic liberal-individualism as early as John Leland. See Thompson, "Re-envisioning Baptist Identity: Historical, Theological, and Liturgical Analysis," *Perspectives in Religious Studies* 27 (2000): 287-302. The most masterful treatment of this theme is Gregory A. Wills, *Democratic Religion: Freedom, Authority, and Church Discipline in the Baptist South, 1785-1900* (New York: Oxford University Press, 1997).

⁴Timothy George, "The Priesthood of All Believers," in Paul Basden and David S. Dockery, eds., *The People of God: Essays on the Believers' Church* (Nashville: Broadman, 1991), 85-98.

⁵"Re-envisioning Baptist Identity: A Manifesto for Baptist Communities in North America," *http://baptiststudiesonline.com/wp-content/uploads/2007/02/reenvisioningbaptistidentity2.pdf.*

⁶A revival of confessionalism, a sort of *ad fontes*, especially among young adults, is discussed in Thomas C. Oden, *The Rebirth of Orthodoxy: Signs of New Life in Christianity* (San Francisco: Harper San Francisco, 2002), and Colleen Carroll, *The New Faithful: Why Young Adults Are Em-bracing Christian Orthodoxy* (Chicago: Loyola University Press, 2002). On confessionalism and Baptists, see Timothy George, "Southern Baptist Ghosts," *First Things* 93 (1999).

⁷J. Matthew Pinson, *Free Will Baptists and Church Government* (Nashville: Historical Commis-sion, National Association of Free Will Baptists, 2008), 6, 10. According to Gregory Wills, even (non-Free Will) Baptists in the American South had similar sentiments: "Populist religious leaders touted private judgment, personal autonomy, and individual conscience over creedal systems. But when John Leland, the most famous Baptist exponent of individual autonomy, exercised his right of private judgment in scripture interpretation, his association disfellow-shiped him. Baptists opposed this kind of individualism. Conscience was not supreme" (Wills, *Democratic Religion*, 33). Conference minutes from the General-Free Will Baptist tradition are replete with such cases of ministerial discipline for the lack of sound doctrine. Wills con-vincingly contends that this mentality eroded in the late nineteenth century among Southern Baptists and was gradually replaced with views of individual autonomy and private judgment.

⁸Timothy George, "Southern Baptist Ghosts," 21. He goes on to say: "But this principle, sa-cred to Baptists through the ages, is fully compatible with voluntary, conscientious adherence to an explicit doctrinal standard. . . . All confessional traditions are liable to lapse into legal-ism. . . . But confessionless Christianity poses an even greater danger. Forsaking the distilled wisdom of the past makes every man's hat his own church."

⁹It is interesting that the postconservative thinker, Arminian, and Baptist Roger E. Olson signed "Re-envisioning Baptist Identity," given his recent comments on confessionalism that sound much like the sort of autonomous individualism the above paragraph of the document is meant to avoid: "In the current lively discussion about these matters conservatives have ar-rogated to themselves the label 'confessional evangelicals.' I wish to affirm that I, too, am a

'confessional evangelical' because I also confess the gospel. A difference lies in the fact that I, like many postconseratives, prefer to confess my own faith for myself rather than affirm or swear allegiance to a historic creed or written confessional statement. My own statement of faith is no less a confession of faith, however, than is another evangelical's signing of the Westminster Confession or the Baptist Faith and Message," (Roger E. Olson, *Reformed and Always Reforming: The Postconservative Approach to Evangelical Theology* [Grand Rapids: Baker Academic, 2007], 75, n. 15).

[10]Michael S. Horton, "Evangelical Arminians," *Modern Reformation* 1 (1992): 15-19.

[11]Two of the more interesting debates about the definition of evangelicalism are those between Donald W. Dayton and George M. Marsden (*Christian Scholar's Review* 23 [1993], 12-40) and Michael S. Horton and Roger E. Olson (*Christian Scholar's Review* 31 [2001], 131-68).

[12]Olson, *Reformed and Always Reforming*: see also Stanley J. Grenz, *Renewing the Center: Evangelical Theology in a Post-Evangelical Era* (Grand Rapids: Baker Academic, 2000). A number of scholars cogently argue for continuity between the early pietism and the theological content of Protestant Orthodoxy. See William G. Travis, "Pietism and the History of American Evangelicalism," in Millard J. Erickson, Paul Kjoss Helseth, and Justin Taylor, eds., *Reclaiming the Center* (Wheaton: Crossway, 2004), 251-79.

[13]Admittedly, many (non-Free Will) Baptists in the nineteenth century, such as the Separate Baptists, eschewed confessional subscription, probably owing to the emphasis of the Disciples of Christ (the Stone-Campbell movement).

[14]Thomas C. Oden, "The Real Reformers Are Traditionalists," *Christianity Today* 42 (February 9, 1998), 46.

[15]Mark Noll, *The Scandal of the Evangelical Mind* (Grand Rapids: Eerdmans, 1994), 48-49, 60-64. The Free Will Baptists of the South were slower to be influenced by the revivalism and social reform characteristic of northern evangelicalism in the nineteenth century. The Free Will Baptists of the late eighteenth and most of the nineteenth century were leery of "new light" revivalism. See Rufus K. Hearn, "Origins of the Free Will Baptist Church of North Carolina" (1880s), reprinted in *The Historical Review* (Summer 1994), 37.

[16]This use of the word *Holiness* here does not exclude the Keswick movement, which George Marsden shows was a milder version of the popular Holiness theology of Charles Finney and others in nineteenth-century America. For one of the best discussions of the Holiness movement in print, see George M. Marsden, *Fundamentalism and American Culture* (Oxford: Oxford University Press, 1980), esp. chs. 8 and 11.

[17]Stephen M. Ashby, "Reformed Arminianism," in J. Matthew Pinson, ed., *Four Views on Eternal Security* (Grand Rapids: Zondervan, 2002).

[18]See the following recent Free Will Baptist works along these lines: F. Leroy Forlines, *The Quest for Truth: Theology for Postmodern Times* (Nashville: Randall House, 2000); Robert E. Picirilli, *Grace, Faith, Free Will: Contrasting Views: Calvinism and Arminianism* (Nashville: Randall House, 2002); Ashby, "Reformed Arminianism" and J. Matthew Pinson, "Introduction," in Pinson, *Four Views on Eternal Security*; Stephen M. Ashby, "Introduction," in *The Works of James Arminius*, 3 vols. (Nashville: Randall House, 2007); J. Matthew Pinson, *A Free Will Baptist Handbook: Heritage, Beliefs, and Ministries*; see also Chapters One and Six of this volume.

[19]Neil Postman, *Amusing Ourselves to Death: Public Discourse in an Age of Show Business* (New York: Penguin, 1985).

[20]Oden, *The Rebirth of Orthodoxy*; Thomas C. Oden, *After Modernity . . . What?* (Grand Rapids: Zondervan, 1990); Thomas C. Oden, "Toward a Theologically Informed Renewal of American Protestantism: Propositions for Debate Attested by Classical Arguments," in Richard John Neuhaus, ed., *The Believable Futures of American Protestantism* (Grand Rapids: Eerdmans, 1988), 72-102.

[21]Timothy George, "The Reformation Roots of the Baptist Tradition," *Review and Expositor* 86 (1989): 9-22; Anthony N. S. Lane, "*Sola Scriptura?* Making Sense of a Post-Reformation Slogan," in *A Pathway into the Holy Scripture*, ed. Philip E. Satterthwaite and David F. Wright (Grand Rapids: Eerdmans, 1994), 297-328; Timothy George, *Theology of the Reformers* (Nashville: Broadman, 1988), 79-86, 314-17.

[22]John Lee Thompson, *Reading the Bible with the Dead: What You Can Learn from the History of Exegesis That You Can't Learn from Exegesis Alone* (Grand Rapids: Eerdmans, 2007).

[23]Nineteenth- and twentieth-century Southern Baptist concepts of soul competency, individualism, and anti-traditionalism are being re-thought by moderate and conservative Southern Baptists alike. See, e.g., Curtis W. Freeman, "A New Perspective on Baptist Identity"; Curtis W. Freeman, "Can Baptist Theology Be Revisioned?" *Perspectives in Religious Studies* 24 (1997): 273-310; George, "Southern Baptist Ghosts" *First Things* 93 (1999): 18-24; George, "Priesthood of All Believers"; Steven R. Harmon, "The Authority of the Community (of All the Saints): Toward a Postmodern Baptist Hermeneutic of Tradition," *Review and Expositor* 100 (2003): 587-621. (For treatments from the perspective of Baptist individualism, see Jeff B. Pool, *Against Returning to Egypt: Exposing and Resisting Credalism in the Southern Baptist Convention* [Macon: Mercer University Press, 1998] and Walter B. Shurden, *Not an Easy Journey*, [Macon: Mercer University Press, 2005]).

For a contemporary Baptist perspective that values tradition with an emphasis on the value of patristic Christianity for the free church tradition, see D. H. Williams, ed. *The Free Church and the Early Church: Bridging the Historical and Theological Divide* (Grand Rapids: Eerdmans, 2002), esp. Williams's Preface and his chapter "Scripture, Tradition, and the Church: Reformation and Post-Reformation," 101-28. Cf. D. H. Williams, *Retrieving the Tradition and Renewing Evangelicalism: A Primer for Suspicious Protestants* (Grand Rapids: Eerdmans, 1999). For a renewed emphasis on the wider Christian tradition and its import for Baptists, see Steven R. Harmon, *Towards Baptist Catholicity: Essays on Tradition and the Baptist Vision* (Waynesboro: Paternoster, 2006). For a Reformed Baptist approach, see Michael A. G. Haykin, *Rediscovering the Church Fathers: Who They Were and How They Shaped the Church* (Wheaton: Crossway, 2011) and his short article, "Why Study the Fathers?" *Eusebia* (2007), 3-7.

[24]See B. R. White, *The English Separatist Tradition: From the Marian Martyrs to the Pilgrim Fathers* (London: Oxford University Press, 1971) for an account of Smyth and Helwys. See also B. R. White, *The English Baptists of the Seventeenth Century* (Didcot, UK: Baptist Historical Society, 1996).

[25]See Chapter Three; see also Alvin J. Beachy, *The Concept of Grace in the Radical Reformation* (Nieuwkoop: B. De Graaf, 1977).

[26]See Chapter Three.

[27]The expression "General Baptist" was in flux during the English Civil War and Interregnum, the period between the unseating of Charles I as king of England and the restoration of the monarchy under Charles II in 1660. For example, general-atonement Baptists and political radicals such as Henry Denne and Thomas Lambe were antinomian and more predestinarian and did not accept the laying on of hands after baptism, as affirmed by the General Assembly and the *Standard Confession, 1660*. Furthermore, General Baptists such as Jeremiah Ives were more politically radical, rejected the imposition of hands, and were more semi-Pelagian in their soteriology than the mainstream General Baptists.

[28]Philip E. Thompson, "A New Question in Baptist History: Seeking a Catholic Spirit among Early Baptists," *Pro Ecclesia* 8 (1999), 61.

[29]Thomas Grantham, *Christianismus Primitivus* (London: Francis Smith, 1678), Book 4, 1.

[30]Freeman, "Can Baptist Theology Be Revisioned?," 283.

[31]Grantham, *Christianismus Primitivus*, Book 4, 11-12.

[32]Ibid., Book 4, 15. *The Baptist against the Papist* (originally written in prison in 1663) is reprinted in *Christianismus Primitivus*, Book 4, 1-42.

[33]Ibid., Book 2, 59.

[34]"An Orthodox Creed," *Southwestern Journal of Theology* 48 (2006), 132.

[35]Joseph Hooke, *Creed-Making and Creed-Imposing Considered . . .* (London: J. Darby and T. Browne, 1729), 9-10; this is the second edition of the book, originally published in 1719.

[36]A. G. Matthews, "The Puritans," in Nathaniel Micklem, ed., *Christian Worship: Studies in Its History and Meaning* (Oxford: Clarendon, 1936), 172-88. See also Davies, *The Worship of the English Puritans* (Morgan: Soli Deo Gloria, [1948] repr. 1997), 46-48, 81-83, 98-114, 273-77.

[37]Grantham, *Christianismus Primitivus*, Book 2, 59-61.

[38]Lumpkin, 326.

[39]This is also true of the American Free Will Baptists of the nineteenth century. See, e.g., Hearn, 35.

[40]Hooke, *Creed-Making and Creed-Imposing Considered*, 6.

[41]"After the first and second admonition, [a heretic] is to be rejected; but we must not suffer him to abide in the Church: but we should suffer him to abide in the World, Math. 13. 30, 38, 39. Not driving him out of it with Fire and Faggot; that is Popish Discipline, but no Discipline of the Church of Christ" (Ibid.).

[42]Ibid., 8.

[43]Grantham, *Christianismus Primitivus*, Book 2, 53. "That place of the Apostle, *Tit*. 3. 10, 11. *A man that is an Heretick after the first and second Admonition reject, knowing that he that is such, is subverted and sinneth, having damnation of himself*; Made some think, that Hereticks being so admonished, can never be received into the Communion of the Faithful. But then it must be only such an obstinate Heretick as these words do set forth: otherwise, the consequence would be dreadful, if all that are led astray by Heretical Doctrine, should be exposed to such a severe Censure. This opinon, with respect to *contumacious Hereticks* seems to be strengthened by 1 Cor. 16. 22. *If any man love not our Lord Jesus Christ, let him be Anathema Maranatha*" (*Christianismus Primitivus*, Book 2, 154).

44Ibid., Book 2, 53.

45Hooke, *Creed-Making and Creed-Imposing Considered*, 8.

46Ibid., 39.

47Oden, *The Rebirth of Orthodoxy*, 128.

48Clint C. Bass, *Thomas Grantham (1633-1692) and General Baptist Theology* (Oxford: Regent's Park College, Oxford University, 2013), 38-39.

49Lumpkin, 297.

50The Free Will Baptists in America differed from the earlier General Baptists in their open communion posture. Free Will Baptists admitted all believing Christians to the Lord's Table regardless of their baptism but required immersion for full church membership.

51An ironic example of this is the *Orthodox Creed*, which quotes Chrysostom on its title page as a proof text for *sola scriptura*: "I beseech you, regard not what this, or that man saith but inquire all things of the Scripture." A. C. Underwood was right when he remarked that Thomas Monck was a "remarkable farmer," because, in the preface of the *Orthodox Creed*, he quoted Ambrose, Augustine, Chrysostom, Gregory the Great, and Bernard of Clairvaux in Latin (Underwood, *A History of the English Baptists*, 107). See also the works of Thomas Monck and Joseph Hooke.

52"Scripture, Tradition, and the Church," 102. Grantham's views were much like sixteenth-century Reformers both in the Magisterial and Radical wings of the Reformation, such as Martin Luther, John Calvin, and Balthasar Hubmaier. See Wolfgang A. Bienert, "The Patristic Background of Luther's Theology," *Lutheran Quarterly* NS 9 (1995): 263-79; Anthony N. S. Lane, *John Calvin: Student of the Church Fathers* (Edinburgh: T&T Clark, 1999); Andrew P. Klager, "Balthasar Hubmaier's Use of the Church Fathers: Availability, Access, and Interaction," *Mennonite Quarterly Review* 84 (2010), 5-65; Phyllis Rodgerson Pleasants, "Sola Scriptura in Zurich?" in Williams, ed., *The Free Church and the Early Church*, 77-99.

53Grantham, *Christianismus Primitivus*, Book 2, 61.

54Lane, 28-29. For example, like Calvin, Grantham tended to cite the fathers when he was arguing with those who give more weight to them. Calvin used much patristic material when arguing with Roman Catholics but little when arguing with Anabaptists. Similarly, Grantham extensively used the fathers against the Church of Rome in *The Baptist against the Papist* but rarely quoted them in *The Baptist against the Quaker*. However, when arguing against his fellow Baptists for the validity of laying on of hands after baptism for the promised Spirit, Grantham cited patristic sources abundantly.

55Lane, 26-27.

56Grantham, *Christianismus Primitivus*, Book 4, 6-7. Ironically, Grantham, again like Calvin, cited fathers like Augustine to prove his *sola scriptura*.

57Grantham chided the Papists for saying, "The Tradition of our Fore-Fathers . . . [is] *the only thing that is unquestionable, and needs no other ground to stand upon, but it self.* And against the Scripture's being received, upon its own Evidence or Authority, they usually do thus object, *That before we can receive what it teacheth, we must be assured of its truth.* . . . And by these, and other-like Objections, they usually in all their Writings, invalidate the Scriptures Certainty, Authority, and Sufficiency, that so they may advance the Authority of their Traditions" (Grantham, *Christianismus Primitivus*, Book 4, 24).

[58]"But now it would be known . . . how much of the Scripture the *Quaker* will own, for a true Declaration, &*c*. What Books by name, what Chapters, and what Verses in these Books will abide his Censure. . . . [The Scriptures are] written by Inspiration of God's Spirit, or the Motion thereof. . . . Otherwise this passage would be doubtful, and all the Historical part of the Scripture also, which declares matter of Fact: For either these things were written in the Book of God, by the Motion and Direction of his Spirit, or else they only rest on Humane Authority, and Conjecture . . . but when God speaketh, we must submit our Reason; by Faith receive, what by Science we cannot understand. . . . for shame never doubt but that he [God] speaketh in the *holy Scriptures*. Now we are sure that the Holy Spirit speaketh in the Scripture; but we are not sure that he speaks in thee. . . . the Spirit speaking in the Scriptures, ought to be heard, rather than you, O *Quakers!* When you speak without, or against the Authority and Truth of them" (Grantham, *Christianismus Primitivus*, Book 4, 46-51. *The Baptist against the Quaker*, originally written in 1673, was reprinted in *Christianismus Primitivus*, Book 4, 43-74).

[59]Grantham rarely ever quoted the medieval scholastics.

[60]J. I. Packer, "A Stunted Ecclesiology?" in Kenneth Tanner and Christopher A. Hall, eds., *Ancient and Postmodern Christianity: Paleo-Orthodoxy in the 21st Century: Essays in Honor of Thomas C. Oden* (Downers Grove: InterVarsity, 2002), 122.

[61]George, *Theology of the Reformers*, 82. The intent of this essay is to deal with the theme "The Will to Believe and the Need for Creed: Evangelicals and the Nicene Faith." Thus, its narrow aim is neither to outline a General-Free Will Baptist theological method nor to probe the question of the sufficiency of Scripture and its relation to tradition, but rather to focus on the value that the General-Free Will Baptist tradition placed on the Christian tradition while always upholding the sufficiency of Holy Scripture for Christian faith and practice.

[62]Bass, 182, n. 19; 205, n. 126.

[63]Ibid., 182.

[64]Thomas Grantham, *A Sigh for Peace* (London: Printed for the Author, 1671), 104-05.

[65]Thomas Monck, *A Cure for the Cankering Error of the New Eutychians* (London: Printed for the Author, 1673). Richard Haines followed in 1674 with *New Lords, New Laws* (London, 1674), another strongly Trinitarian work.

[66]Grantham was responding to heterodox General Baptists as well as to the wave of anti-Trinitarianism in the Church of England and among the Presbyterians during that time.

[67]Bass, 184; Adam Taylor, *History of the English General Baptists* (London: T. Bore, 1818), 1:364-76, 463-80. Taylor, W. T. Whitley, and others have traditionally argued that anti-Trinitarian sentiments among the General Baptists were limited to Kent and Sussex, where even there they were strongly opposed. See W. T. Whitley, *A History of the British Baptists* (London: Charles Griffin, 1923), 172-74. See also Underwood, *A History of English Baptists*, and Crosby, *The History of the English Baptists*.

[68]Christopher Cooper, *The Vail Turn'd Aside: Or, Heresie Unmask'd, Being a Reply to a Book Entituled The Moderate Trinitarian* (London: J. Marshal, 1701), 116-20. By law, Parliament required all Baptist and other dissenting ministers to subscribe to the Thirty-Nine Articles of

the Church of England (with the exception of the articles that dealt with distinctive Baptist doctrines). Cooper said that the Caffynites were deceivers, because they publicly subscribed to this confession under oath in court, and publicly subscribed to the 1691 edition of the *Standard Confession* in the General Assembly, but still propagated anti-Trinitarian heresy privately.

[69]Cooper also accused Caffyn and his group of dishonesty because they forged a copy of the 1691 *Standard Confession*, making changes to its third article on the person of Christ yet keeping the orthodox Joseph Wright's name at the top of it. Furthermore, Cooper stated, the "pretended Tryal" of Caffyn in London in 1700 was "just like the rest," with Caffyn denying that he was heretical and his group drawing up "a paper in *Ambiguous* words, which looked like Orthodox" (Ibid., 120-21). There was always confusion and misperception about what exactly Caffyn believed. For example, the orthodox group alleged at one point that Caffyn had told an anti-Trinitarian that his truths were "precious," but Caffyn's followers said that he had said they were "pernicious truths" (but this attempt at a defense is dubious—how can a truth be said to be pernicious?).

[70]Bass, 11-12.

[71]Curtis W. Freeman, "God in Three Persons: Baptist Unitarianism and the Trinity," *Perspectives in Religious Studies* 33 (2006), 326. Freeman mistakenly conflates Grantham with Allen. Freeman avers that Allen is representative of "the moderate position" in his work, which was a response to Joseph Taylor. Yet Grantham's views align with Taylor's, not with Allen's unorthodox views. Cf. Bass, 201.

[72]Bass, 187-93, 197-99.

[73]Ibid., 203.

[74]Adam Taylor, *History of the English General Baptists*, 1:364-76, 463-80. See Taylor for a careful, point-by-point defense of the orthodoxy of the mainstream of the seventeenth century General Baptists.

[75]Grantham, *Christianismus Primitivus*, Book 2, 40.

[76]Ibid. (emphasis added).

[77]George, *Theology of the Reformers*, 182.

[78]There is no better defense of Grantham's robust Trinitarianism than that of Clint Bass in his new monograph on Grantham's theology. While Bass misunderstands some of the nuances of Grantham's soteriology, his study is otherwise stellar.

[79]Bass, 196.

[80]Thomas Grantham, *St. Paul's Catechism, Or a Brief Explication of the Six Principles of the Christian Religion . . .* (London, 1687).

[81]W. T. Whitley, ed., *Minutes of the General Assembly of the General Baptists* (London: Kingsgate, 1909), General Assembly, 1691.

[82]Ibid.

[83]Other charges were brought against Caffyn in 1692 (Whitley, *Minutes*, General Assembly, 1692). The General Assembly apparently adjourned for three years, reconvening in 1696.

[84]Whitley, *Minutes*, General Association, 1697.

[85]See, e.g., Whitley, *Minutes*, General Assembly, 1686, 1693, 1700, 1702, 1704, 1705. Taylor, *History of the English General Baptists*, 477-78. The early Baptist historian Thomas Cros-

by even believed that Caffyn himself was orthodox and simply "var[ied] a little in some abstruse *unrevealed* speculations" (Thomas Crosby, *The History of the English Baptists* [London: John Robinson, 1740], 280-83).

[86]Underwood, *A History of the English Baptists*, 126-28.

[87]As is seen in works by Joseph Hooke, Christopher Cooper, Joseph Taylor, and William Russell.

[88]The American denomination, the General Association of General Baptists, is an Arminian Baptist movement that arose spontaneously in the Midwest in the middle nineteenth century but had no organic ties to the English General Baptists.

[89]Michael R. Pelt surmises that Palmer might have been a General Baptist "messenger," the third, itinerant office of the English General Baptists (in addition to elder [i.e., pastor, bishop] and deacon) for planting churches and helping settle church disputes and ordain ministers, whose counsel could be disregarded by local congregations. See Pelt, *A History of Original Free Will Baptists* (Mount Olive: Mount Olive College Press, 1998).

[90]George Stevenson, "Benjamin Laker," in *Dictionary of North Carolina Biography*, ed. William S. Powell (Chapel Hill: University of North Carolina Press, 1991), 4:3-4.

[91]William F. Davidson shows that this was the church in the Perquimans Precinct of North Carolina where Laker had exerted his influence. (Davidson, *The Free Will Baptists in History* [Nashville: Randall House, 2001], 34-35). Pelt (24) concurs, as does George Stevenson, "Benjamin Laker." The only other scholar to discuss this was W. T. Whitley, who mistakenly assumed that the plea could have come from either the Perquimans group or the Charleston, South Carolina, church. But the Charleston church already had a pastor, William Screven (since 1696), and was Calvinistic in doctrine. (See W. T. Whitley, "General Baptists in Carolina and Virginia," *The Free Will Baptist* 75/29 [1960]: 12-14).

[92]Whitley, *Minutes*, General Association, 1702.

[93]Whitley, "General Baptists in Carolina and Virginia," 13.

[94]Elizabeth Smith, "The Former Articles of Faith of the North Carolina Free Will Baptists," *The Free Will Baptist* 75/29 (1960): 9-11; Davidson, 92-99; Pelt, 109-13.

[95]Stevenson, 3-4.

[96]Davidson, 25-47; Pelt, 33-67.

[97]Hearn, 37.

[98]*An Abstract of the Former Articles of Faith Confessed by the Original Baptist Church Holding the Doctrine of General Provision with a Proper Code of Discipline*, 2nd ed. (New Bern: Salmon Hall, 1814).

[99]*Abstract* (1855), 12, 16, 17.

[100]Davidson, 175. See, e.g., *Minutes of the Thirty-Third Annual Convention of Free Will Baptists* ([Cumberland Association, Middle Tennessee] 1876), 14.

[101]Pelt, 140; Charles C. Ware, *Tar Heel Disciples* (New Bern: Owen G. Dunn, 1942), 36.

[102]Pelt, 135; Ware, 22-24.

[103]Pelt, 137.

[104]See Pelt, 128-43, for the best documentation and analysis of this controversy.

181

[105]J. Matthew Pinson, "E. L. St. Claire and the Free Will Baptist Experience, 1893-1916," *Viewpoints: The Journal of the Georgia Baptist Historical Society* 17 (2000): 28-29.

[106]See, e.g., minutes, issues of the weekly magazine *The Free Will Baptist*, which began to be published in 1873, books such as Thad F. Harrison and J. M. Barfield, *History of the Free Will Baptists of North Carolina* (Ayden: Free Will Baptist Press, 1897, repr. 1959), and the many works by E. L. St. Claire.

Appendix One

INTRODUCTION TO CLASSICAL ARMINIANISM

by F. Leroy Forlines

F. Leroy Forlines has been at the forefront of a growing movement that many are calling "Reformed Arminianism."[1] During his college days at Welch College in the late 1940s and early 1950s, Professor Forlines began to develop his views on Classical Arminianism. Key to his early theological development was a course entitled "Arminian Theology" taught by President L. C. Johnson.[2] During that course, Forlines began to read the works of Jacobus Arminius. He was particularly struck by Arminius's disputation on the threefold office of Christ. In that disputation, Arminius, in a discussion of Christ's priesthood, advocated a penal satisfaction view of atonement. He painstakingly argued that Christ's penal sacrifice on the cross satisfied the just demands of a holy God against sinful human beings.

How different Arminius was, Forlines concluded, from Arminian authors such as Charles Finney or John Miley or Orton Wiley.[3] They had taught a governmental view of atonement similar to that of Hugo Grotius. That theory held that God could freely pardon sinners without any satisfaction for the violation of divine law, because such a pardon was within God's discretion as governor or sovereign. Thus, the sacrifice of Christ is accepted by God as governor or ruler rather than as judge. The death of Christ, in this view, is a symbol of the punishment sin may induce. God uses this symbol as a deterrent.

183

The penalty for sin is therefore set aside rather than paid. So, upon faith, the believer is pardoned as a governor would pardon a guilty criminal, and all past sins are forgotten.

However, in Arminius's oration on the priesthood of Christ, he plainly articulated a more Reformed understanding of atonement that accorded with the Belgic Confession of Faith and the Heidelberg Catechism, to which he eagerly subscribed.[4] For Arminius, Christ, in His execution of the role of priesthood, becomes the human victim that is offered up to God to appease His justice. Indeed, as the priest-sacrifice, Christ offers Himself up as an oblation to God. This oblation, this offering, consists of the sacrifice of His body—His shedding of blood and subsequent death. Arminius described this oblation as a payment that Christ renders to God as the price of redemption for human sin. In Christ's oblation, Arminius argued, Christ as priest and sacrifice suffers the divine punishment that is due for human sin. This suffering constitutes the satisfaction or payment to the divine justice for redemption of humans from sin, guilt, and divine wrath. Thus, Arminius presented an understanding of atonement in the context of his view of the priestly office of Jesus Christ that is consistent with the penal substitution motifs regnant in sixteenth- and early seventeenth-century Reformed theology.[5]

Professor Forlines had heard this approach to atonement preached, in less articulate form, while growing up as a Free Will Baptist in rural eastern North Carolina.[6] In Arminius, he now found a theological expression of it from a non-Calvinist vantage point. And on this view of atonement hinged an entire system of theology that was at once Arminian but also Reformed in important ways. That system was Arminian in the sense of how one *comes to be* in a state of grace (predestination, free will, grace). But it was Reformed on the *meaning* of sin and redemption. Put another way, Reformed Arminians agree with Augustinian-Reformed theology on the sinfulness of humanity and the way God has accomplished redemption through Christ and applied it in justification and sanctification. Yet they see the issue of *just how* redemption is applied in a different way than Calvinists do.[7]

At the same time that Forlines began teaching this kind of Arminian theology in the 1950s, Carl Bangs (whom Forlines never knew personally) was working out a historiography of it.[8] Bangs argued that Arminius, far from being a former supralapsarian Calvinist as many earlier historians had mistakenly held, simply reflected and systematized a non-Calvinist undercurrent that had been present in the Reformed churches since before Calvin's time. Bangs presented "Arminius as a Reformed Theologian," positing a milieu within the continental Reformed churches in the late sixteenth century that was broader than Calvinist predestinarianism.[9]

From this Reformed/Arminian posture on atonement, Forlines extrapolated a Reformed doctrine of justification through faith alone by the imputed righteousness of Christ alone, similar to that articulated by Arminius. This account of atonement and justification affected many doctrines that had traditionally separated Arminians from Calvinists. For example, Forlines's doctrine of atonement presupposes the seriousness of sin and the complete depravity and inability of people to desire God without a radical intervention of divine enabling grace.

Forlines's Reformed understanding of justification as the imputation of the active and passive obedience of Christ shifts the focus from the believer's good works to the merit of Christ. His merit alone clothes believers and gives them their righteous position before God the judge. Reformed Arminians do not resort to a doctrine of entire sanctification to deal with the problem of sin in the believer's life. They see a lack of assurance in much Arminian thought and piety that necessitates a doctrine of entire sanctification or Christian perfection. They also see an attenuated doctrine of justification—more in terms of simple forgiveness or pardon rather than imputation—as being at the heart of predominant Arminian views on perseverance, which focus on the believer's good works, rather than faith, as necessary for maintaining God's forgiveness.

By contrast, Professor Forlines presents believers as secure in Christ because they have been imputed with the active and passive obedience of Christ. Forlines's view of perseverance holds that believers maintain the freedom to cease to be believers and thus to decline from salvation.[10] Like Arminius as

185

well as Calvin, Forlines believes that justification results in sanctification, that true faith will produce "works befitting repentance" (Acts 26:20). Yet believers are "kept by the power of God through faith" (1 Pet 1:5), not through works. This approach militates against the lack of assurance characteristic of much Arminianism, in which believers can lose their salvation again and again by committing sins and must regain it through repentance to maintain their justification before God.[11]

Thus, there is in Forlines's theology a logical outgrowth from the Reformed doctrines of atonement and justification. In short, an Arminian acceptance of a Reformed account of atonement and justification affects one's doctrine of perseverance. Believers persevere solely in union with Christ, imputed with His righteousness; thus, continuance is not grounded in forgiveness of post-conversion sins. Apostasy is a once-for-all, irremediable event, a complete shipwreck of saving faith. This *sola fide* approach to perseverance and apostasy bases assurance on the believer's position in union with Christ rather than on one's efforts. If an Arminian does not accept this perspective, entire sanctification is more compelling as a way to achieve full assurance of salvation.

Another unique feature of Forlines's Classical Arminianism that arises from a more Reformed understanding of theology is his focus on the election of individuals rather than on corporate election. Unlike many Arminians, Forlines "camps out" in Romans 9 for fifty pages. He does not shrink from the concept that Paul in that chapter is describing the personal election of individuals, not the election of the church or people of God as a corporate entity. Long before E. P. Sanders's concept of covenantal nomism became commonplace, Professor Forlines was teaching his students in his courses on Romans that Paul in Romans 9 was dealing with the tension in Jewish thought between salvation by works of the law on the one hand and salvation by corporate election of the people of God on the other. In a careful way, Forlines articulates nuanced crosscurrents with aspects of Sanders's thought. Yet at the same time, Forlines explicates a thoroughgoing penal substitutionary view of atonement together with a doctrine of justification that posits the imputation of Christ's righteousness to the believer.

186

In this work Professor Forlines presents the traditional Arminian view of God's simple, exhaustive foreknowledge of all future events. Thus, he eschews the novel attempts of open theists—so-called "free will theists"—who grant the Calvinists/determinists their argument that God can foreknow only those events He foreordains. Against both determinism and open theism, Forlines posits God's exhaustive foreknowledge of all events alongside the significant freedom of personal beings created in His image. However, he also avoids the idiosyncratic views of the Jesuit theologian Luis de Molina known as "middle knowledge." Forlines believes this construct to be unhelpful and overly speculative as an account of the divine foreknowledge.

Forlines engages in a helpful and extensive discussion of the value of an "influence-and-response" model of divine-human relations as opposed to the "cause-and-effect" model of determinist metaphysics, with which he classes Calvinistic views of divine sovereignty. He has a thorough knowledge of Calvinistic approaches to sovereignty, different types of determinism, including Calvinistic attempts at defending a compatibilist or "soft" determinist account of free will. His discussion of these issues will illuminate them for readers on both sides of the libertarian-determinist debate. Calvinists will be pleased with the way Forlines strives to be eminently fair in representing and interacting with their views despite his respectful disagreement with them.

In 2000, Randall House published F. Leroy Forlines's systematic theology, *The Quest for Truth*. Evangelical scholars such as I. Howard Marshall, Jonathan Wilson, Fisher Humphreys, and L. Igou Hodges praised the book as a model of Arminian scholarship. Forlines's combination of theological clarity with a winsome, conversational style has gained the book many devotees. The volume's growing importance for the Arminian-Calvinist dialogue has been noted many times in various reviews and online discussions. Since its publication, *The Quest for Truth* has been used as a text in Arminian schools and even in moderate Calvinist ones.[12]

One reason that more and more people outside Free Will Baptist circles are reading *The Quest for Truth* and *Grace, Faith, Free Will*, by Forlines's long-time colleague Robert E. Picirilli, is that classical Calvinism is on the rise.[13] Traditional Calvinism is so aggressive in its growth that it has become the leading view at many Southern Baptist seminaries. The "New Calvinism" even made it into a *Time* magazine cover story entitled "Ten Ideas That Are Changing the World Right Now" (even *Time* thinks traditional theology can still change the world—it was number three on the list!). In this environment, Arminians of all denominations desire theologically solid resource material from an Arminian vantage point, and Calvinists need works that will acquaint them with perspicacious Arminian scholarship. *The Quest for Truth* is, as I. Howard Marshall said, probably the best of such resources.

However, a number of non-Free Will Baptist scholars and teachers—both Arminian and moderate Calvinist—have wished that the material on salvation from *The Quest for Truth* could be extracted from it and put under a different cover for a shorter book just on the topic of Arminianism. Many readers will purchase and read a smaller monograph on a specialized topic who are not interested in reading a larger systematic theology.

Thus, this new volume is a revised and completely reformatted version of the soteriological material in *The Quest for Truth*, arranged in an order that is more conducive to the contours of the Arminian-Calvinist conversation. The result is a smaller, more topic-specific book that will find an entirely new audience among Arminians and Calvinists alike. It is published in the hopes that readers from diverse confessional backgrounds will realize F. Leroy Forlines's maxim, which has characterized him personally and professionally, that biblical truth is for the whole of life.

---

[1]See Stephen M. Ashby, "Reformed Arminianism," in J. Matthew Pinson, ed., *Four Views on Eternal Security* (Grand Rapids: Zondervan, 2002). The term was coined by Robert E. Picirilli, who used it in his 1987 preface to Professor Forlines's theological commentary on the epistle to the Romans. See F. Leroy Forlines, *Romans* in the *Randall House Bible Commentary*, ed. Robert E. Picirilli (Nashville: Randall House, 1987). Picirilli later began to use the term "Reformation Arminianism." Forlines uses the term "Classical Arminianism," which he sees as an Arminianism similar to that of Arminius.

[2]F. Leroy Forlines, *The Quest for Truth* (Nashville: Randall House, 2000), 507, n.5.

[3]Professor Forlines found more affinity with the moderate Calvinist evangelical theologian Henry Clarence Thiessen (*Lectures in Systematic Theology* [Grand Rapids: Eerdmans], 1949).

Forlines disagreed with Thiessen's soteriology only on the question of the eternal security of the believer. It is interesting that Thiessen's book was later revised, after his death, to teach four-point Calvinism.

⁴Jacobus Arminius, *The Works of James Arminius*, trans. James Nichols and William Nichols (Nashville: Randall House, 2007), Public Disputation 14, "On the Offices of Our Lord Jesus Christ," 2:211-25. See 2:690 for Arminius's agreement with the Belgic Confession and Heidelberg Catechism.

⁵See Chapter Two.

⁶This pre-Wesleyan approach to Arminianism had been taught by the forefathers of American Free Will Baptists, the seventeenth-century English General Baptists. Their most outstanding theologian, Thomas Grantham, summed up their theory of atonement in the title of Section V in book two, chapter three of his book *Christianismus Primitivus*, which reads, "According to the Will of God, and his Eternal Wisdom, Christ did, in the place and stead of Mankind, fulfil that Law, by which the whole World stood guilty before God." In this section, Grantham explained "how deeply Mankind stood indebted to the Righteous God of Heaven and Earth, and how unable he was to pay that score; and how consequently he must inevitably undergo the eternal displeasure of God, with the malediction of his Righteous Law." He later said: "That God imputes Righteousness to Men without Works, is so plain, that it can never be denied. What is thus imputed, is not acted by us, but expressly reckoned as a matter of free Gift, or Grace; and this can be the Righteousness of none but Christ . . . because no other way can the Righteousness of God be made ours . . . there is none righteous, no not one. Except therefore the Righteousness of Christ be laid hold on, there is no Righteousness to be imputed to Sinners." Grantham's theory of active and passive obedience as essential aspects of the atonement is brought directly to bear on his doctrine of justification: "Now whether the Passive Righteousness of Christ only, or his Active Righteousness also, be that which is imputed to Sinners, is doubtful to some; but for my part I take it to be both. . . . The whole Righteousness of Christ, Active and Passive, is reckoned as ours through believing" (Thomas Grantham, *Christianismus Primitivus, or The Ancient Christian Religion* [London, 1678], Book 2, 62, 67, 68). See also Grantham's *St. Paul's Catechism* (London, 1687), 28. A more in-depth discussion of Grantham's soteriology and how it contrasts with that of the Arminian Puritan John Goodwin can be found in Chapter Five.

⁷I give a much fuller description of the ways in which Arminius defies both modern Calvinistic and Arminian interpretations in Chapter One.

⁸Carl Bangs, "Arminius and Reformed Theology," doctoral dissertation, University of Chicago, 1958; Carl Bangs, *Arminius: A Study in the Dutch Reformation* (Nashville: Abingdon Press, 1971); Carl Bangs, "Arminius as a Reformed Theologian," in *The Heritage of John Calvin*, ed. John H. Bratt (Grand Rapids: William B. Eerdmans Publishing Company, 1973).

⁹See J. Matthew Pinson, "Introduction," in *Four Views on Eternal Security*, 14.

¹⁰Cf. Arminius, 1:742.

¹¹See, e.g., Wesleyan theologian Steve Harper's comments that, for Wesley, Christ's atonement "totally accomplishes our deliverance, but the efficacy of that deliverance must include our ongoing appropriation of it." Harper later states approvingly that, for Wesley, "vol-

untary sins—deliberate violations of the known laws of God—do, however, become mortal if we do not repent of them. The subject of eternal security rests (in both categories of sin [involuntary and voluntary]) on the matter of ongoing repentance." "A Wesleyan Arminian View," in *Four Views on Eternal Security*, 226, 240. For more on traditional Wesleyan soteriology, see Chapter Six.

[12]When I say "moderate Calvinist," I am referring to the *via media* of many Baptists and other evangelicals who have emerged from a Calvinistic theological heritage but have moderated their Calvinistic soteriology to include many elements of Arminian thought. For an excellent example of this, see the first edition of Henry C. Thiessen's *Lectures in Systematic Theology* (Grand Rapids: Eerdmans, 1949). For a more recent example of this from a Southern Baptist perspective, see David Allen and Steve Lemke, eds., *Whosoever Will: A Biblical-Theological Critique of Five-Point Calvinism* (Nashville: B&H Academic, 2010).

[13]Robert E. Picirilli, *Grace, Faith, Free Will: Contrasting Views of Salvation—Calvinism and Arminianism* (Nashville: Randall House, 2002).

Appendix Two

WHOSOEVER WILL: A BIBLICAL-THEOLOGICAL CRITIQUE OF FIVE-POINT CALVINISM[1]

A REVIEW ESSAY

It was interesting growing up Free Will Baptist in the religious culture of the South in the 1970s and 80s. It was dominated by the Southern Baptist Convention, which Martin Marty once called the "Catholic Church of the South," owing to its ubiquity in Southern religious life. If you were an intellectually curious and theologically oriented Free Will Baptist, the finer points of soteriology were always forced to the forefront of your thinking. There was no way to avoid it: When a Southern Baptist asked you what church you were a member of and you said "Free Will Baptist," it was unremarkable. The Southern Baptist said, "Everybody believes in free will. What makes you different?"

You braced yourself, because you knew what was about to happen. Before you could blurt out all the words "Free Will Baptists believe Christians can fall from grace," your Southern Baptist friend would react in horror at the prospect that there were people who actually believed in the possibility of apostasy from the faith. But no Southern Baptist would react negatively to your belief that God had granted all people the freedom to resist His gracious, universal calling in salvation.

In those days, at least in my neck of the woods, Southern Baptists didn't mind being called Calvinists. They just said they were "mild" Calvinists. Some joked about being "Calminians," but it was unsurprising that "Missionary Baptists" had moderated their Calvinism. But they would never have thought of themselves as Arminian. After all, Arminians believed—horror of horrors—that a believer could apostatize!

So when I read *Whosoever Will*, it seemed uncontroversial. It seemed very familiar to me—much like the "mild" Calvinism of the "Catholic Church of the South" in whose theological shadow I grew up—and from whom I was a friendly but persistent dissenter.

Whosoever Will is a fascinating and thought-provoking book. Of course, like many such works that arise out of church conferences, there is some unevenness both in style and scholarly perspicuity. Some of this seems to be by design, with some of the authors, for example Paige Patterson and Richard Land, taking on a more pastoral and conversational tone, and others, for example David Allen and Steve Lemke, tending more to utilize scholarly conventions. However, it appears that the whole book is designed to be read by pastors and other church leaders who are interested in Christian theology, not just professional scholars. So while I think some of the chapters could have gone into more depth, on the whole the work strikes a good balance between practical and scholarly, especially given its intended readership.

In this essay I do not intend to give a summary or systematic analysis of the book. Rather, I would like to contemplate the general tenor of the book, emphasizing certain features of chapters that stood out to me. The first three chapters—the sermon on John 3:16 by Jerry Vines, and the chapters on total depravity and election by Paige Patterson and Richard Land respectively—represent a pastoral sort of interaction with these themes that will no doubt create interest among younger Southern Baptist scholars to probe more deeply the doctrines they discuss. Vines preaches the sort of universal-grace sermon one would hear in most evangelical Protestant pulpits, expounding the text of John 3:16. He emphasizes, through winsome exposition and exhortation, that God's love is global, sacrificial, personal, and eternal.

I appreciate Patterson's appeal to a basic Augustinian-Reformed framework for understanding original sin and depravity, as represented by the late nineteenth-century Baptist thinker Augustus Strong.[2] Despite Patterson's desire to espouse Reformation approaches to original sin and total depravity, I wish he had gone to greater lengths than he did to articulate a consistent Reformed approach to these crucial doctrines. For example, at one point Patterson asks, "Are humans born guilty before God?" to which he replies, "That cannot be demonstrated from Scripture. Humans are born with a sin sickness—a disease that makes certain that humans will sin and rebel against God" (38).

In another place, Patterson tells the story of a World War II sailor, blinded from an explosion on a sinking ship. Floating in the water, and nearly deaf, the soldier faintly heard the sound of a helicopter and began to cry for help. The helicopter dropped the collar, but the sailor was too weak to put it on. A corpsman took the initiative to go and save the sailor. The disoriented sailor began fighting off the corpsman, but eventually the corpsman overcame the sailor and rescued him. Patterson says, "The Heavenly Father is the Admiral who saw our hopeless condition and sent that helicopter. That helicopter with the whirring blades is like the Word of God. The Lord Jesus is like the corpsman; He came to earth and leaped into the water to save us even while we resist him" (43).

The problem with this story is that the sailor was injured and not so incapacitated as not to be able to cry out for help. It might be helpful to note that this is an internecine debate among Southern Baptists who are not strong Calvinists. For example, Kenneth Keathley, in his excellent new book, *Salvation and Sovereignty* (for which Patterson wrote the foreword), provides what I think is a much better illustration of the biblical approach. He cites Richard Cross's "ambulatory model," according to which the sinner is like an unconscious person who is rescued by EMTs and wakes up in an ambulance and does not resist the EMTs' medical actions to save his life.

Incidentally, Jacobus Arminius himself would have liked Keathley's illustration better than Patterson's. Several Free Will Baptist scholars (including Leroy Forlines, Robert Picirilli, Stephen Ashby, and myself) have been attempting in their teaching and writing to revive many of the views of Arminius, especially on depravity, atonement, and justification (this viewpoint is often dubbed "Reformed Arminianism"). They argue that it is possible to subscribe to a genuinely Augustinian-Reformed approach to original sin and depravity while still maintaining the resistibility of divine drawing grace.

Arminius espoused the Augustinian view of original sin and taught that "the free will of man towards the true good is not only wounded, maimed, infirm, bent, and (*attenuatum*) weakened; but it is also (*captivatum*) imprisoned, destroyed, and lost: And its powers are not only debilitated and useless unless they be assisted by grace, but it has no powers whatever except such are excited by divine grace."[3] Fallen humanity, Arminius argued, has no ability or power to reach out to God on its own. Arminius explained that "the mind of man in this state is dark, destitute of the saving knowledge of God, and, according to the apostle, incapable of those things which belong to the Spirit of God."[4] He goes on to discuss "the utter weakness of all the powers to perform that which is truly good, and to omit the perpetration of that which is evil."[5] Arminius's approach to depravity and inability is the sort I would commend to Baptists who affirm the sort of *via media* soteriology *Whosoever Will* espouses.

Richard Land's brief chapter on "congruent election" is interesting, interpreting divine foreknowledge of individuals as being in Christ or outside of Christ as a result of belief, in terms of an eternal-now sort of approach to God and time. In essence, Land is arguing that God has an omniscient grasp on what *is* in ontological reality, and part of that is His knowledge of those who are His by faith and those who are separated from Him through unbelief. His election and reprobation are based on this knowledge. Land presents some interesting ideas here about the relation of divine foreknowledge to election (which seem to me to have more fruitful possibilities than the *avant-garde* approach Keathley takes to divine knowledge in *Salvation and Sovereignty* with his Molinist approach to *scientia media*). One wonders if Land has to embrace an "eternal now" approach to God and time to articulate the kind of perfect knowledge that is demanded by his "congruent election" approach. At any rate, Land's ideas are far too brief and need to be expanded on by a doctoral student at a Southern Baptist seminary.

Perhaps most compelling about Land's chapter are his historical remarks, which seem to be an attempt to rebut the arguments of classical Calvinists in the Southern Baptist Convention (SBC) that true, historic Southern Baptist theology is Calvinist theology. I have long found convincing the views of Tom Nettles and others that historic Southern Baptist theology is really Particular Baptist theology brought over from England and later institutionalized by people like John Leadley Dagg and James Petrigru Boyce. Yet a more developed account similar to Land's has the potential to give non-classical Calvinists in the SBC a historical grounding that challenges the formidable Calvinist Baptist historiography of scholars such as Nettles and Michael Haykin. I am not yet convinced, but there are the makings of such an argument, for example, in Land's discussion of John Leland, whom he quotes (in a statement made as early as the 1790s) as saying, "I conclude that the *eternal purposes* of God and the *freedom of the human will* are both truths, and it is a matter of fact that the preaching that has been most blessed of God and most profitable to men, is *the doctrine of sovereign grace in the salvation of souls, mixed with a little of what is called Arminianism*" (46).

Chapters Four and Five—Allen's defense of universal atonement and Lemke's critique of irresistible grace—constitute the heart of the book. The most important part of Allen's chapter is his historical consideration of Calvinists who believed in some form of universal atonement, whom the vast majority of his readers would assume were five-point Calvinists. Allen makes a cogent case for the fact that many Calvinists whom most people would assume were adherents of limited atonement actually held some form of universal atonement. His readers will be shocked to hear that people like Calvin, Bunyan, and Edwards, as well as many of the members of the Synod of Dort, did not support limited atonement. Some of the arguments Allen employs regarding Calvin's views on the extent of the atonement are dealt with at greater length in Chapter Seven, Kevin Kennedy's "Was Calvin a Calvinist?"

Allen makes a convincing case for unlimited atonement without ever appealing to any non-Calvinist or Arminian writers. He probes the doctrine of the extent of the atonement utilizing both exegesis and systematic theology, and argues convincingly for universal atonement. Especially helpful is his handling of the objection of five-point Calvinists—best represented by John Owen—that for Christ to atone for the sins of all people, and then for the reprobate still to be punished for their sins, would constitute a "double payment" for sins. Allen handles this argument well, strongly supporting a penal satisfaction view of atonement at the same time.

Interestingly, most Arminian theologians reject the penal satisfaction account of atonement in favor of some other theory of atonement (most often, historically, the governmental view), using the same double-payment argument. They simply choose not to believe that Christ paid the penalty for sin on the cross and safeguard the atonement's universality, whereas Owen's and other Calvinists' way of dealing with the problem is to safeguard the penal satisfaction nature of the atonement and reject its universality. In this regard, Reformed Arminians like me would agree with Allen's view that the universality of atonement is consistent with a full penal-satisfaction view of Christ's atonement.[6]

Lemke's chapter on the resistibility of divine grace in salvation is thought-provoking and, all-in-all, cogent. I deeply appreciate his commitment to the Remonstrants' notion that "the only way for anyone to be saved is for God's grace to come before, during, and after justification, because even the best-intentioned human being can 'neither think, will, nor do good' apart from God's grace" (110). For Lemke, libertarian free will does not detract from human beings' utter depravity and inability to save themselves, nor from God's utter graciousness in salvation. "Humans do not do anything to earn or deserve salvation. Humans are too sinful in nature to seek God independently or take the initiative in their own salvation. Humans can come to salvation only as they are urged to by the conviction of the Holy Spirit, and they are drawn to Christ as He is lifted up in proclamation" (157).

Libertarian free will for Lemke is not a human-centered concept that makes man the author of his own salvation. Instead, it is set in opposition to meticulous sovereignty, whereby God ordains all things that come to pass. In other words, to say that "man has free will" is simply to say that God gives humans creaturely freedom to make significant decisions as personal beings made in God's image who think, feel, and make authentic decisions. But such freedom does not imply absolute free will: the ability to desire God or to think, will, or do good apart from divine grace. According to Lemke, God graciously draws and enables human beings, without which they would never yearn for God. But he graciously gives them the ability to resist that gracious drawing. This is what I see as the drift of Lemke's account, although at times some of the things he says (for example, his allusion to Patterson's floating-sailor illustration) seem unclear and inconsistent with his overall anti-Pelagian line of thought.

I believe Calvinists need to take Lemke's reflections on the definition of divine sovereignty seriously. He argues that Calvinism's view of divine sovereignty arises more from philosophical than biblical considerations, and that sovereignty from the Bible's point of view is more about God's reign and submitting to it or risking negative consequences by one's lack of submission. This, Lemke argues, is how the Bible views sovereignty—not as God's "micromanaging creation through meticulous providence . . . [ruling] in such a way that nothing happens without His control and specific direction" (153). Lemke shows that Calvinists do not have a corner on God's sovereignty and glory. He extols John Piper's emphasis on the sovereignty and glory of God, but he asks,

> Which gives God the greater glory—a view that the only persons who can praise God are those whose wills He changes without their permission, or the view that persons respond to the gracious invitation of God and the conviction of the Holy Spirit to praise God truly of their own volition? So the question is not, Is God powerful enough to reign in any way He wants? Of course, He is. God is omnipotent and can do anything He wants. As the Scripture says, "For who can resist His will?" (Rom 9:19, HCSB). But the question

197

> is, What is God's will? How has God chosen to reign in the hearts of persons? If God is truly sovereign, He is free to choose what He sovereignly chooses. So how has He chosen to reign? (155).

I believe young non-Calvinists need to come to grips with the sovereignty and glory of God and articulate a more robust doctrine of them. Non-Calvinists can stand to learn from Piper's Edwardsean emphasis on the "God of grace and glory." Yet they must find a more biblical way to affirm those beautiful truths that avoids the deterministic tendencies of Piper and the New Calvinists. I hope Lemke's account of these things will spur some of them on in that direction.

I was intrigued by Lemke's discussion of R. C. Sproul's view that God "woos" and "entices" people to come to Christ. Sproul says that this wooing and enticing is a necessary but not sufficient condition for salvation, "because the wooing does not, in fact, guarantee that we will come to Christ." Sproul argues that the term "draw" in John 6:44 is more forceful than "woo" and "entice" and instead means "to compel by irresistible superiority" (113). The question in the Arminian's mind is akin to the question why God would offer free grace to people He does not enable to appropriate it (i.e., the general call as distinguished from the effectual call). The question is: Why does God woo and entice people to come to Him if He has determined that they are among the reprobate and will hence be unable to come to Him? This concept involves, not just an external Word-based call to the non-elect—a general preaching of the Word of the gospel to all—but rather the Holy Spirit working diligently with people, convicting them, wooing them, enticing them to come to God. Yet He does this realizing that they will never come, because He has eternally foreordained them to damnation to the praise of His glory. This is a rather difficult concept for modern-day Calvinists. It was discussed a great deal in Puritan literature, and especially in Jonathan Edwards, but it is not dealt with openly by most contemporary Calvinists.

Lemke's discussion of Jesus's lament over Jerusalem in Matthew 23:37 is illuminating. That text reads: "How often I wanted to gather your children together, as a hen gathers her chicks under her wings, yet you were not willing!" Lemke correctly comments that the Greek verb *thelō* (to will) is used twice in the verse: "I willed . . . but you were not willing." He notes that Jesus is not referring only to the elect within Jerusalem but for all Jerusalem over many generations. Thus, Jesus's will (*thelō*) is for all the children of Jerusalem to come to Him, yet they frustrate His will and do not come because of their will (*thelō*). This is difficult to square with the Calvinistic concept of irresistible grace. I also think it is more than a curiosity when Lemke emphasizes that the use of "all" (*pas*) in "all scripture is given by inspiration of God" (2 Tim. 3:16), "All things were made by Him" (John 1:3), and so on, cannot submit to the same use Calvinists place on "all" when describing God's salvific will. This is a stock non-Calvinist argument, but Calvinists need to be reminded of it.

Another important argument Lemke makes concerns placing regeneration prior to faith. F. Leroy Forlines argues in his book *Classical Arminianism* that there is a problem for the coherence of Calvinism when it places regeneration before faith, because, as the Calvinist theologian Louis Berkhof states, "Regeneration is the beginning of sanctification." It is a problem, logically, to place regeneration prior to faith in the *ordo salutis*, because, if regeneration is the beginning of sanctification, and if justification results from faith, then logically Calvinism is placing sanctification prior to justification. Lemke parallels Forlines's argument when he quotes Lorraine Boettner as saying, "A man is not saved because he believes in Christ; he believes in Christ because he is saved," to which Lemke replies, "Clearly, being saved before believing in Christ is getting 'the cart before the horse.' This question can be divided into three questions about which comes first: Regeneration or salvation? Receiving the Holy Spirit or salvation? Salvation or repentance and faith? Many key texts make these issues clear" (136, 138). Lemke asks, "When does the Spirit come into a believer's life? . . . What do the Scriptures say about the order of believing and receiving the Spirit?" (137). This is particularly poignant, Lemke argues, in view of Peter's statement in Acts 2:38: "Repent, and each of you be baptized in the name of Jesus Christ for the forgiveness of your sins; and you will receive the gift of the Holy Spirit" (NASB). If Berkhof and Boettner are correct, and regeneration is the beginning of salvation and sanctification, then the Calvinist *ordo salutis* that places regeneration before saving faith, which in Scripture is prior to justification and the gift of the Spirit, is problematic.

Arminians will agree with Lemke when he argues that the two callings God gives, according to Calvinism ("outward and inward, effectual and ineffectual, serious and not serious") necessitate two wills in God, a secret and a revealed will, and this dichotomy presents problems for people's knowledge of the will of God. For example,

> The revealed will of God issues for the Great Commission that the gospel should be preached to all nations, but the secret will is that only a small group of elect will be saved. The revealed will commands the general, outward call to be proclaimed, but the secret will knows that only a few will receive the effectual, serious calling from the Holy Spirit. The God of hard Calvinism is either disingenuous, cynically making a pseudo offer of salvation to persons whom He has not given the means to accept, or there is a deep inner conflict within the will of God. If He has extended a general call to all persons to be saved, but has given the effectual call irresistibly to just a few, the general call seems rather misleading. This conflict between the wills of God portrays Him as having a divided mind. In response to this challenge, Calvinists appeal to mystery. Is that a successful move? (144-45).

Lemke's concerns are encapsulated by some quotations he provides from the early Remonstrants, who he says were concerned that the perspective of the Synod of Dort "portrayed God as riddled by inner conflict" (145):

> 8. Whomsoever God calls, he calls them seriously, that is, with a sincere and not with a dissembled intention and will of saving them. Neither do we subscribe to the opinion of those persons who assert that God outwardly calls certain men whom he does not will to call

inwardly, that is, whom he is unwilling to be truly converted, even prior to their rejection of the grace of calling.

9. There is not in God a secret will of that kind which is so opposed to his will revealed in his word, that according to this same secret will he does not will the conversion and salvation of the greatest part of those whom, by the word of his Gospel, and by his revealed will, he seriously calls and invites to faith and salvation.

10. Neither on this point do we admit of a holy dissimulation, as it is the manner of some men to speak, or of a twofold person in the Deity (145).

Lemke is correct to argue that the most coherent, biblically consistent theodicy is provided by the doctrine of libertarian freedom. Determinism, whether in a hard or soft (compatibilist) sense, provides a troubling solution to the problem of evil—why there is so much evil in the world if there is a loving God. Lemke invokes a form of the classic free will theodicy—that evil results largely because God created people free so that they could genuinely love Him, freely, not because they are caused or determined to love Him. Lemke quips,

Babies do not come home from the hospital housebroken. They cry all night. They break their toes, and they break your hearts. But when that child of his or her own volition says, "Daddy, I love you," it really means something. The parents are more glorified with a real child than with a doll that could not have praised them had they not pulled its string. So, then, which gives God the greater glory— a view that the only persons who can praise God are those whose wills He changes without their permission, or the view that persons respond to the gracious invitation of God and the conviction of the Holy Spirit to praise God truly of their own volition? (154-55).

Regarding compatibilism, Lemke is right to argue that someone's merely *willing* (wanting) to do something does not constitute a free action. There are too many examples in human life of people being willing to do something but not having the choice to do otherwise. Indeed, the way human freedom is normally defined, even when compatibilists use it of everyday human circumstances, is as the power of alternative choice. Furthermore, "the human analogies that come to mind about God changing our will in irresistible grace, whereby others change our minds irresistibly and invincibly, are unpleasant phenomena such as hypnotism or brainwashing. Obviously, these are not pleasant phenomena, and are not appropriate when applied to God" (150).

Lemke's chapter is not without its problems. I think he is stretching when he appeals to David Engelsma's hyper-Calvinism and avers that irresistible grace might make conversion unnecessary and infant baptism might result (132). Engelsma is not representative of Calvinism on the necessity of conversion. Lemke also erroneously conflates the issue of infant baptism and salvation with the issue of Calvinism vs. Arminianism (133). I think the following statement is unnecessary and somewhat beside the point in a work on Calvinism and Arminianism:

> Hopefully, very few Calvinistic Baptists are tempted to practice nonconversionist Calvinism in the manner of Engelsma. When Baptists go out of their way to organize fellowship with such Presbyterians rather than fellow Baptists, or when they push to allow people christened as infants into the membership of their own church without believer's baptism, or when they speak of public invitations as sinful or as a rejection of the sovereignty of God, seeing much difference between them is difficult (134).

Also, Lemke's reasoning is fallacious when he cites John Calvin's view that some people can be saved without preaching and then conflates it with Terrence Tiessen's views, which are certainly unrepresentative of Calvinism.

I think Lemke goes too far in trying to paint Calvinism with the brush of hyper-Calvinism. This will do more to rally the non-Calvinist troops than to win over Calvinists. Still, I think he is onto something in pointing out the inconsistency of mainstream Calvinism in affirming irresistible grace and a distinction between a universal, ineffectual calling and a particular, effectual calling—and the resultant distinction between God's revealed will and secret will—while at the same time affirming the free offer of the gospel. What he is trying to do, like Engelsma, is get mainstream Calvinists to see the inconsistency of their particularistic soteriology with a general call of the gospel. I think he is right. Both Arminians and Calvinists have errors that they are liable to, and Lemke, even though he takes his rhetoric too far in places, is right to remind Calvinists of the peculiar errors to which they are liable, errors that Calvinists have sadly repeated at various points in their history (hyper-Calvinism).

Chapter Six by Kenneth Keathley argues a position on perseverance and assurance that is Calvinist in its assertion that genuine believers cannot cease to be believers and hence fall away from a state of grace. However, Keathley is critical of post-Reformation Reformed (especially Puritan) views of assurance that predicate it on sanctification rather than justification. He argues that "good works and the evidences of God's grace do not provide assurance. They provide warrant to assurance but not assurance itself" (184).

Keathley spends much of his chapter critiquing the view of Thomas Schreiner and Ardel Caneday. They argue that the warning passages in the New Testament are genuine warnings that God uses as a means of helping the elect to persevere. Keathley rightly sees the difficulty with saying that God is threatening people with the possibility of apostasy—which, for the Calvinist, is not in reality a threat since it cannot occur—to help them persevere—which they cannot keep from doing.

Yet in his critique of Schreiner and Caneday's misuse of the warning passages, Keathley fails to provide his readers with an understanding of how they are to treat the warning passages. I assume this is because his Southern Baptist audience is not an Arminian one (i.e., believing in the genuine possibility of apostasy), and so he sees no need to do this in the context of this book. Still, it would have been helpful if Keathley had provided a brief explanation of how someone who argues for unconditional perseverance should explain warning passages such as Hebrews 6:4-6. In other words, how can a Southern Baptist say "Amen" to a responsive reading in church, without comment, on, say, Hebrews 6:1-12?

It is gratifying to see that Keathley explicitly eschews the easy-believism views of Charles Stanley, which are shared by Zane Hodges and the Grace Evangelical Society. This is what I believe SBC people who are not classical Calvinists need to be on vigilant guard against: "preaching people into heaven" just because they walked the aisle one time decades ago, even though their lives have been characterized by the consistent practice of sin and not progressive sanctification. Thus, it was refreshing to hear Keathley say:

> The genuinely saved person hungers and thirsts for righteousness, even when he is struggling with temptation or even if he stumbles into sin. In fact, I am not as concerned about the destiny of those who struggle as I am about those who do not care enough to struggle. Indifference is more of a red flag than weakness.
>
> The absence of a desire for the things of God clearly indicates a serious spiritual problem, and a continued indifference can possibly mean that the person professing faith has never been genuinely converted (184-85).

I would add, of course, that it could also possibly mean that the person has ceased to believe in Christ, is no longer in union with Christ, and thus, has apostatized from saving faith. However, I believe that Keathley's approach can help Southern Baptists avoid the ever-present temptation of an easy-believism that places all the emphasis on a one-time, past decision—a sinner's prayer— and not on hungering and thirsting for righteousness in the here and now.

All the chapters I have just discussed comprise Part One of the book. Those were chapters that were plenary sessions at the conference from which these essays originated. Part Two of the book consists of five additional essays that complement the general argument of the book. I will spend less time discussing these well-written essays. I have already made reference to Kevin Kennedy's excellent discussion of Calvin's views on the extent of the atonement.

Chapters Eight and Nine—Malcolm Yarnell's discussion of the potential impact of Calvinism on Baptist churches and Alan Streett's consideration of Calvinism and public invitations—raised more questions in my mind than they answered. Yarnell argues in his chapter that embracing Calvinism lays Baptists open to Calvinist ecclesiological tendencies—things like moving away from *sola scriptura* toward an exaltation of the ancient church, specifically Augustine, and an aristocratic-elitist church polity. Malcolm Yarnell is one of the brightest evangelical scholars writing today. What he is doing in his writings and the journal he edits is brilliant. I look forward to his future writings and have learned a great deal from his writings thus far. However, I have a disconnect with him that seems to arise from historiographical differences: He tends to exaggerate the Anabaptist influence on Baptist thought and radically discount Reformed and Puritan influences. I exalt the Reformed and Puritan influence on Baptist thought while believing that the continental Anabaptist movement did exert modest influence on early Baptist thought.

It is ironic that I am a full-fledged Arminian who comes from a faith community that has always seen itself as self-consciously and integrally connected with Arminius and with the General Baptist tradition. Yet I have far more appreciation for the Reformed tradition and the Puritans than Yarnell does. I think this arises from the fact that I see "Reformed" as being not chiefly a soteriological word but an ecclesial one.

The English General Baptists of the seventeenth century claimed to be "reformed according to the Scriptures" every bit as much as the Particular Baptists. Both General and Particular Baptists were Radical Puritans who inherited the Puritan desire to reform and purify the church according to the Scriptures. Just as there were both Calvinist and Arminian baptistic Puritans (Baptists) who wanted to reform the church according to the Scriptures, there were Calvinist (John Owen) and Arminian (John Goodwin) paedobaptist Puritans who wanted to reform the church according to the Scriptures. There were also

Calvinist (Calvin) and Arminian (Jacobus Arminius) paedobaptist continental Reformed churchmen. Neither do I think "Reformed" is about church government.

I view being "Reformed," as my ancestors did, as being about (1) the reformation of the church along New Testament lines and (2) the gospel—atonement and justification, by grace alone, through faith alone, in Christ alone, to the glory of God alone. I think some of the people doing more than anyone else for ecclesial renewal and the gospel are "Reformed." I think it makes more sense to see Baptist identity as having developed out of a Puritan-Reformed sensibility—albeit with important influences from continental Anabaptism—than as an Anabaptist movement.

I am not as concerned with Calvinist tendencies on Baptist churches as Yarnell is, unless by "tendencies" one is referring to unconditional election, particular redemption, irresistible grace, and the perseverance of the saints as conceived by Calvinism. I am not worried about Calvinism in the Kuyperian sense having a negative influence on Baptists, or Calvinist theological method having a negative influence on Baptists. The only thing that worries me is that Baptists will become Calvinists in the soteriological sense. I am not any more worried that Southern Baptists are going to become non-baptistic in polity and baptismal theology by reading Calvin than I am that Free Will Baptists will do the same by reading Arminius. I am hoping to see more people who are reforming the church according to the Scriptures in ways similar to John Calvin and Jacobus Arminius, John Owen and John Goodwin, Hanserd Knollys and Thomas Grantham.

Yarnell raises two other issues on which I feel the need to comment. First, he says that Calvinism is guilty of ecclesiological antinomianism, not holding closely enough to the scriptural pattern in polity and other matters. I am sympathetic to Yarnell, and believe that this can be said of many of us modern evangelicals. However, I think much of Reformed confessional ecclesiology forms the basis for Baptist views on the sufficiency of Scripture for the life of the church, including its polity, worship, and other practices. This explains why both the Orthodox Creed of the General Baptists and the Second London Confession of the Particular Baptists relied heavily on the Westminster Confession for many of their statements on the sufficiency of Scripture, and of the divinely ordained means of grace, for the life of the church. Second, Yarnell argues against the concept of the worldwide, invisible church. Yet many historic Baptists have shared this commitment (I subscribe to it because of my own Free Will Baptist confessional commitments). Thus, I do not believe that subscription to the idea of a universal, invisible church is a problem of non-Baptist Calvinists.

Streett has done a great deal of work defending the idea of a public invitation biblically, theologically, and historically. His fear is that the reason for many Calvinists' rejection of the public invitation is they do not really believe in the free offer of the gospel—there is a tension in their thought on the free offer of the gospel that keeps them from thinking people can respond to that free offer in a public invitation.

I am not opposed to non-manipulative public invitations for people to come forward for prayer and counseling with the hope that they will be converted. However, I do not see this as a Calvinist-Arminian issue. There are many Arminians who argue against the use of public invitations because they think it does not have warrant in Scripture. Or they argue that it is manipulative and goes against the free human response to the offer of the gospel and the mysterious conviction of sin that is taking place between the Spirit and the individual. For example, Wesleyan writer C. Marion Brown writes in *The Arminian Magazine*, "Gospel preaching at its best is aided and abetted by the Holy Spirit convicting and convincing men of sin. When men are shown their sins and convicted of the same, they need not be begged, cajoled, or subjected to second rate psychology to induce or entice them to prayer."[7] Joseph D. McPherson, in a later issue of the same magazine, pointed out some similar concerns in an article entitled "Modern Altar Methods: An Inadequate Substitute for the Methodist Class Meeting."[8] (These perspectives remind me of fundamentalist Wesleyan author Jeff Paton's indictment of "Decisional Regeneration."[9]) I also know Arminian Anglicans, synergistic Lutherans, and traditionalist Mennonites who would never dream of offering a public invitation.

At the same time, I must admit I am intrigued by the reasons my Calvinist friends sometimes give for not offering public invitations. I have often wondered the following: Calvinists all admit that the Spirit uses means to convert the elect. So why could the Spirit not use the means of a public response to an invitation to receive prayer and counseling with the hope that one will be converted? How is inviting people to respond publicly during a church service and have someone pray they will be converted, with the hopes they will, any different from doing the same thing in another setting? I can understand if there are other reasons—similar to the Wesleyan Arminian brothers I cited above—that Calvinists would want to do things differently. But why all the concern over offering public invitations *per se* to respond to the gospel? In the end, I do not think this is a Calvinism-Arminianism issue. I know too many Calvinists who offer public invitations and too many Arminians who do not.

Along with the chapters by Lemke and Allen, those by Jeremy Evans and Bruce Little represent the most substantive and incisive chapters in the book. If the SBC produces young scholars along the lines of Evans and Little, then it is sure that the *via media* soteriological approach of this book will experience a renaissance.

Jeremy Evans's chapter contains some penetrating reflections on determinism and libertarian free will that attempt to remain biblical and anti-Pelagian. In that vein, Evans makes approving reference to Richard Cross's excellent article in *Faith and Philosophy*, "Anti-Pelagianism and the Resistibility of Grace."[10] He cites Keathley's book, which goes into much more detail biblically and theologically than Cross's article. Cross asks, "Suppose we do adopt . . . that there can be no natural active human cooperation in justification. Would such a position require us to accept the irresistibility of grace?" (Evans, 260). Cross and Evans think it would not, and Evans calls this "Monergism with resistibility of grace." Evans reminds me of Arminius's desire to maintain "the greatest possible distance from Pelagianism."[11] Evans remarks that this approach means that "the only contribution the person makes is not of positive personal status, as strands of Pelagianism and Semi-Pelagianism hold," because salvation is "wrought by God (Eph 2:8-9)." So people do not "pull [themselves] up by [their] own bootstraps." Instead, saving faith is a "gift freely given from above and does not reside in any natural capacity of the person (Phil 1:28-29)." Furthermore, Evans maintains, affirming monergism together with resistible grace "helps explain how God desires that none perish (1 Tim 2:3)" (261).

Expanding on some of the themes in Lemke's chapter, Evans explains that this account of saving grace helps deal with the logical problem of placing regeneration before faith as Calvinism does. So, instead of new life leading to saving faith, saving faith brings about new life. This seems to accord better with straightforward scriptural statements about salvation and new life: "Jesus provides forgiveness of sins for those who believe in Him (Acts 13:38); the one who hears the words of Christ and believes passes from death to life (John 5:24). Notice that the verse does not say 'the one who passes from death to life believes' but 'the one who believes passes from death to life.' The New Testament is replete with other instances where new life is brought from faith (John 20:31; 1 Tim 1:16)" (261).

Evans is most helpful at the intersection of the disciplines of theology and philosophy of religion, and this comes to bear in his clear discussion of determinism and free will. He gets to the heart of the difference between libertarian freedom and various forms of determinism—whether hard or soft (compatibilism)—in his argument that we can be held responsible for something only if it is a genuinely free action. He explains: "I concur with Robert Kane, that ultimate responsibility . . . resides where ultimate cause is. If I am *never* the original force behind my choices, then I am not responsible for the contents of my choices. At some point in the causal chain, I must have contra-causal freedom (the ability to do otherwise)" (263).

In fleshing out his argument, Evans does a superb job of exposing the problem of classical Calvinism's views of the will. For example, he states, "The strong Calvinist's claim hinges on the notion of complete psychological determinism—that humans *always* act on their strongest desires or motives" (263). However, this perspective seems to be contradicted by passages like Romans 7 (regardless of whether it is interpreted as pre- or post-conversion): "Rather than taking Paul as saying, 'I have the desire to do what is right,' he must have meant, 'But I have a greater desire for something else.' Clearly, however, Scripture does not make this statement but provides the opposite one—he does the things he hates" (263-64).

No matter how much softening modern Calvinists do of their determinism, what they are still left with is the fact that God causes all things that come to pass. "Anyone who wants to grant God the type of sovereignty proposed by strong Calvinism, which is a causal account of human willing and acting, yet wants to say that the world is not as it should be (sin) is under a particular burden to explain how they can make these claims in conjunction with one another" (267).

Another problem with Calvinism is that it necessitates that the present world is the "Best Possible World." Yet, if the best possible world is the one we are in, how can the Calvinist say that many of the things that are, ought not to be (i.e., sin)? If God foreordains all things, therefore being causally responsible for all things, "and we say the world is not as it ought to be (which is conceptually entailed by sin, and in this case the rejection of Jesus [by human beings]), then we are explicitly saying that God should not have caused the world to be as it is." These ideas are not merely mysterious, Evans insists, "they are contradictory" (269).

The most difficult-to-understand section of Evans's chapter is also perhaps one of the most fruitful lines of argument he presents: on speech-act theory and problems it presents for Calvinist soteriology. Calvinist theologians and philosophers need to wrestle with this argument, because many conservative Calvinists ground their theory of plenary-verbal inspiration in speech-act theory.

In speech-act theory, an *illocution* is a speaker's intent revealed in what he speaks—his speech. The *perlocution* is the effect the speech has, or is intended to have, on the speaker or the hearer. Evans applies this construct to the statement that God "commands all people everywhere to repent" (Acts 17:30). Evans says that the command is morally binding on everyone. However, when one follows the Calvinist line of reasoning, every detail of reality is determined by God for His purposes, "including the damnation of some for His good pleasure." How then are individuals to understand the command to repent? "It seems God has commanded something (repentance and faith from everyone) that He has not willed." This seems to drive a wedge between God's commands and His will, "and human beings are morally accountable for the content of God's will and not His commands" (270).

Thus it appears that God has no intention for His speech (His command) to change the reprobate. In Calvinism, God's intention was that the elect repent and be saved, but His intention for the nonelect was that they not repent and be damned. Yet He commanded them all to repent. "The same message, but two divine perlocutions, was given," Evans concludes (271).

Why is this problematic? Evans asks. His answer is that, if God gives the command to repent to inform people and direct them away from sin, He "*intends* to command human beings for the purpose of change" (271). However, this proposition cannot be true for Calvinists. It means "God will still hold persons accountable for patterns of thought and action that He never intended to correct by His command. Indeed, if God knew that He had not elected many, then His intention in the illocution for the non-elect would not be for a corrective course of action. If divine commands are not intended to correct a course of thought and action, then the non-elect are not morally obligated to that course of action (God never intended them to change their status)" (271).

In his conclusion, Evans states he moved away from classical Calvinism while in seminary, despite the fact that most of his professors were Calvinistic. He felt he needed to do this "to avoid what I considered to be problems bigger than those faced by non-Reformed views of the will" (274). He believed that both deterministic and libertarian views entail difficulties, but the difficulties with libertarian views of freedom dealt more with mystery regarding the infinite attributes of God, not problems with God's character as just, righteous, and holy. Many of us have made the same choice, and I think we have been right to do so.

In the book's final chapter, Bruce Little presents an incisive study of the implications of Calvinist views of determinism and free will for the problem of evil. He opens his essay with two illustrations of gratuitous evil. He refers, for example, to John Piper's statements surrounding a plane crash in 2009, in which Piper said that God can take down a plane anytime He pleases and wrong no one because we're all guilty and deserve judgment (279). Piper said the entire event was "designed" by God (288). Little remarks, "This assertion can only mean that God in His sovereignty designed it before the world began to fit His purposes. If that is so, God does not merely *allow* this; God designs and executes it. . . . God is responsible but not morally culpable" (288).

Little refers to the case of a young Florida girl named Jessica whom a convicted sex offender abducted, tortured, raped, and buried alive. According to the meticulous account of sovereignty and determinism of strong Calvinism advocated by Piper, Little argues, because this child was guilty before God, God did not owe her anything and thus had the right to ordain the state of affairs that led to and entailed her abduction, torture, rape, and burial alive (279).

Little rightly says, "Piper seems to confuse suffering in time with suffering in eternity." He argues that it does not follow that God would ordain Jessica's torture because she is a sinner. Furthermore, he argues, according to this Edwardsean-Calvinist account, Jessica's torture and death are the only way things could have turned out, because they were ordained by God. He makes it clear this "means more than simply saying God allowed it to happen" (279).

Little explains that, according to Calvinists such as Piper, God is not blameworthy even though He caused the chain of events to occur. This necessitates God operating under two categories of moral order—one for Himself and another for people created in His image. It makes God the author of the evil He commands people not to perform. If all events are ordained by God, Little argues, then not only is Jessica's torture and death ordained, but also her murderer's motives and actions. Still, however, he points out, according to the Edwardsean view, her murderer is still fully responsible for the act, even though he could never have done otherwise because the act was divinely preplanned. "Understand the logical force of this view: there is no way for Jessica to be raped except for *someone* to rape her. If the rape is ordained, then so is the *rapist* ordained to act" (279-80).

Little is concerned that Calvinism of this sort does not achieve the proper balance between God's right to do what He pleases and His commitments or promises by which He constrains Himself (which self-constraint does not detract from His sovereignty). "Christians are commanded to do good to all people, especially those of the household of faith (Gal 6:10). Should God do less—especially the sovereign God?" (280).

Little is quick to point out that all except perhaps open theists would agree all that happens in the world happens either because God ordains or allows it. He argues that the purpose of allowing evil will never be the greater good, because this would entail consequentialism, or an ends-justifies-the-means mentality. Some Arminians and other advocates of libertarian free will would not join Little in this assertion. However, the important point is that the sort of determinism he is considering does not simply have God allowing evil but ordaining it, being the causal agent of it, yet still holding individuals responsible for the evil.

According to this strong Calvinist view, Little stresses, God's purposes cannot be obtained unless He controls every aspect of reality. If He does not, then He cannot achieve His purposes. It is all or nothing. Either every aspect of reality has a purpose or all is chaotic. A core part of God's purpose in bringing about evil, according to this view, is to glorify God. In response to these notions, Little poses two questions: "(1) Does divine sovereignty require this strong view in order to maintain a biblical view of sovereignty? (2) If God ordains or wills all things, in that way do persons, not God, stand morally responsible for their acts?" (283). Little distinguishes between purpose and reason. There is a reason why all things happen, because God has ordered His universe in a careful way. But that does not mean God has a purpose in every event that occurs (285).

Little's distinction between the Calvinist view of sovereignty and the biblical view is compelling. He suggests that exhaustive control or determination of every act in reality is not the biblical view of how a sovereign maintains control of that over which he is sovereign: "Another way to understand God's control is that of the man who is in control of his family. He ensures that everybody follows the established rules. This form is called *simple sovereignty* and is the one displayed in Ancient Near Eastern texts referring to the suzerain and his vassal" (287).

So why, according to Calvinists like Piper, does God ordain every evil that comes to pass? It is "to make the glory of Christ shine more brightly" (289). But Little, in classic libertarian fashion, points out that, if this is true, "then it seems that people need the ugly in order to appreciate beauty. That would mean that the beauty and glory of God could not be fully appreciated until there was the ugly—evil. So Adam in the garden could not appreciate the beauty and glory of God. Does that not necessitate the fall in the garden?" (289). This is one of the most common reasons people have left Calvinism in the past—because they think it necessitates a supralapsarian approach to the divine decrees or a "fortunate fall." This is precisely why Thomas Helwys left Calvinism, as seen in his work, *A Short and Plaine Proofe*, the first Baptist treatise on predestination.[12]

Little avers that "the logic of this argument says that the more evil there is, the brighter Christ's glory will shine." But he points out that this seems to contradict Paul's statement, "What shall we say then? Shall we continue in sin that grace may abound? Certainly not!" (Rom 6:1-2). According to this system, Little argues, it appears that "God not only ordained evil but actually needs evil if Christ is to get the greater glory. In fact, it makes the fall in the garden necessary, which in the end means Adam had no choice. So why is God not the one morally responsible even if for a good cause—the glory of Christ?" (291-92).

Finally, according to Little, the Scriptures make it look as if people can make significant free choices and are then solely responsible for those choices. He refers, for example, to Deuteronomy 28, where God discusses His blessings and curses on His people because of their obedience and disobedience. I think we must reckon with his observation that, "if it was not a free choice, then moral responsibility cannot be imputed. . . . To say they chose but were not free is to void the meaning of 'to choose,' and then language means nothing. Not only that, but it destroys the entire notion of justice. The man who raped Jessica and buried her alive could not have chosen to do differently. In the plain sense of language, that choice means he should not be held accountable" (297). Little's logic is compelling: If God ordains all evil actions and is not considered morally responsible for them, but rather the person whom He determined to perform the action is considered solely morally responsible, this presents a problem that cannot be solved simply by appealing to mystery. Little concludes that "the logical end of the Calvinist position on the question of sovereignty leads to a strong form of determinism, which is not the necessary outcome of biblical sovereignty. In addition, moral responsibility for sin must find its final causal agent to be God" (296). His reasoning is consistent with classic, non-determinist accounts of God's action in the world.

Whosoever Will is an absorbing book that needs to be read by Calvinists and non-Calvinists alike, not only in the Southern Baptist Convention, but also in the broader evangelical community. It is ironic that sometimes debate on important differences can bring people together on other important issues. I believe that healthy debate on this issue can bring Calvinist and Arminian evangelicals together by clarifying the essence of the gospel and the importance of theology in the life of the church and its proclamation. This volume has the potential to further such healthy debate so that evangelicals on both sides of it can unite for the proclamation of the gospel of Christ's kingdom.

<hr/>

[1]David Allen and Steve Lemke, eds., *Whosoever Will: A Biblical-Theological Critique of Five-Point Calvinism* (Nashville: B&H Academic, 2011).

[2]Strong is joined in his Augustinian naturalism by his late nineteenth-century Presbyterian colleague William G. T. Shedd, who goes to great lengths to demonstrate that federalism is a later development in Calvinism and that the "elder Calvinism" was naturalist/realist (see William G. T. Shedd, *Dogmatic Theology*, esp. 2:39-40). Strong exerted a commanding influence on subsequent Baptist evangelical thought, mediated through the work of the influential Wheaton College professor Henry Clarence Thiessen. Yet Thiessen moderated Strong's four-point Calvinism considerably. His 1949 book *Lectures in Systematic Theology*, which was used widely in Bible colleges and seminaries as an introductory text, had a strong influence on many evangelical theologians and preachers and is perhaps the most outstanding example of the sort of Baptist *via media* between Calvinism and Arminianism represented in *Whosoever Will*. Curiously, after Thiessen's death, the book was revised to teach four-point Calvinism. Thus the work's original mediating position has had less influence on recent generations. The first edition can be found only in libraries and used bookstores.

[3]Jacobus Arminius, *The Works of James Arminius,* 3 vols. Trans. James Nichols and William Nichols (Nashville: Randall House, 2007), 2:192.

[4]Ibid.

[5]Ibid., 2:193.

[6]Arminius would concur. See Chapter Two.

[7]C. Marion Brown, "Some Meditations on the Altar Call," *The Arminian Magazine,* Vol. 4, No. 1 (Fall, 1983), *http://www.fwponline.cc/v4n1/v4n1cmbrown.html.*

[8]See also Joseph D. McPherson, "Modern Altar Methods: An Inadequate Substitute for the Methodist Class Meeting," *The Arminian Magazine,* Vol. 15, No. 2 (Fall, 1997), *http://www.fwponline.cc/v15n2/v15n2joemac.html.*

[9]*http://www.biblical-theology.net/decisional_regeneration.htm.*

[10]"Anti-Pelagianism and the Resistibility of Grace," *Faith and Philosophy* 22:2 (2005), 204.

[11]Arminius, 1:764.

[12]See Chapter Four.

ARMINIAN THEOLOGY: MYTHS AND REALITIES

by Roger E. Olson

A REVIEW

Rare indeed is the book that discusses traditional theological issues in a way that respects tradition yet brings fresh, constructive insight to the contemporary theological scene. Roger E. Olson's pathbreaking *Arminian Theology: Myths and Realities* is such a book. One reason that Olson is able to bring such freshness to the Arminian-Calvinist debate is that Arminius, the progenitor of the theological system that bears his name, has been so neglected. In his revival of the theology of Arminius, Olson joins recent thinkers such as Leroy Forlines (*The Quest for Truth*) and Robert Picirilli (*Grace, Faith, Free Will*) in a "return to the sources," in which Arminius is rescued from obscurity and Arminianism is rescued from some of its later historical development.

Free Will Baptists interested in Arminianism need to read this work. Yet readers from across the spectrum, Calvinists and Arminians alike, will greatly benefit from it. Reading this book will help Calvinists to move beyond the caricatures of Arminianism in Calvinistic theological literature. Arminians and other non-Calvinists will be introduced—most for the first time—to a more grace-oriented stream of Arminianism with which they were formerly unfamiliar.

217

In his exposition of what he calls "classical Arminianism" (this is much broader than Leroy Forlines's use of the phrase in *The Quest for Truth*, which puts it at odds with much of Wesleyan Arminianism), Olson argues there are some issues on which Arminians and Calvinists cannot compromise (as in "Calminianism") and maintain the coherence of either of their systems. Yet Arminianism has much more in common with Reformed Christianity than most Calvinists realize. Indeed, Arminianism is more a development of Reformed theology than a departure from it.

Some of Olson's best passages are those in which he quotes contemporary Calvinists caricaturing Arminians and then shows how real Arminian theologians do not fit those caricatures. He is correct in criticizing, for example, the Alliance of Confessing Evangelicals for excluding Arminians (though many confessional Arminians wholeheartedly agree with the Alliance's approach except for their Calvinism). If advocates of infant baptism and adherents of believer's baptism can work together for the mutual progress of the kingdom, Olson asks, then why can't Calvinists and Arminians? This gets back to the irresponsible ways that many well-known Calvinists characterize their Arminian brothers and sisters—associating Arminianism with heresy and liberalism and suggesting that it is closer to Roman Catholic than to Protestant theology. Olson provides numerous examples of Arminians past and present who defy such categories.

Olson contends it is a mistake to think that free will is the guiding principle for Arminianism, when in reality free will for most Arminian theologians results necessarily from the goodness—for Arminius, the "justice"—of God. That is, they do not want to make God the author of sin, which they see divine determinism (that is, God's foreordaining every event down to a "tee," thus precluding human freedom) as logically doing.

Olson also dispels the notion that Arminianism does not believe in the sovereignty of God. It is not judicious, he argues, for Calvinists to define divine sovereignty in their own deterministic terms, and then suggest that Arminians do not believe in divine sovereignty just because the latter do not define it deterministically. Most sovereigns in this world have maintained rule over their realms without controlling every detail of them, he argues. Why must God's sovereignty be interpreted as control of every detail of reality? More importantly, the Bible does not present God's sovereignty and providence in this deterministic manner. However, it will surprise many Calvinist readers when they see how serious a doctrine of divine sovereignty these traditional Arminians held.

Calvinists often describe Arminianism as a human-centered theology with an optimistic doctrine of man and his natural spiritual abilities. However, as Olson shows, Arminius's doctrines of original sin, total depravity, human inability, the bondage of the will, and the absolute necessity of divine grace for salvation cannot be described as human-centered. That caricature is more the result of what Olson calls "vulgarized" American Arminianism which Jonathan Edwards encountered and Finney later popularized. Popular Calvinists also argue that Arminians cannot "give God the glory" for their salvation but take the glory themselves because their act of faith is a work. Olson shows how classical Arminian theologians argue that faith is a gift. Furthermore, a beggar simply receiving a gift from a rich man does not detract from the rich man's glory nor give it to the beggar.

Another common myth is that predestination is a Calvinistic doctrine and that Arminians do not believe in it. Olson gives an excellent exposition of the Arminian account of election and reprobation conditioned on exhaustive divine foreknowledge of free human acts. He shows how Arminians have defended their viewpoint exegetically and how the classical Arminian approach is different from Calvinism as well as open theism.

The last two chapters of the book, in my judgment, contain the most important argument of the book. In them, Olson dispels the commonly held notion that all Arminians hold views of justification and atonement that are inconsistent with those of the Protestant Reformers. He shows that it is a myth to believe all Arminians deny the imputation of Christ's righteousness to the believer in justification and hold the governmental view of atonement. On the contrary, many Arminians, like Arminius himself, subscribe to the penal satisfaction theory of atonement and the imputation of Christ's righteousness to the believer as the only meritorious cause of the believer's justification before God.

The strengths of this book are many. It is the first book ever published to survey the field of historical Arminian theology so exhaustively. Yet it does so in a way that is accessible not only to scholars but also to college and seminary students, pastors, and interested laypeople. Those looking for an exegetical-theological defense of Arminianism will not be satisfied with this book. That is not the book's purpose. Olson's work is historical theology at its best. He paints a picture of the theology of classical Arminians past and present. This sets certain limits for his work. He insists that he is not defending any particular Arminian viewpoint, though his views do shine through at certain points. His aim is simply to present accurately Arminian soteriology so as to correct current misunderstandings and encourage more fruitful dialogue between Calvinists and Arminians.

In compelling and readable prose, Olson ranges over a great deal of territory. He discusses Arminius, the Remonstrants Simon Episcopius and Philip Limborch, John Wesley, nineteenth-century Wesleyan theologians such as Richard Watson, William Burton Pope, Thomas Summers, and John Miley, as well as twentieth-century and contemporary Arminians such as H. Orton Wiley, Thomas Oden, F. Leroy Forlines, Jack C. Cottrell, and H. Ray Dunning. He also makes frequent use of two fine dissertations recently written by John Mark Hicks and William G. Witt.

Olson cogently makes several important points that will add significantly to the discussion of Arminianism and that recent works in Arminian theology have not adequately discussed. For example, he clears up the misunderstanding of Arminianism as semi-Pelagianism by discussing Arminius's disavowal of the label and the latter's theological reasons for vigorously distancing himself from semi-Pelagianism. His terminology that the act of faith is the free "non-resistance" to the drawing power of the Holy Spirit is valuable.

He correctly speaks of individual election as the classical Arminian view. According to this perspective, the New Testament speaks of a personal election of individuals to salvation based on divine foreknowledge of them in their believing status. His emphasis that, for Arminius and other classical Arminians, this is individual election as opposed to corporate election is a welcome change to the overwhelming view of "corporate election" among contemporary Arminians. In this way, Olson echoes recent grace-oriented Arminians such as Thomas Oden, Leroy Forlines, and Robert Picirilli. Corporate election, according to classical Arminians, is the unconditional election of the church as the people of God. Individual election is the personal election of believers to salvation.

Olson accurately describes Arminius as a covenant theologian. This should gain the attention of traditional Reformed thinkers, who tend to be friendlier with Calvinist Dispensationalists than with non-Calvinists who share approaches to the covenants and eschatology that are closer to Reformed views.

He states clearly that classical Arminianism is completely different from open theism (or limited omniscience), because the former demands absolute divine foreknowledge of future free actions for its entire system of predestination to cohere. He is also to be commended for discerning that Arminius did not accept middle knowledge. Olson cogently argues that the idea of middle knowledge results in just another kind of divine determinism. Thus it does not help the Arminian cause but in essence is incompatible with libertarian free will. He correctly says the classical Arminian contends that middle knowledge is illogical because the concept of counterfactuals of freedom is illogical.

Because this is such an excellent book, I will keep my criticisms to a minimum. However, there are a few. These are mostly internecine Arminian issues but are extremely important to the core argument that Olson is making. Olson is vague on certain details that seem to mitigate the points he is trying to make in getting Calvinists to reconsider Arminianism. Perhaps this is because he is attempting to present a united front for evangelical Arminians. In some places, Olson seems to minimize the distinctions between Arminius and later types of Arminianism, particularly Wesleyanism.

Wesleyan Arminian theologians tend to take the view that either Christ's atonement or the drawing power of the Holy Spirit (or both—the reader is left confused over which it is) reverses inherited guilt (33) or even releases all people from the condemnation for Adam's sin (34). Olson seems to disagree with this, but he leaves too many loose ends for those Arminians who want to follow Arminius more stringently.

Arminius simply believed that original sin, total depravity, and inherited guilt were the lot of all those born into the human race and the Holy Spirit draws them individually by His grace. Thus he would have disagreed with what Stephen M. Ashby has called the "scattergun" Wesleyan approach to grace. This view seems to aver that Christ's atonement automatically renders the will free, rather than the Holy Spirit's convicting power applied in his own time to individual sinners' hearts and minds. Olson would no doubt agree, but he would have done well to have made this clearer. Calvinist authors like Robert A. Peterson and Michael D. Williams, whose book *Why I Am Not an Arminian* Olson cites, are right to think that this view would mean that "in Arminian theology nobody is actually depraved! Depravity and bondage of the will is [sic] only hypothetical and not actual" (154). Furthermore, one might wish that Olson had spent more time talking about how most Arminians after Arminius have differed with him on the imputation of Adam's sin to the race, a Reformed view that Arminius vigorously upheld.

Another place where one might wish for more clarity is Olson's discussion of prevenient grace as partially regenerative. He argues that classical Arminians see those under the sway of prevenient grace as partially but not completely regenerated. Thus, there is an "intermediate stage" between being completely unregenerate and fully regenerated, when the will is "freed to respond to the good news of redemption in Christ" (164). Most Arminian theologians will be ill at ease with this concept, preferring to say that saving faith logically precedes regeneration in the *ordo salutis* (order of salvation). An obvious, related question is, why is prevenient grace necessary if Christ's atonement reverses inherited guilt and releases people from the condemnation for Adam's sin? Would this not mitigate total depravity, rendering prevenient grace unnecessary?

Many Arminians, with Calvinists, will be uncomfortable with Olson's view that divine love is the "guiding vision" of Arminian theology (72-73). They, along with Arminius, would say that God's justice or holiness is the guiding vision in Arminianism as much as in Calvinism. This is the view of recent Arminians such as Forlines, Oden, and Picirilli.

Olson is quite clear that classical Arminianism is incompatible with open theism and that he disagrees with the latter. Still, traditional Arminians will be concerned about Olson's footnote regarding open theism: "I consider open theism a legitimate evangelical and Arminian option even though I have not yet adopted it as my own perspective" (198, n. 65).

A few comments are in order regarding Olson's treatment of justification and atonement in Arminianism. Olson correctly notes that Wesleyans in the nineteenth century and afterward have disagreed with the imputation of the righteousness of Christ as the sole meritorious cause of the believer's justification, as well as the penal satisfaction doctrine of atonement that accompanies it. He states clearly that he regrets this development and prefers the contemporary Wesleyan theologian Thomas Oden's approach, which defends both these doctrines. The difficulty is that Olson seems to hope fondly that these doctrines are not at the core of Wesleyan Arminianism and that Wesleyans can choose between the mainstream Wesleyan view and Oden's view. This hope seems to root itself in one of the few profound misunderstandings in Olson's entire book: Wesley's doctrines of atonement and justification.

While Wesley uses imputational language in his discussion of justification, he falls far short of a Reformed understanding of the imputation of Christ's righteousness as the meritorious cause of the believer's justification before God. Furthermore, Wesley melds satisfaction and governmental motifs in his doctrine of atonement, arguing that Christ's death atones only for the believer's past sins. Thus Olson's interpretation of Wesley's views on atonement and justification is flawed. This likely accounts for what seems to be his hope that Wesleyans can recover from these theological views by going back to Wesley himself.

One historically rooted criticism may account for why Olson misunderstands Wesley: The only period of Arminian theology of which Olson does not take account is seventeenth-century English Arminianism. Yet this is the most crucial period for the development of subsequent (largely Wesleyan) Arminian thought. In other words, seventeenth-century English Arminianism, from the Arminian Puritan John Goodwin to thinkers such as Jeremy Taylor and Henry Hammond of the Anglican "Holy Living" school, provided the context for Wesley's development of his Arminianism. These are the people he read and studied and re-published, not Arminius. Understanding the historical context of Wesley's soteriological development would have helped Olson's treatment. Yet it makes clearer the divide that really does exist between Reformed theology (as well as Arminius) and Wesleyan theology on such issues as the actual total depravity (in the here-and-now) of sinners, the satisfaction view of atonement, and the imputation of the righteousness of Christ.

Finally, Olson fails to deal with sanctification and perseverance. Perhaps this is because he wants to bring together all non-Calvinists in a united voice against the determinism, unconditional predestination, and limited atonement of classical Calvinism (a noble aim and something that needs to be done). Dealing with these issues would have shown the consequences of many Arminians not believing in the imputation of Christ's righteousness and the satisfaction view of atonement: that is, a belief in the possibility of entire sanctification or sinless perfection, which dovetails with the notion that only past sins are forgiven and hence one can lose salvation by committing acts of sin and regain it by repenting. Olson failed to deal with these crucial doctrines, repeating the view that Arminius is not really sure if once-regenerate people can lose their salvation.

Despite these criticisms, if Olson's purpose is to provide a united front for all non-Calvinists, help Calvinists get past their unfair caricatures of Arminian theology, and help breathe new life into the Calvinist-Arminian debate, then he has fulfilled his purpose grandly. Olson says that, while Calvinists and Arminians, like advocates of infant baptism and adherents of believer's baptism, will have a difficult time being members of the same congregations, they can do great things together for evangelical theology and the kingdom of God. One hopes this view can be reflected in reality, and I believe that *Arminian Theology: Myths and Realities* can play a significant role in making it so.

SUBJECT INDEX

80N25, 90, 103-04, 115, 159, 178N54, 205-06

ANALOGY OF FAITH, 162

ANALYSIS OF THE NINTH CHAPTER OF ST. PAUL'S EPISTLE TO THE ROMANS, 14, 55

ANCIENT CHRISTIAN FAITH, 103, 124N16, 133, 150N47, 158, 161, 164, 179N60, 189N6, 205

ANGELS, INNOCENCE OF, 71, 126N62

ANGLICANISM, 29N8, 58, 79, 102, 124N14, 131-41, 143, 148, 149N13, 149N15, 207, 224

ANTE-NICENE CHRISTIANITY, 158, 164

ANTHROPOCENTRISM, 132

ANTI-CALVINISM, 4, 61, 64, 66, 78-79

ANTI-CONFESSIONALISM, 153, 160

ANTINOMIANISM, 105, 140, 177N27; ECCLESIOLOGICAL, 206

ANTIPAEDOBAPTISM, 61-62

ANTI-PELAGIANISM, 34N93, 197, 208, 216N10

ANTIQUITY, 161

ANTI-TRADITIONALISM, 153, 158, 160, 164, 176N23

APOLOGY AGAINST THIRTY-ONE DEFAMATORY ARTICLES, 13, 19, 26, 28N27, 30NN44-45, 33N92

APOSTASY, IX, 6, 30N17, 119-22, 130, 144-48, 158, 162, 186, 191-92, 203-04

APOSTLE'S CREED, 161-62

APOSTOLIC, XIII, 158, 161

APPEASEMENT, 39, 42-43, 50, 74, 138, 184

APPLICATION, OF REDEMPTION, 20, 23, 98, 104, 141-42, 184

APPREHENSION, OF RIGHTEOUSNESS, 75, 77-78, 116, 119

ARMINIAN BAPTISTS, IX, XI, 84, 99, 101, 129, 173, 181N88, 205

ARMINIANISM: ANGLICAN, 28N8, 58, 79, 124N14, 132-36, 138-39, 141, 143; CLASSICAL, IX, XIIN1, XIIN3, 32N54, 34N86, 101, 183-90, 199, 218-23; EVANGELICAL, 58, 149N14, 175N10, 221;

NEW, 105; RADICAL, 105; REFORMATION, IX, XIIN3, 188N1; REFORMED, IX-XII, 30N17, 35N107, 58, 108, 116, 129-30, 148N1, 148N3, 157-58, 175N17, 175N18, 183-85, 188N1, 194, 196; "VULGARIZED" AMERICAN, 219

ARTICLE, OF FAITH, 5, 19, 24, 35N107, 39, 52N12, 68-69, 71-72, 75-77, 80N31, 82N58, 84, 123N3, 124N16, 139-40, 150N39, 162, 164, 168, 171, 179N68, 180N69, 181N94, 181N98

ASSEMBLY, 35N107, 159, 161, 166, 168-70, 177N27, 179N68, 180N81

ASSEMBLY, GENERAL, 159, 168-70, 177N27, 179N68

ASSENT, 42, 70, 155, 161, 171

ASSOCIATIONS, 102, 155, 168-70, 173, 174N7, 180N84, 181N88, 181N92, 181N100

ASSURANCE, 29N10, 30N17, 51N4, 95, 130, 143, 185-86, 203

ATHANASIAN CREED, 162

NAME INDEX

ADAM, 13, 17-19, 33N68, 45, 68-71, 73, 85-91, 95-98, 106-09, 124N16, 214, 222

AINSWORTH, HENRY, 60

ALLEN, DANIEL, 167, 180N71

ALLEN, DAVID, 190, 192, 195-96, 215N1, 218

ALLISON, C. F., 132, 135, 149N14, 149N25

ALTHAUS, PAUL, 81N55

ANSELM OF CANTER-BURY, 41, 126N62, 138

APOSTLE PAUL, THE, 15-16, 26, 32N55, 52N9, 112, 114, 118, 124N18, 125N22, 126N56, 126N61, 144, 161, 168, 180N80, 186, 189, 209, 214

ARMINIUS, JACOBUS, X-XII, 1-55, 57-58, 64-67, 71, 73, 77-78. 81. 84. 89-90, 99, 101-03, 105-06, 108, 110, 112, 114, 118, 123-27, 129-30, 148, 157, 159, 175, 183-85, 188-89, 193-94, 205-06, 208, 216-24

ASHBY, STEPHEN M., X, XI-XII, 15-16, 28N3, 30N17, 32NN53-54, 32N57, 148N5, 175NN17-18, 188N1, 193, 222

AUGUSTINE OF HIPPO, 10, 17-19, 36N112, 67-68, 70-71, 73, 81N35, 89, 91, 95-96, 127N86, 164, 178N51, 178N56, 184, 193-94, 205, 215N2

BAGNALL, WILLIAM, 54N64

BAKER, MARK D., 51N9

BANCROFT, BISHOP RICHARD, 58

BANGS, CARL, 2, 4, 6-8, 28N3, 28N8, 29NN9-11, 30N13, 30N18, 31NN22-23, 31NN28-29, 31N32, 33N75, 33N83, 34N85, 37-38, 50N1, 51N4, 185, 189N8

BARFIELD, J. M., 182N106

BARKER, WILLIAM, 34N107

BARO, PETER, 79, 80N25

BARROW, REUBEN, 172

BASDEN, PAUL, 174N4

BASS, CLINT C., 123N4, 127N86, 167, 178N48, 179N62, 179N67, 180NN70-73, 180NN78-79

BATHSHEBA, 146

BAXTER, RICHARD, 126NN64-65, 136-39, 141, 143, 149N14

BEACHY, ALVIN J., 124N7, 176N25

BEILBY, JAMES K., 52N9

BELLARMINE, CARDINAL ROBERT, 4

BERKHOF, LOUIS, 199

BERNARD OF CLAIR-VAUX, 178N51

BEVERIDGE, HENRY, 81N54

BEZA, THEODORE, 3-4, 6-7

BIENERT, WOLFGANG A., 178N52

BLACKETER, RAYMOND, 29N12

SCRIPTURE INDEX

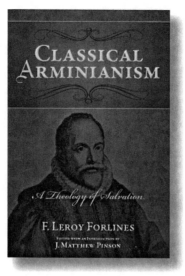

"In this book Leroy Forlines presents a lively, relevant, biblical restatement of classical Arminian theology. In a time when the choice seems to be Calvinism or "free will theism," his classical Arminianism is most welcome. Believing that theology is for life, Forlines writes for every Christian, not just for other theologians. His work appeals to the whole person, sets before us a powerful vision of God's holiness, and calls us to holy living. Every Christian who seeks to be biblically faithful will grow by reading and digesting this nourishing work."

Jonathan R. Wilson
Pioneer McDonald Chair of Theology
Carey Theological College

"Leroy Forlines is an accomplished and seasoned scholar who is the face of Reformed or Classical Arminianism, which is closer to the actual teachings of Jacob Arminius than the more widely known Wesleyan Arminianism. Forlines is, above all, faithful to careful biblical exposition as the foundation of his theology. The perspective offered by Forlines, along with like-minded theologians such as Robert Picirilli and Roger Olson, deserves to be heard on these crucial issues. Although our own perspective differs at points, we have used their books profitably at our seminary."

Steve W. Lemke
Provost
New Orleans Baptist Theological Seminary

randall house

To order, call 800-877-7030
or visit www.randallhouse.com.

What is D6?

BASED ON DEUTERONOMY 6:4-7

A **conference** for your entire **team**

A **curriculum** for every age at **church**

An **experience** for every person in your **home**

Connecting
CHURCH & HOME
These must work together!

D6 CONFERENCE ONCE A YEAR

DEFINE & REFINE Your Discipleship

www.d6family.co

ONE HOUR A WEEK

POWER OF PARENTAL INFLUENCE

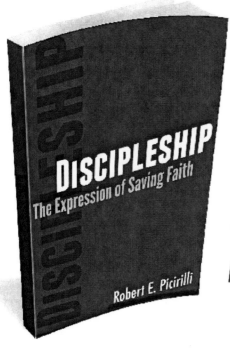

CPSIA information can be obtained at www.ICGtesting.com
Printed in the USA
LVOW10s0719130515

438194LV00003B/3/P

3670824

9 780892 656967